BY THE SAME AUTHORS
The Botanical Art Files - Composition

Rita Parkinson ©Copyright 2016

First edition published in 2016 by The Botanical Press
3/7 Beachcomber Place. Victoria. Australia
www:thebotanicalpress.com

Amazon.com/The Botanical Art Files - Narratives

Parkinson Rita
The Botanical Art Files - Narratives
Subject: Botanical Art
Illustrations. R. Parkinson and Dolores Sk-Malloni
Printed by Createspace: An Amazon Company
ISBN 978-0-9925624-4-1

Cover illustration Rita Parkinson. *Ipomoea Indica. I. lacunose*
Title Page. Dolores Sk-Malloni. *Ranunculus lingua*. Anenomes

BOTANICAL ART FILES
narratives
A guide to sources and styles for botanical artists

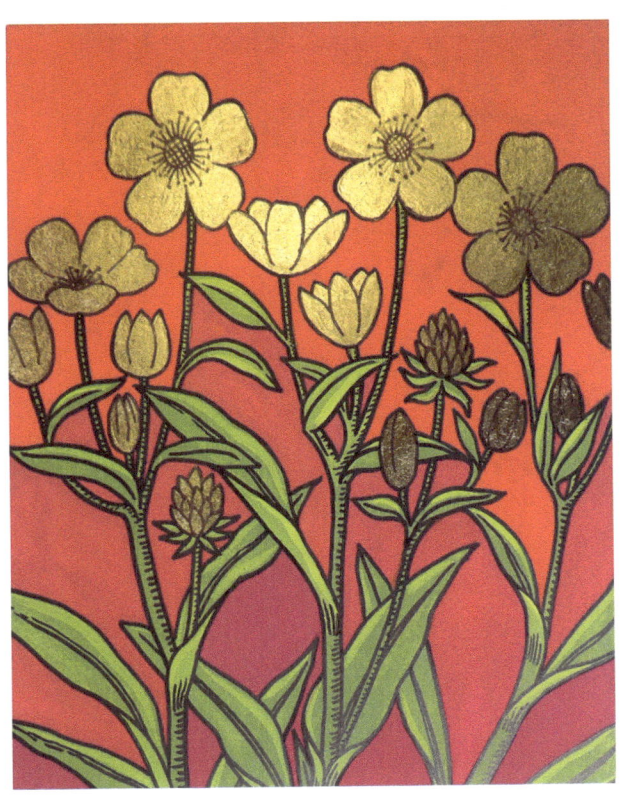

Rita Parkinson

Illustrations by Dolores Sk-Malloni and Rita Parkinson

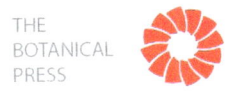

THE BOTANICAL PRESS

CONTENTS

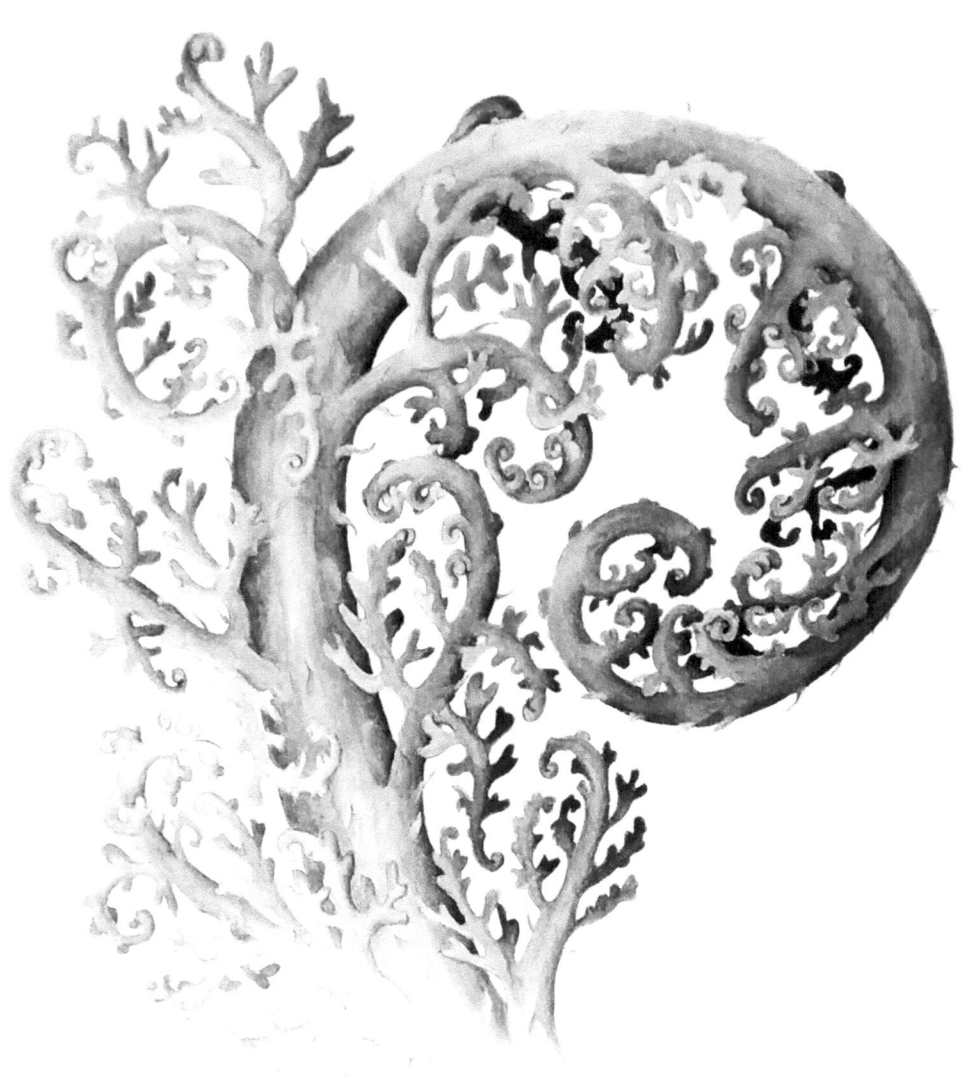

R. Parkinson.
Asplenium bulbiferum
Watercolour

Introduction

There is more than one reason to be a botanical artist. There is more than one path to follow and more than one goal to aspire. Botanical artists have many different objectives and enthusiasms. Some are fascinated by fungi and others are inspired by their local indigenous species. Some prefer to draw than to paint and of course some simply love to paint flowers, the more colorful the better. So, at the Geelong School of Botanical Art where I am a tutor, we aim to give our students a wide experience that helps them to develop their own unique path. For this reason we take a broad view of the skills needed and of the subjects that we explore.

This book is about the various narratives of botanical art. It starts from the premise that to be able to render an image that replicates the subject skillfully is absolutely essential. This is a worthy prime goal and takes time to accomplish, but it is not everything. If your contribution to the field can bring something of yourself, it will be the stronger for that.

The customary style of botanical illustration harks back to the golden age of Botanical Art in the 17th C. It is called the Linnaean Style and was developed by illustrators such as Georg Dionysius Ehret, Ferdinand Bauer and other great illustrators of that era. They were working in a pivotal time that brought together several important new factors. There was the new science of plant classification, the exploration of new lands and the global trade expansion that went with it. New techniques of printing were developing and made publications available to a wider audience.

Much as we admire these paintings, it is impossible to get the same sense of surprise and excitement that would have occurred on seeing such different and exotic plants for the first time. Our world is very different. We live in a time that is saturated with visual imagery and our work has to compete in this contemporary explosion of media. That means we need to be discerning in our narratives and understand how to promote them.

There are new priorities in the plant world. There are two main themes, one is the need to maintain bio-diversity and the second is that very little of the total mass of plant life has actually been described so far. Fungi for instance make up a considerable percentage of the organic biomass of the earth and to date only a very small part has been described. This book is an exploration of the breadth of influences and purposes that have made up the botanical illustration narrative traditions- and their relevance today. We need to make sure it is a genre that can take on board all our contemporary knowledge and amalgamate it with the traditions of the past.

THE SCOPE OF BOTANICAL ILLUSTRATION

Anyone studying botanical illustration today should understand that there can be a wider field of interest to develop than many expect. It is sometimes assumed that the main purpose of botanical illustration has always been for classification purposes. But that is not the case, the history of botanical illustration shows us that it has functioned for different purposes at various times. Its primary use has been as a complement to science with its emphasis on classification and taxonomy. But it has also played a significant part in the history of the horticultural industry, providing illustrations for plant catalogues, periodicals and magazines. The plant world has often been a subject for the publishing industry, providing illustrations in the early days for magnificent portfolios and later in gardening magazines. At the present time botanical art is forging a new place in the world of fine arts. Today you could see large Botanical Art exhibitions, small group shows, solo exhibitions and more specialized thematic exhibitions. Eg. Endangered Plants.

HERBALS Medicinal, Culinary, Hallucinatory, Aromatic, Magical Texts.
BOTANY Taxonomy, Classification, Education, Field Guides, Floras.
HORTICULTURE Magazines, Plant catalogues, Periodicals.
PUBLISHING Portfolios, Garden magazines, Florilegia, Flower books.
CONTEMPORARY ART Botanical Art Exhibitions.

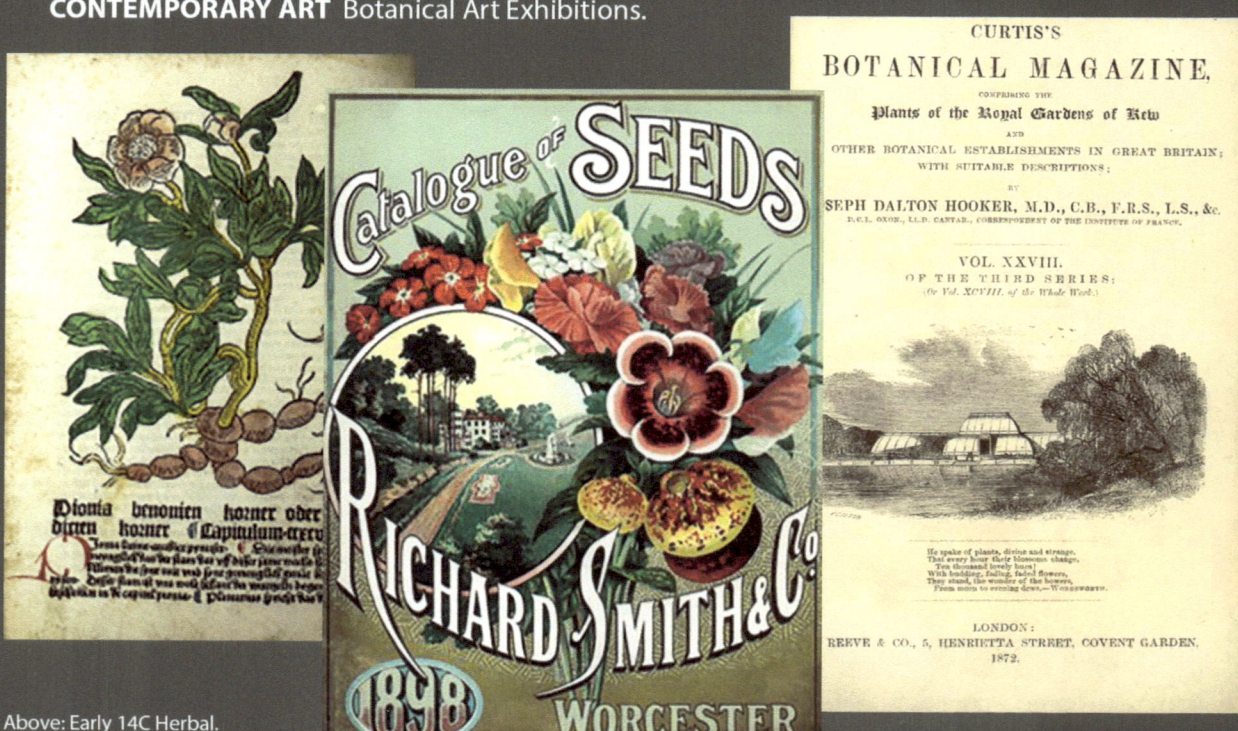

Above: Early 14C Herbal.
Right: Seed catalogue. 1898
Far right: Front cover. Curtis Botanical Magazine. 1872

A SHORT HISTORY

Early manuscripts from the classical world, the Middle East, India and China survived in libraries and monasteries in Europe through to the Middle Ages. Initially they were hand copied. The medieval herbals came into existence with the development of the woodblock prints. They were initially intended to list the curative effects of the featured plants, but they could also be illustrated for their culinary, hallucinatory, aromatic and magical qualities. As the influence of the Renaissance turned into the Age of Enlightenment, the needs of science with its emphasis on classification became the main intent of Floras, as the systematic account of plants from a particular area supplanted the old herbals. The developing horticultural Industry relied on the specialized skills of plant selection and hybridization and therefore needed plant catalogues for a growing public. Advances in printing technologies grew this audience for horticultural publications, portfolios and periodicals such as the William Curtis's Botanical Magazine. Garden magazines appeared for the general public when 'new' plants poured into Europe from far-away exotic places. They were as exciting to the Empress Josephine of France as they were to a growing leisured middle class, so she commissioned Pierre-Joseph Redouté to produce port-folios of portraits of her favorite flowers from her garden in Malmaison.

A Florilegium is a treatise on flowers where the typical emphasis is more on the aesthetic qualities. The tradition of Florilegia began in the 17 and 18th C. when wealthy owners of exceptional gardens were enthusiastic to show off their collections of rare plants. The practice continues today. Advances in printing techniques have always been at the forefront of the reproduction of botanical illustration and is dependent on the need to reproduce images as accurately as possible. In the western tradition beginning with the early primitive woodblock prints, advancement came through the development of various engraving techniques, culminating in the mezzotint. Then came the subtleties of lithography. In the present day most print is photo-lithography. But we also have digital images, digital image manipulation such as Photoshop, digital reproduction and all the various social media contexts that go with it. All of which must be beneficial, as it can bring our specialized work to a global audience.

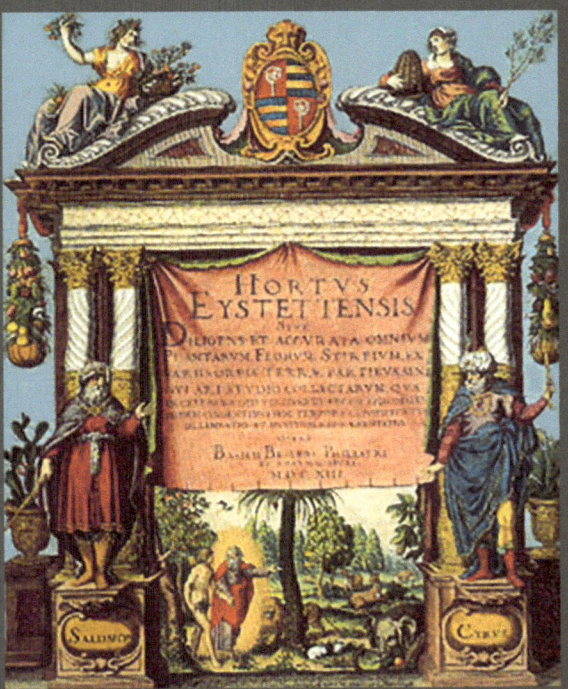

Above: Front cover. **Hortus Eystettensis 1613. Basilius Besler**

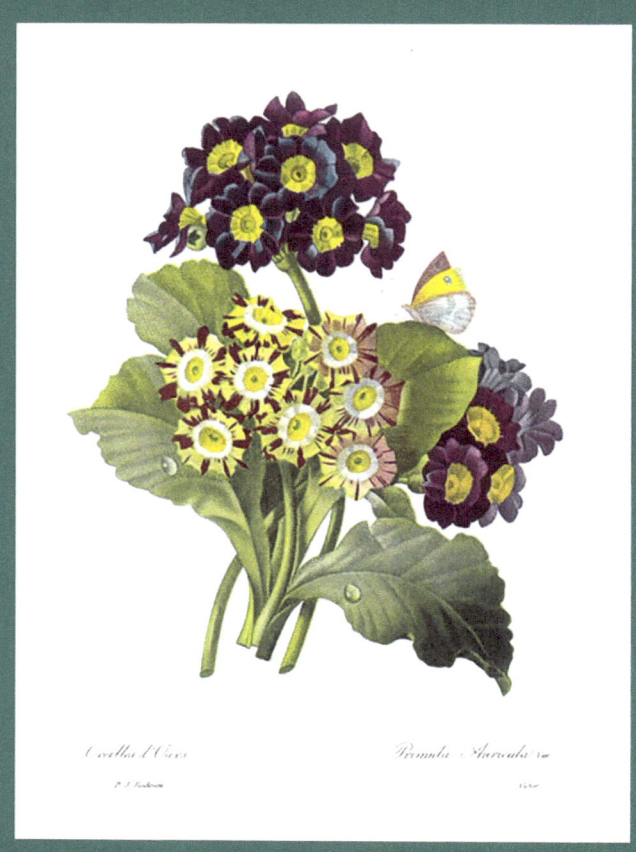

Primula auricula
Pierre-Joseph Redouté

THE GOLDEN AGE OF BOTANICAL ART
MASTERS OF BOTANICAL ART

THE TRADITIONS

FERDINAND AND FRANZ BAUER

PIERRE-JOSEPH REDOUTÉ

SYDNEY PARKINSON

MARIA SIBYLLA MERIAN

GEORG DIONYSIS EHRET

TRADITIONS FROM THE GOLDEN AGE

A chapter devoted to the styles and scope of botanical illustrations would have to begin at the Golden Age of botanical illustration. The 17th century heralded this era as a time when many factors came together to create the conditions that eventually produced some of the most iconic works of botanical illustration. There were be many illustrators that you could include who would demonstrate this point, but depicted here are five who exemplify the various forces that came together to create these unique conditions. The factors included the new technologies of printing, and the subsequent development of a publishing industry. This in turn depended on an expanding and educated middle class. It was an age of science and the need for classification. It was also the age of empire building and all the associated desire for trade and information.

Maria Sibylla Merian 1647-1717
Maria Sibylla Merian was a German-born naturalist and scientific illustrator. Incredibly for a woman of this period, she managed to revolutionize both botany and zoology. She was way ahead of her time and was the first to look at the plant world in its ecological context.

George Ehret 1708 - 1770
Georg Ehret was the first artist to illustrate Carl Linnaeus' system of plant classification, and in the process created the conventions of the Linnean style still in use today.

Sydney Parkinson 1745 - 1771
Sidney Parkinson in his short life was a voyager on great expeditions. He sailed with Captain Cook on the Endeavour. He was the first botanical artist to draw and paint plants collected in Australia and he lost his life in the process.

Pierre-Joseph Redouté 1759 -1840
Pierre-Joseph Redouté, probably the most recognized botanical artist of all time. He understood the importance of publishing and took the time to understand and master himself the new engraving techniques of the time and he knew how to exploit them.

Franz Bauer 1758 -1826 and Ferdinand Bauer 1760 -1826
The Austrian brothers Ferdinand and Franz Bauer were born into an age of great geographical and botanical exploration and were both key figures in the of the Golden Age, leaving behind a wonderful visual record. Franz Bauer spent much of his professional life at Kew Gardens at the centre of the scientific plant community. Ferdinand was at the forefront of the scientific community of the time, some of his best work coming from the major expeditions that he accompanied.

Front Cover illustration. Florae Graeca. Vol 8

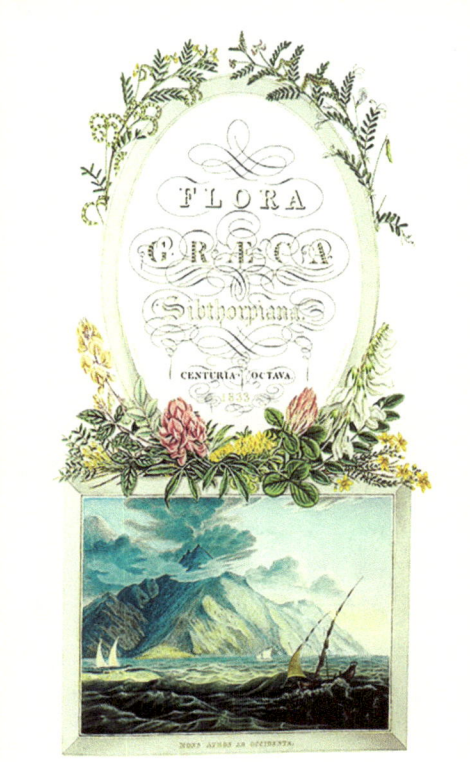

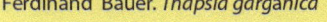

Ferdinand Bauer. *Thapsia garganica*

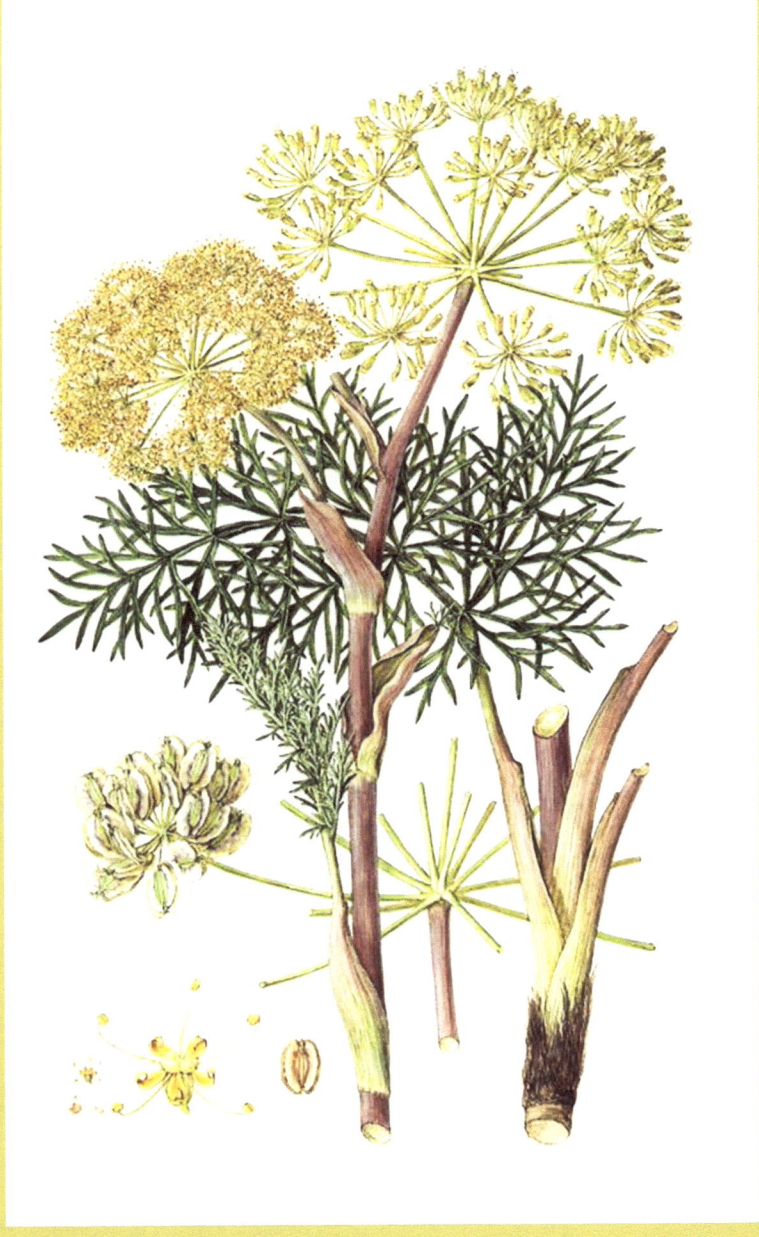

THE AGE OF DISCOVERY

The image of *Thapsia garganica* is an illustration completed for 'Florae Graeca', a publication released in ten volumes over a span of more than three decades from 1806-1840. It contained John Sibthorp's plant descriptions illustrated by 966 color engravings based on Ferdinand Bauer's accurately executed drawings. Ferdinand Bauer's career as an expeditionary artist began in the retinue of John Sibthorp, the Professor of Botany at the University of Oxford, during his faunal and floral tour of Greece and the eastern Mediterranean from 1786 to 1787.

 The Brother Gardeners: Botany, Empire and the Birth of an Obsession. Andrea Wulf. 2009

FERDINAND AND FRANZ BAUER

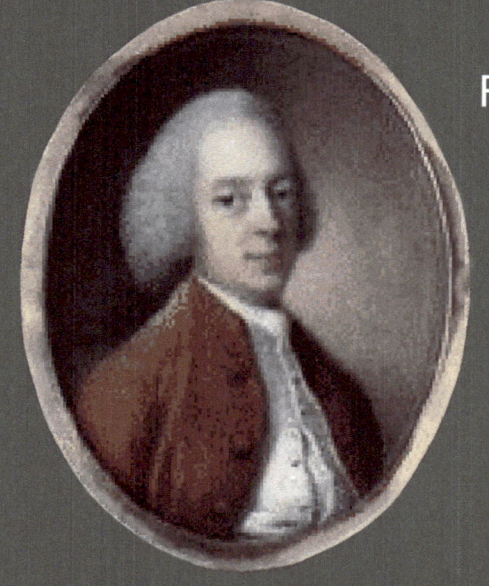

Ferdinand Bauer 1760-1826

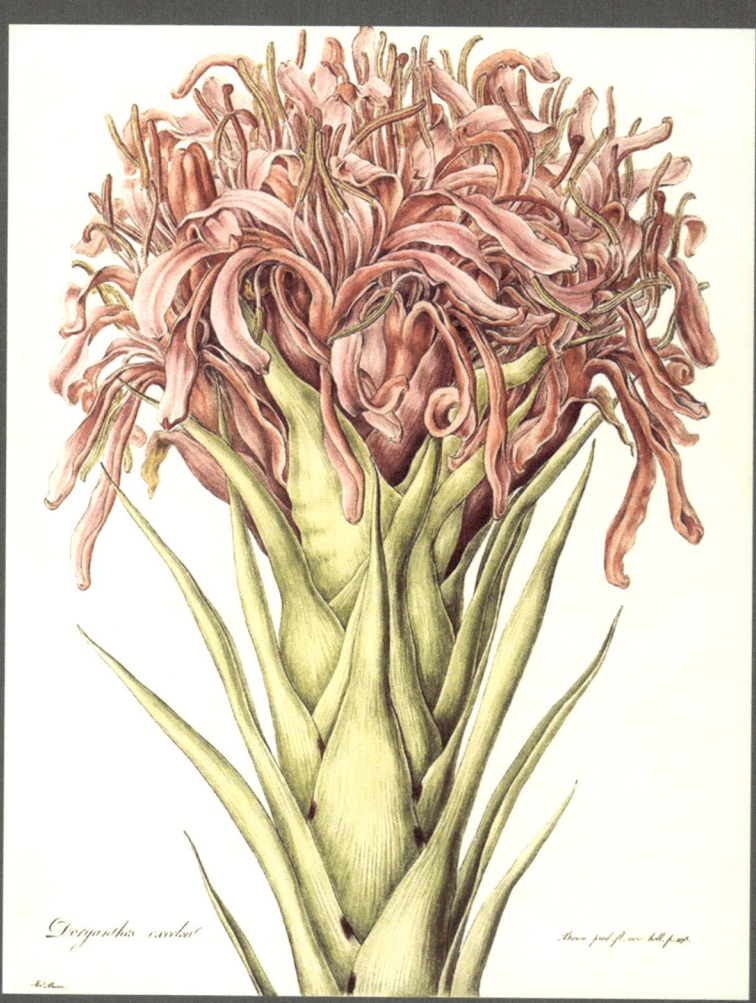

Ferdinand Bauer. *Doryanthus excelsa*

Ferdinand and his brother Franz Brauer were born into an artistic Austrian family. This was an age of great geographical and botanical exploration. They were both extremely talented and became regarded amongst the most pre-eminent botanical illustrators of all time. Both brothers began their careers employed as flower painters in Vienna. Ferdinand Bauer is best known for his role as botanical artist on expeditions to explore and record the flowers and natural history of Greece and the coastline of Australia. In 1801 Ferdinand was chosen by Joseph Banks to be the botanic draftsman to work under the direction of expedition naturalist Robert Brown, to complete the study of fauna and flora on the voyage under the command of Matthew Flinders.

Publications:
1806 - 1828. Flora Graeca Sibthorpiana
1813. Illustrationes Florae Novae Hollandiae.
        The first detailed account of the natural history of the Australia.
        He also contributed ten plates to Flinders' Voyage to Terra Australis.

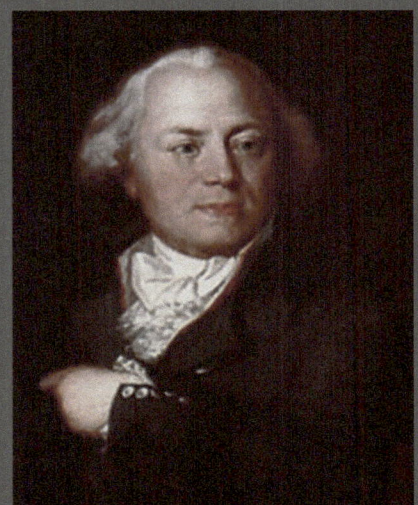

Franz Bauer 1758 - 1826

Franz Bauer relied on his skills as a microsco-pist to further his skills as a botanical artist. He is best known for his work at Kew Gardens where he illustrated works of the great bota-nists and naturalists of the time, including William Hooker, John Lindley and Sir Joseph Banks. He was introduced to Sir Joseph Banks in1790 on a visit to London, who immediately recognizing his talent and secured him a position as the first botanical illustrator at the Royal Botanic Gardens. Kew, where he stayed for the rest of his life. He was immensely gifted, making use of detailed paintings and drawings of flower dissections, often at the microscopic level. He appreciated just how important it was to progress his work to good reproductions and took great care in the hand-coloured lithographic copies of his work. He became a member of the Royal Society and was appointed 'Botanick Painter ' to His Majesty' King George III.

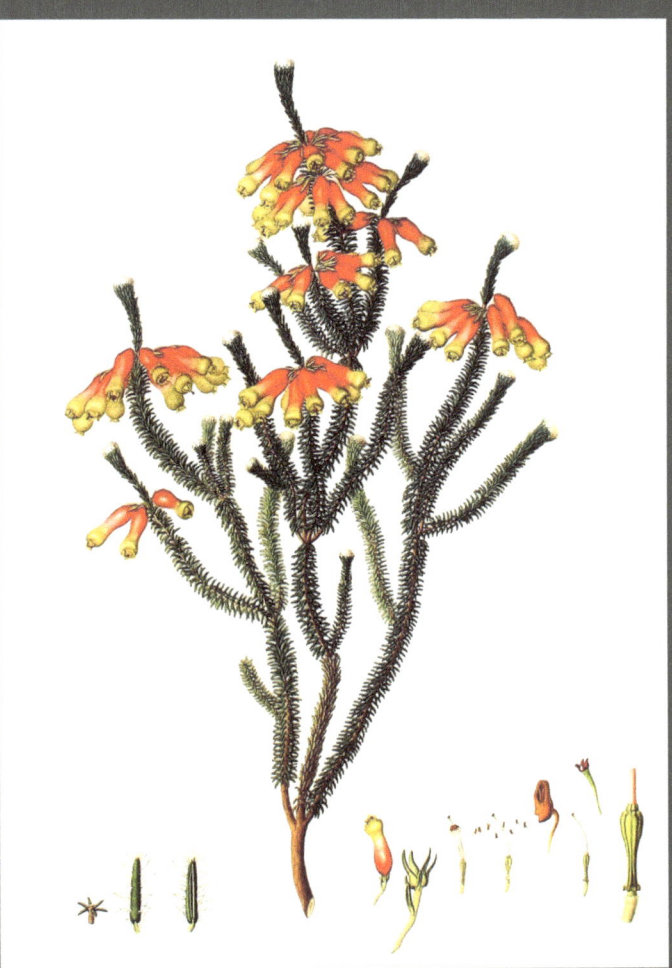

Franz Bauer. *Erica massonii*

Publications
1796–1803. Delineations of Exotick Plants cultivated in the
          Royal Garden at Kew.
1830-1838. The Genera and Species of Orchidaceous Plants,
          John Lindley. London.
1842. Genera filicum; Illustrations of the ferns, and other
          allied genera. William Jackson Hooker. London.

Pierre - Joseph Redouté 1759-1840

Pierre Joseph Redouté was born into a Flemish painters' family. In 1782 he went to Paris, where he initially worked as a decorative painter. He frequently drew in the Jardin du Roi, where he caught the attention of the botanist Charles Louis L'Héritier, who encouraged him to produce anatomical plant studies. His life was remarkable in that he lived and prospered in such turbulent times. He was an official court artist of Queen Marie Antoinette. He continued painting through the French Revolution and the Reign of Terror, and afterwards in the Napoleonic period. He then managed to maintain his career under the Restoration of the Monarchy in 1814. Not only did he survive these chaotic political upheavals but he prospered, gaining international recognition in the process. He collaborated with the greates botanists of his day and participated in nearly fifty publications depicting both the familiar flowers of the French court and plants from places as distant as America, South Africa, Japan, and Australia. In his life time he produced over 2,100 published plates that depicting over 1,800 different species, many never rendered before.

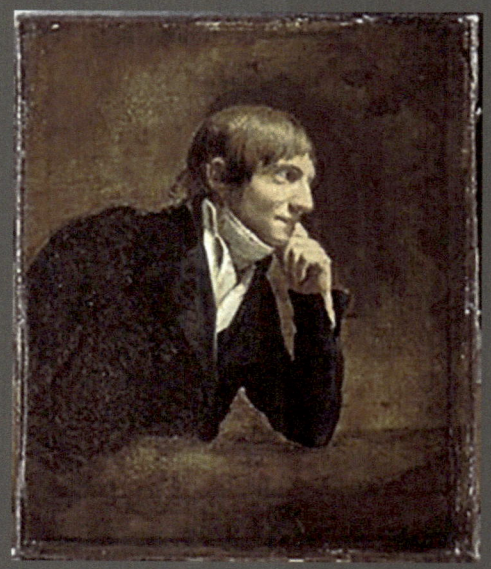

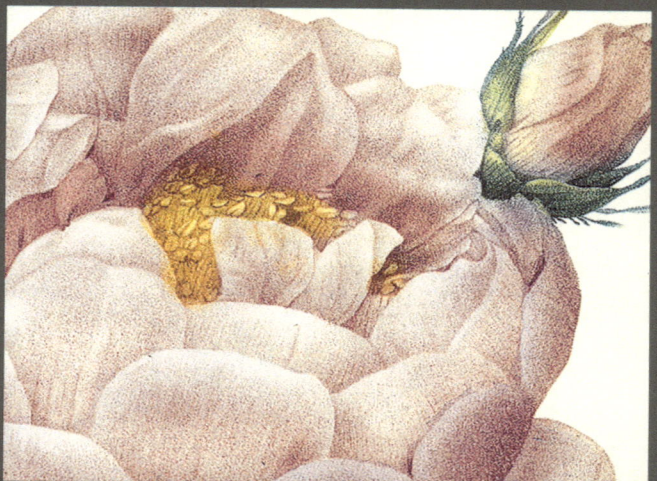

Pierre-Joseph Redouté is the most widely known of all flower painters. What is not so appreciated is that his success depended to a large extant on his knowledge and mastery of the new techniques of reproduction and the publishing opportunities that were opening up at the time. He was well aware that the quality of his reproductions was vital. He took the time to not only understand the new stipple process, but to become a master and improve the technique in the process. The stipple technique was an engraving process which involved the engraving of dots on the copper plate whose density varied to reflect shading. It could be worked to achieve very subtle effects. Fine lines could then be engraved for the outlines and details. The engraved plate was then painted with the 'en poupé' method where with the correct colours were applied with ink and would adhere to the specific dotted areas and engraved lines.

THE EMPRESS

Redoutés most famous patron was the Empress Josephine, Napoleon Bonaparte's first wife. In 1798, Josephine acquired a substantial estate, Malmaison and she set out to create a botanical garden of the rarest and most beautiful plants obtainable. In Josephine's time, the garden at Malmaison had more than 250 varieties of plants. Roses were of particular interest and she intended to grow all known varieties. There were over 200 species and cultivars at Malmaison, many of which Pierre Joseph Redouté immortalized. Redoutés 'Les Roses' contains many roses from Malmaison, as well as from other significant gardens. From 1802 he published his 'Les Liliacées', in which he largely applied the technical possibilities of colour printing to the large and evenly colored leaves and blossoms. In this work he also abandoned the flower painters' tradition of framing the plants with an outer contour line.

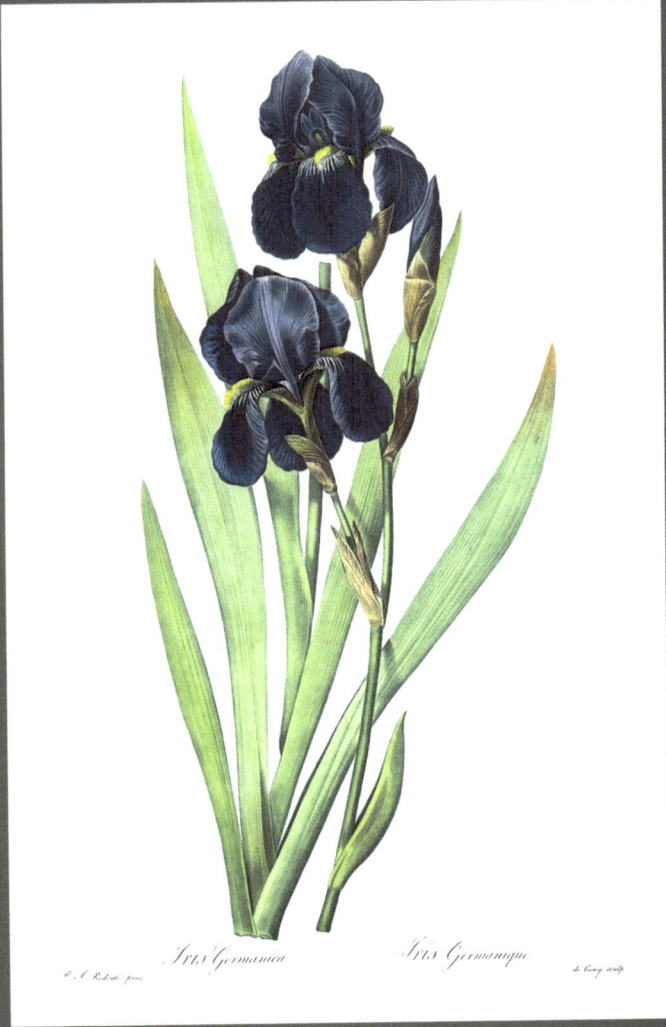

Iris Germanica   Iris Germanique

His masterpieces are considered to be:
Les Liliacées, 8 vols. 1802–1816.
Les Roses, 3 vols. 1817–1824
Choix des plus belles fleurs et de quelques branches des plus beaux fruits. 1827. An anthology of his selection of his finest botanical illustrations.

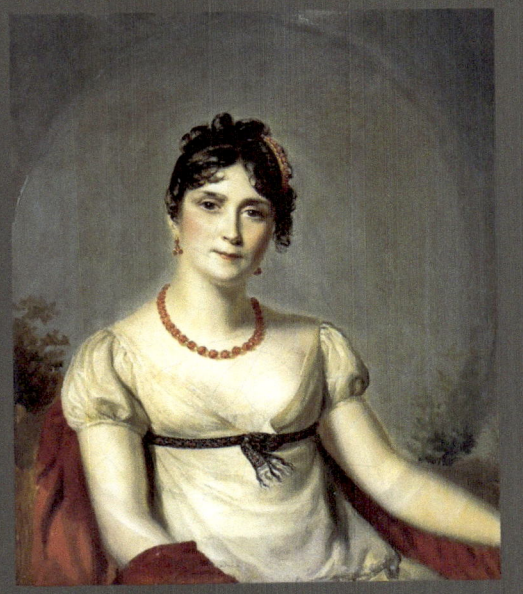

Above: *Iris germanica*. Engraving from original painting by Redouté. Watercolour
Left: The Empress Josephine Buonaparte
Left above: Pierre-Joseph Redouté. Oil on canvas. Louis Leopold Boilly
Left below: Detail of a rose illustration using the stipple technique

Sydney Parkinson 1745 - 1771

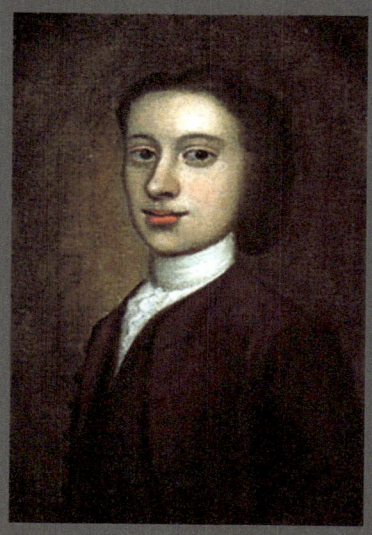

Sydney Parkinson was born in Edinburgh and from an early age became very proficient at drawing plants and flowers. He travelled to London to develop his career as a botanical artist and was discovered by Joseph Banks. The botanist Joseph Banks was the great sponsor of plant discovery and botanical illustration in general. He eventually developed the Royal Botanic Gardens at Kew. Parkinson was highly skilled in botanical drawing, and worked with Joseph Banks in London before joining him and Daniel Solander on James Cook's Endeavour journey (1768-1771) as one of two botanical draughtsmen - a voyage of historical significance and scientific discovery. This became his claim to artistic fame and sadly his epitaph.

THE ENDEAVOR

Life onboard a ship in those days must have been hard. And trying to do professional work that involved microscopes, keeping specimens, creating working drawings and watercolours. Sydney Parkinson started the voyage on the Endeavour as one of two botanical artists taken by Captain Cook to draw and paint plants collected on this exploratory voyage. Neither survived this experience. The other artist Alexander Buchan died of epilepsy in Tahiti. On the return voyage, Sydney Parkinson died at sea after picking up dysentery and malaria in Java. During the first part of the voyage Parkinson had time to work his drawings into full watercolours, either immediately in situ or aboard later in the voyage. He made sketches of hundreds of specimens collected by Joseph Banks and Daniel Solander. He made at least 1,300 drawings and paintings during the journey. This meant that Parkinson became the first European artist to set foot on Australian soil. The first artist to draw an authentic Australian landscape, and the first non-indigenous artist to portray the Aboriginal people of New Zealand and Australia from direct observation. Some of his work was turned into completed watercolours by others on their return. The watercolours made by Sydney Parkinson were engraved by several engravers under the patronage of Banks, but were not published at the time. On Banks' death they went to the Natural History Museum. They were eventually published the 1980s in full colour, using the original engraved plates.

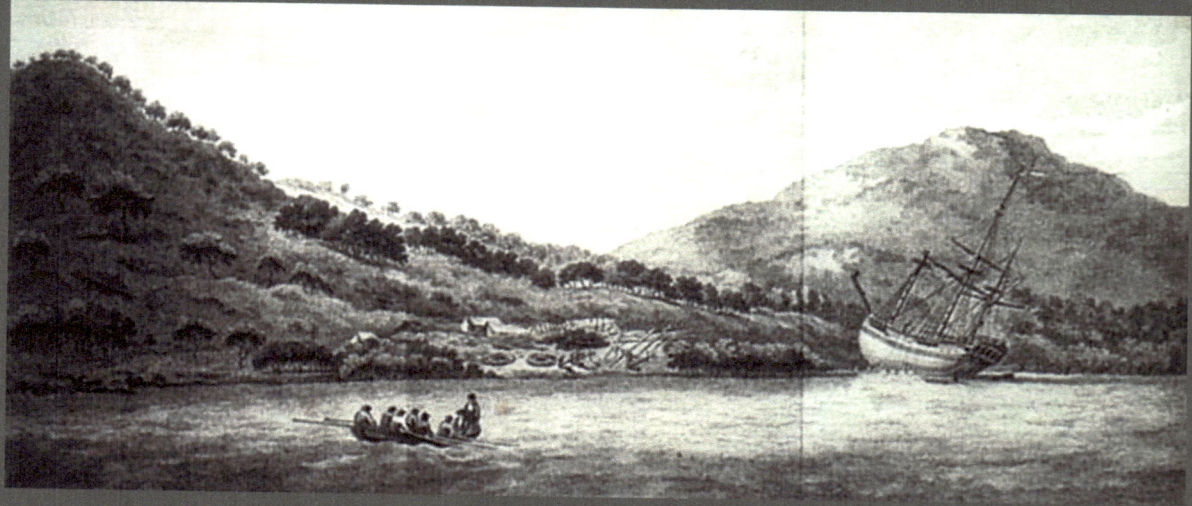

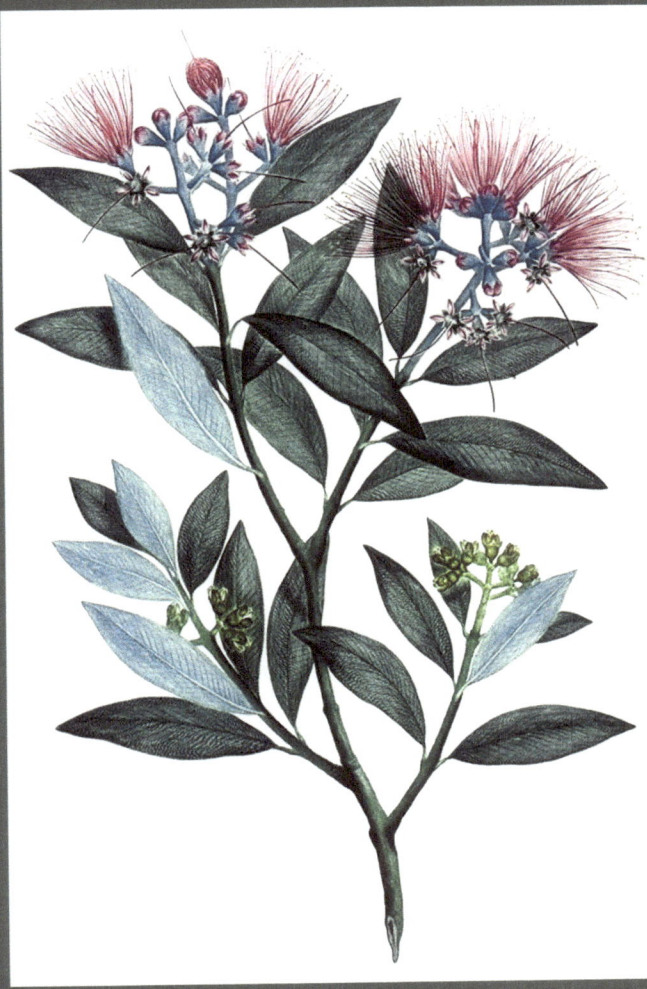

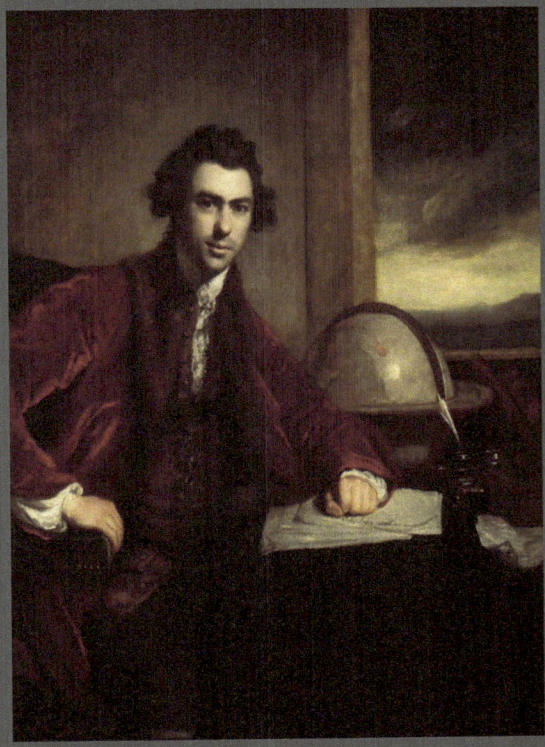

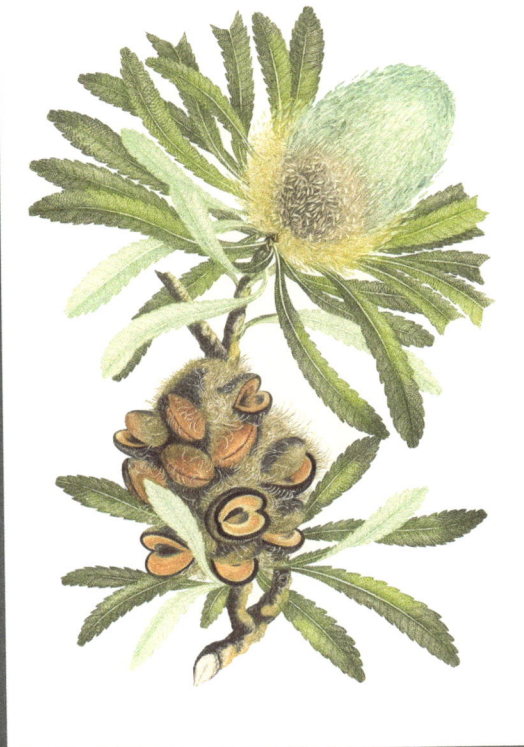

Above. *Metrosideros excelsa*. From a painting by Gabriel Smith from drawings and watercolour notations by Sydney Parkinson.

Above right. Portrait of Sir Joseph Banks by Joshua Reynolds.

Right. *Banksia serrata*. Plate no 285 of Banks' Florilegium.
    Produced from original drawings made by Sydney Parkinson
    on the first voyage of Captain Cook. 1768-1771.
    The flowering plant *Banksia serrata* is one of a genus of plants
    named after Joseph Banks.

Left above. Sydney Parkinson. Self portrait.
Left below. Engraving of the Endeavor

 Banks Florilegium. Alecto Publishing 1980

Maria Sibylla Merian 1647 -1717

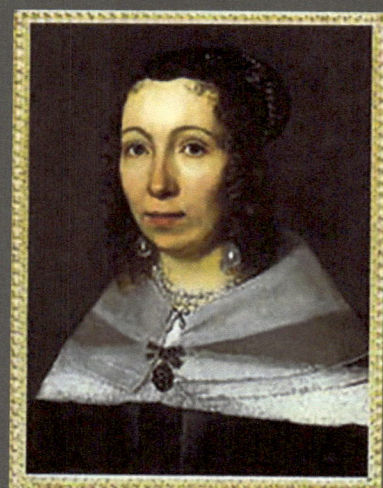

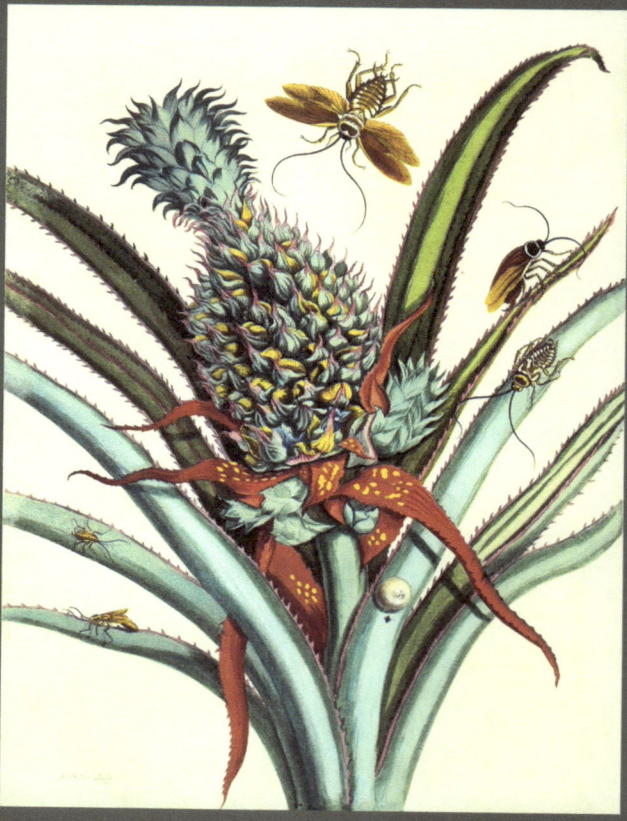

Ananas comosus. Pineapple.
Periplanata austrasia. Blatell germanica. Cockroaches

Maria Sibylla Merian was a German born naturalist and scientific illustrator, a descendant of the Swiss Merian family, one of Europe's largest publishing houses. From early childhood she was interested in the drawing of insects and plants. In 1670 she and her husband moved to Nuremberg, where Merian published and illustrated her first illustrated book, a catalogue of European moths, butterflies and other insects.

She was a remarkable woman for her time. In 1685 Merian left her husband, and with her two daughters set sail for the Dutch province of West Friesland. At some point she saw some dried specimens and was inspired to study them in their natural habitats -South America. At the age of 52, Merian and her youngest daughter embarked on the dangerous trip to the Dutch colony of Surinam in South America. She spent two years there studying and drawing plants and fauna.

Maria Sibylla Merian revolutionized both Botany and Zoology. She was a pioneer in the field of depicting symbiotic relationships, in particular the metamorphis of insects. Rather than working from preserved specimens she favored working from living material, by collecting, propagating and observation. Interestingly she didn't subscribe to the convention of drawing everything to the correct scale. She was a firm believer that using a visual hierarchy to create her emphasis was more important than keeping to the relative scales.

The pineapple depicted above is the first illustration in her famous publication. Merian described the pineapple, as the "most outstanding of all edible fruits." She noted that cockroaches are attracted to the sweet fruit and cause devastation to all the inhabitants by "spoiling their wool, linen, food and drinks."

Maria Sibylla Merian
Metamorphosis insectorum Surinamensium. 1705

Georg Dionysius Ehret 1708 - 1770

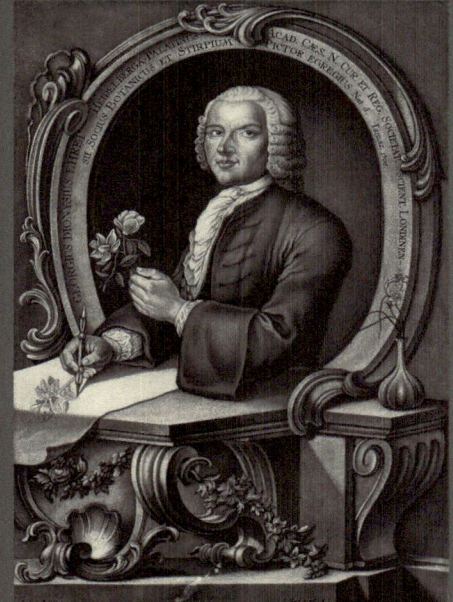

Selinicereus grandiflrus. Queen of the Night

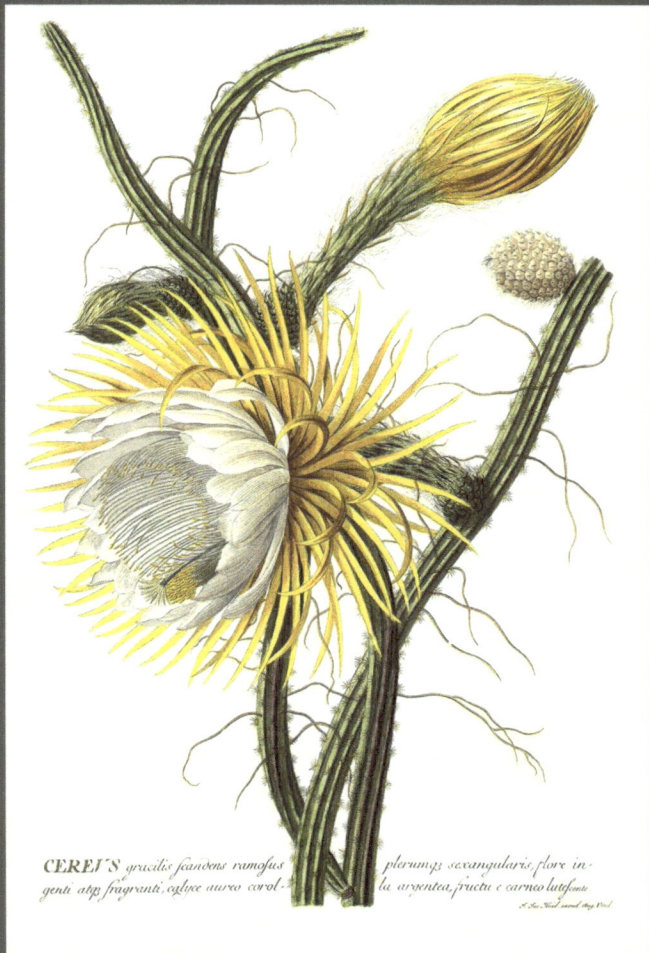

Georg Dionysius Ehret was another German born artist who became one of the most influential botanical artists of all time. He was born in Heidelberg in Germany. As a young man he spent two years in France, including a brief time at the Jardin des Plantes in Paris before moving to Belgium. It was here that he worked with Carl Linnaeus at Georg Clifford's estate, De Hartecamp. From here he helped to produce and publish the Hortus Cliffortianus in 1738, a critical and influential example of early botanical litera-ture. By working with Linnaeus, he needed to developed a style of botanical illustration that was capable of illustrating the Linnaeus system of plant classification. It needed to be in a compact form suitable for publication as a single plate. This development was highly influential and became the preferred style and is still in use today.

Ehret usually worked with bodycolour on vellum. He used sketchbooks to record his plants from life before producing larger paintings in his studio. Ehret lived at a time of scientific discovery and enlighten-ment in Europe, a golden age for botanical art. His unique style and clarity of plant illustration was im-mediately useful and sought out by specialists. He later moved to England and spent most of his career working there. In 1757 Ehret was made a Fellow of the Royal Society. London.

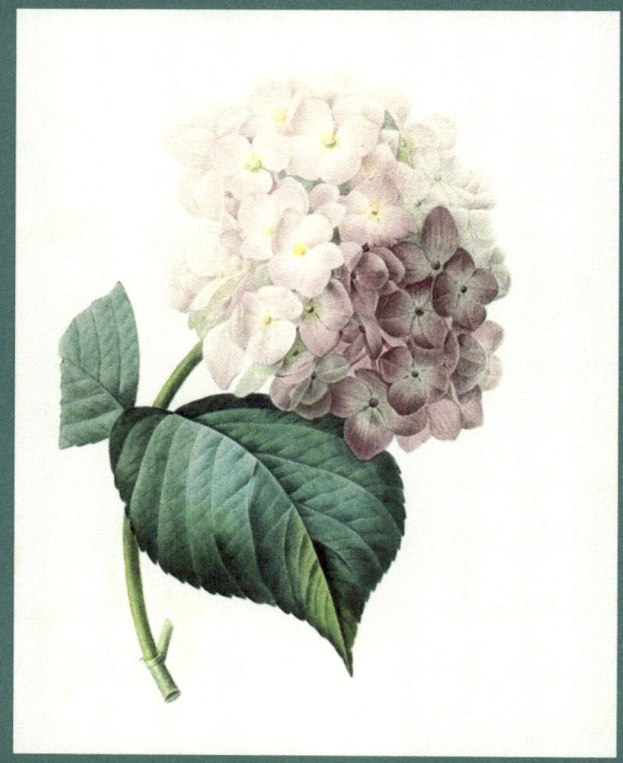

Pierre-Joseph Redouté. *Hortensia.*
An image from the publication "Choix des Plus Belles Fleurs"

HORTICULTURE

THE STUDY OF A SINGLE SPECIES

THE EXOTIC AND RARE

CULTIVARS AND VARIATIONS

FLORILEGIA
Famous Florilegia
Contemporary Florilegia
A Florilegium of Trees

PASSIONS AND MANIAS
Fern Fever
Tulipomania

EXPLORING THE SPECIES

When people mention botanical illustration often the first name that comes to mind is Pierre-Joseph Redouté. Some of the most famous series of all time are his monographs of a single species. The most well known is 'Les Roses', printed in three volumes between 1817 and 1824. Each new volume of the finished color copperplates engraved by Firmin Didot was received with a storm of enthusiasm and soon sold out. The original paintings no longer exist, as tragically they were destroyed in a fire in the Library of the Louvre. But their reputation lives on in the prints that have been reproduced time and time again, to inspire future generations. The publication of 'Les Roses' was a high point in the technical execution of its production and could not be faulted, with its combination of Redouté's plates and the erudite text by Claude Antoine Thory. It remains not only a great artistic achievement, but also a valuable scientific record. Its author, Thory, was a dedicated botanist with his own collection of roses. 'Les Roses' describes many forerunners of today's flowers, and includes details of a number of species and cultivars that have since disappeared. Many of the flowers were novelties in Redouté's day. The roses used as specimens for the work were taken from Thory's own collection, the gardens at Malmaison, and other collections around Paris.

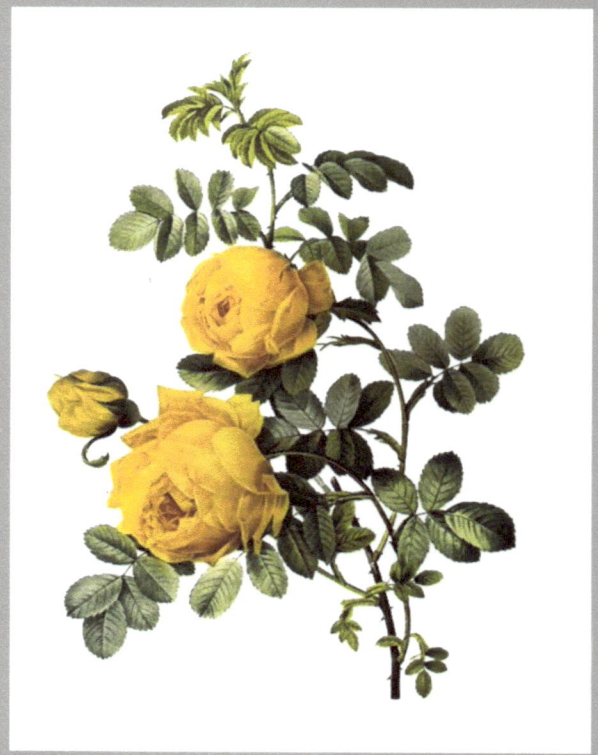

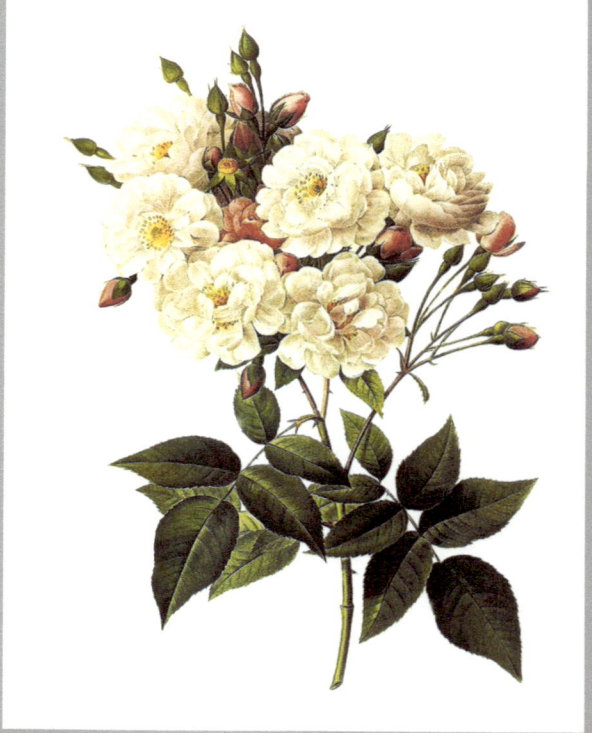

 Les Roses. Three Volumes. 1817 - 1824
Pierre-Joseph Redouté (1759-1840)
Claude Antoine Thory (1759-1827)

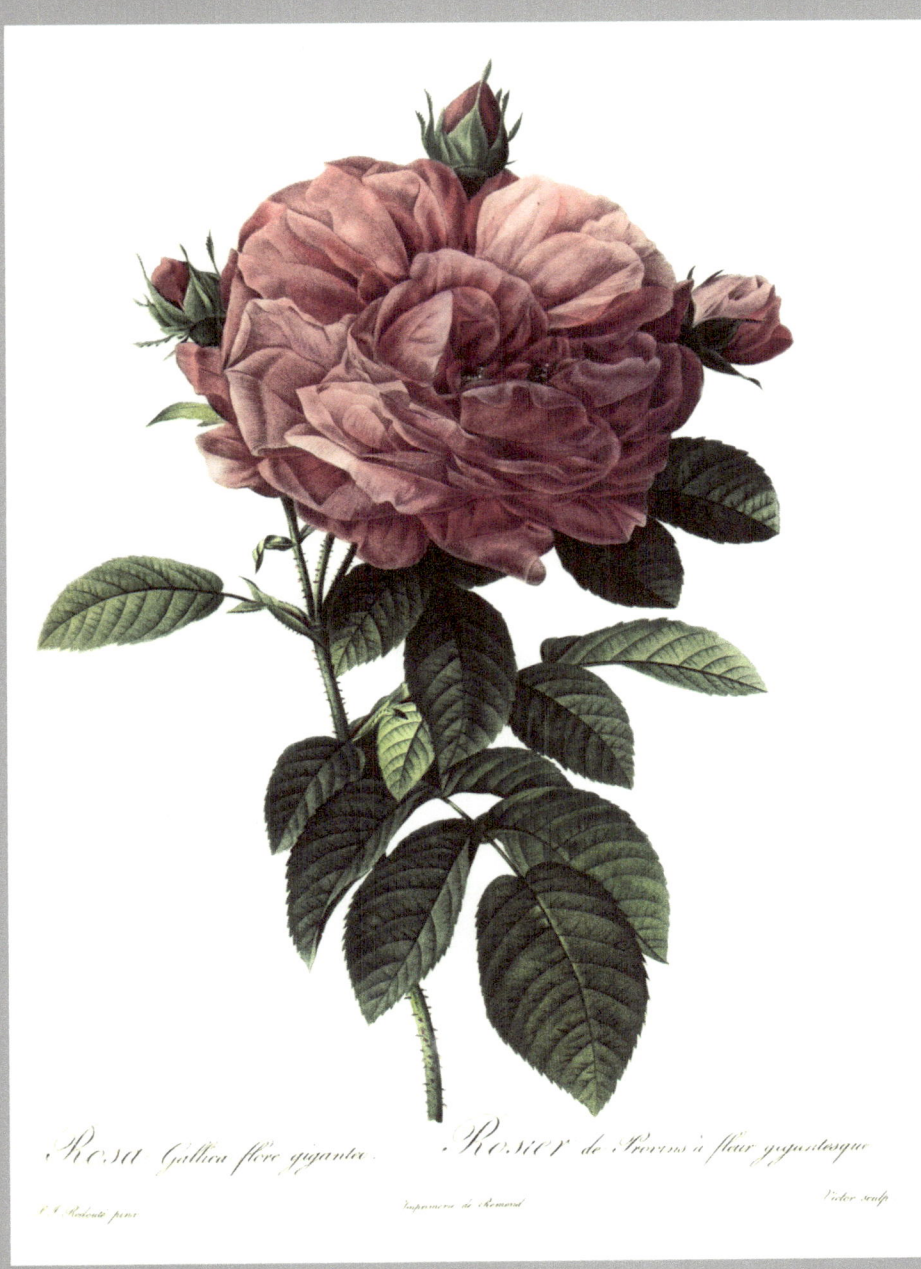

Rosa Galica flore giganteo

Rosier de Provins à fleur gigantesque

Left: *Rosa Galica flore giganteo*
Far left above: *Rosa sulphura*
Far left below: *Rosa noisettiana*

The series of paintings of Roses is still held by many to be the benchmark by which all others are compared. The dynamic realism he achieved surpassed all artists who preceded him in function, economy and vivacity. Since these times the single species study has been a mainstay in botanical art. It will always work towards the goal of classification and general knowledge, and has the personal benefit of time spent on a species you love.

A SINGLE SPECIES

It can be a great advantage to develop a consistent body of work. Most artists will appreciate the theory, but when it comes to actually creating that body of work, some are not sure where to begin. The best place for most would be to follow their natural preferences, and we all have those. That could mean an in depth study of a favorite species. There are several factors that any illustrator needs to consider to develop their work– quality, creativity, and confidence are all important– but consistency is one of the most important, as it often speaks to the other factors.

   Concentrating on one species has always been a favorite theme for botanical artists to explore. It can be an obvious choice, as it allows you to expand your knowledge and technique on your natural preferences. But it does call on a degree of focus to maintain the interest, over the amount of time needed to develop a number of works on a single subject.

NOTE: The Royal Horticultural Society. London. UK specifies in their exhibition guidelines, that each artist must show a collection of works built around a theme, with a minimum of eight pieces. This implies that they consider this number a minimum amount to demonstrate the degree of focus needed to be considered for their medal awards.

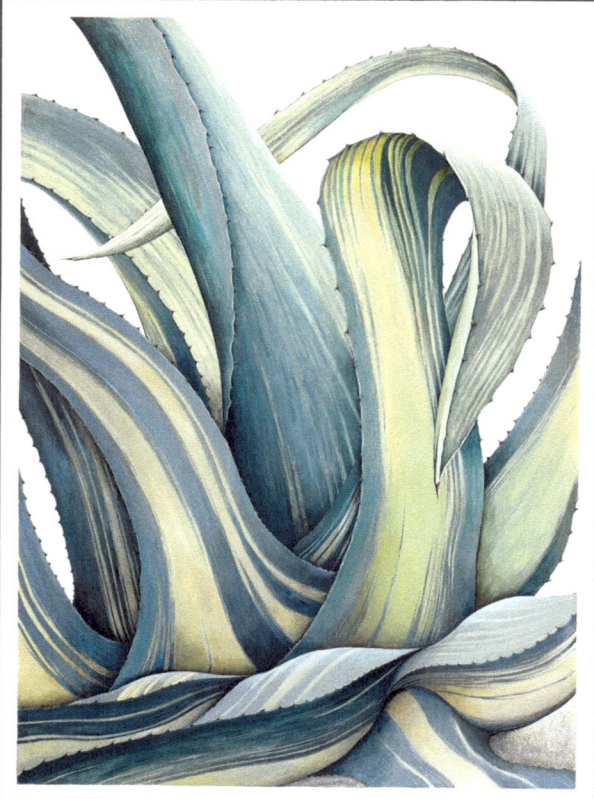

THE ADVANTAGES

For many illustrators it can seem easier to start afresh each time they confront that pristine sheet of white paper. It can just seem simpler to leave behind the perceived flaws in the last work and start all over.

But exploring one species in detail has great benefits. Favoring depth as opposed to breadth, implies a level of purpose and commitment.

   Creating a number of works on one subject can have benefits in the exhibition field, particularly in group shows. Showing a number of paintings of the same subject can carry more weight than works of separate subjects. If these works can be shown together, they create a mini exhibition within an exhibition, and then have a much greater chance of holding a viewer's attention, particularly in large group shows.

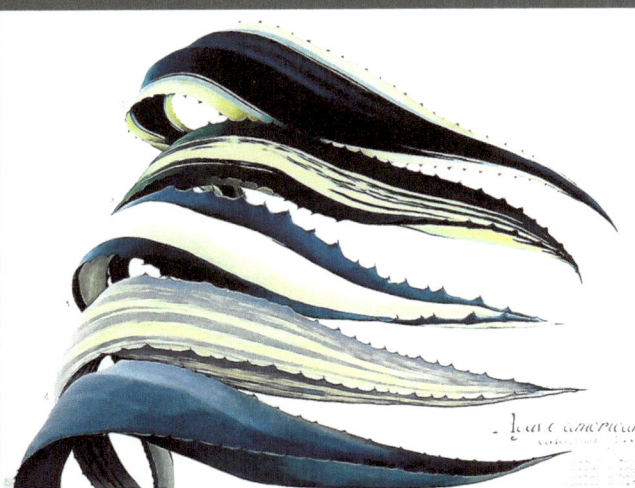

THE AGAVES

The Agave species have an inherent architectual aspect in their form and reveal an obvious evolutionary response to their harsh desert environments. The species illustrated here are all from the Agave Americana species, the century plant. They are native to Mexico but have become naturalized in many places, due in part to the fact that they are cultivated as an ornamental for the strong dramatic forms they add to a landscape. The ones illustrated here are all variegated forms that visually exaggerate their robust curving forms.

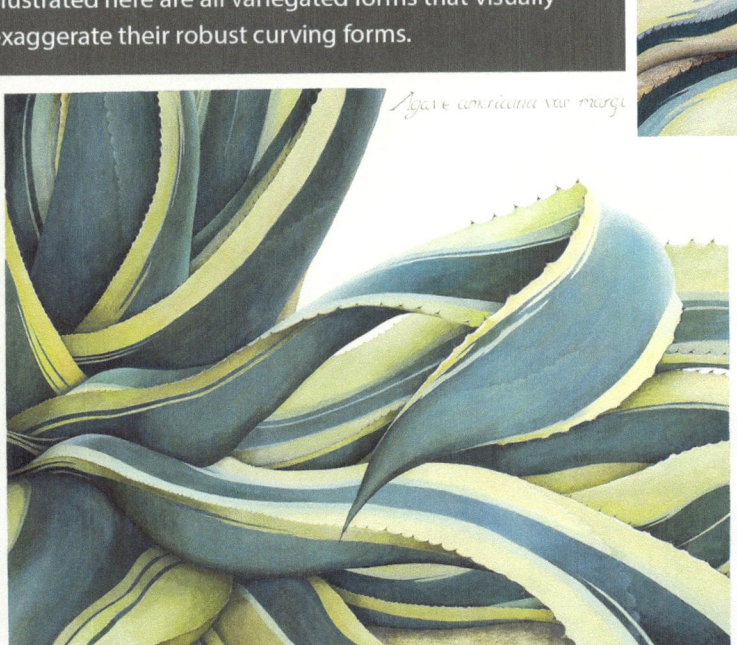

Illustrations: Rita Parkinson
Agave series. Gouache

Above. *Agave americana* var *medio-picta*
Above left. *Agave americana*. Study in variagation
Left. *Agave americana*. var *marginata*
Far left. *Agave americana* var. *striata*

THE RARE AND EXOTIC

A plant could be considered rare because it is uncommon in numbers or it could be simply hard to find. Or it could be endemic, from a place that is remote to us. Rare plants have always been an important subject in the the development of horticulture and in the history of botanical art. Plant discovery meant, among other things, economic advantages that would lead to the expansion of trade and the wealth. As newly discovered plants were introduced to Europe, their images, were created by botanical artists and circulated by the publishing industry, where they caused much excitement and of course influenced art and horticulture.

THE UNFAMILIAR

Images of unusual plants will always have appeal in the world of botanical art. But what is exotic to one can be an everyday subject to another.

The appeal of curiosity is very strong, it is an intrinsic part of human nature. But the very idea of rare or exotic can be a subjective concept. Coconuts, for example, would have been unusual to those who lived in cold climates. The old cold world would have been fascinated by these imported oddities, and coconut palms came to represent the very idea of the exotic to many. Of course if you live on a Pacific Island it is just the local flora.

The Nīkau palm pictured here is unique to New Zealand, where it is the only native palm species.

* In the plant world the word 'exotic' is defined as 'introduced from abroad', rather than synonymous with 'unusual'.

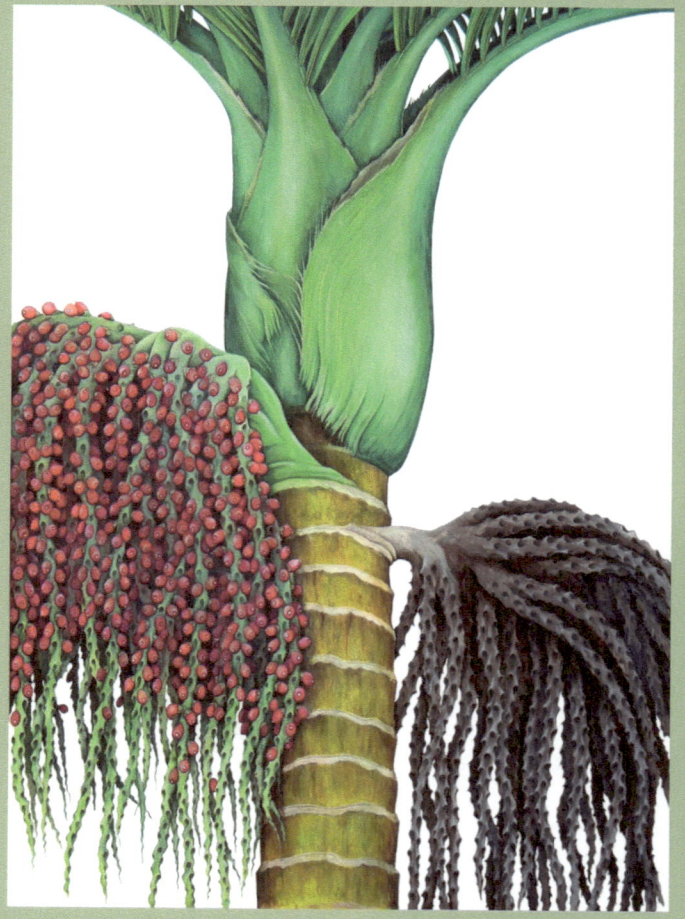

Rita Parkinson. *Rhopalostylis sapida*. The Nikau palm
Gouache on board

A WONDER TO BEHOLD

The *Victoria amazonica* is the largest *of* the Nymphaeaceae family of water lilies. The first published description of the genus was by John Lindley in 1837, based on specimens of the plant brought from British Guiana by Robert Schomburgk. John Lindley named the genus *Victoria regia* after the newly ascended Queen Victoria, but the name was superseded by *Victoria regina*.

The species is renowned for its very large leaves, which can be up to 3 metres in diameter. They float on the water's surface on a submerged stalk, 7–8 m in length. It is native to the waters of the Amazon River basin. The flowers are white on the first night they are open, but become pink on the second night. The flowers are up to 40 cm in diameter, and are pollinated by beetles.

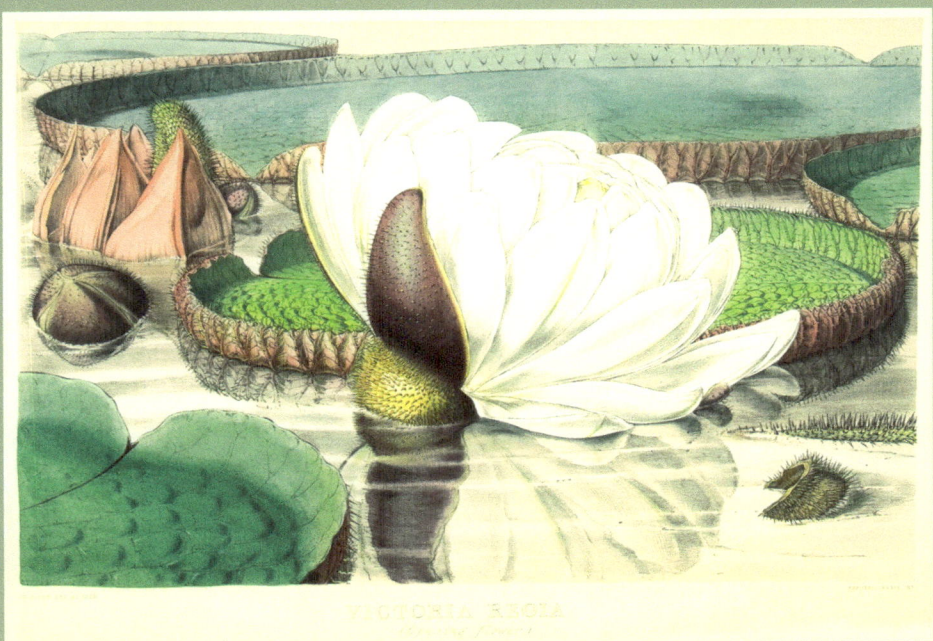

The discovery of *Victoria amazonica* in Victorian times caused rivalry between the proprietors of the great gardens of England to see who could propagate and grow them first. The original name *of Victoria regina* was eventually superceded by *Victoria amazonica* .

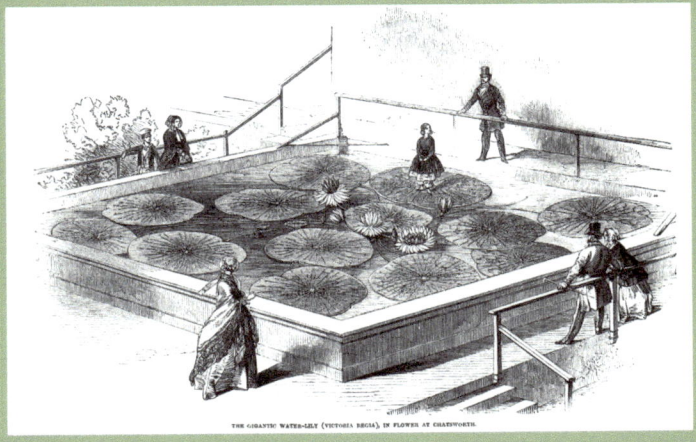

Above: *Victoria regina* . Walter Fitch. 1851. Lithograph
Right: An illustration of *Victoria regia* growing at
　　　Chatsworth House. Derbyshire. UK.

CULTIVARS AND VARIATIONS

Plants are developed from different horticultural techniques to provide new forms. Selective breeding can be used to produce different visual outcomes, a variation of patterns or colours or other attributes. Or it can be from a desire to improve in some other way. It could be to make it more productive, or for the fruit to be sweeter or better shaped. Other reasons could be to have a longer fruiting period, or to increase resistance to disease.

THE CULTIVAR

When a plant is a 'cultivated variety' it is called a cultivar. It means that human intervention has worked on the plant to improve it through selective reproduction either by seed selection, plant cuttings, mixing varieties and other means of human manipulation.

THE VARIETY

A plant is named a variety when a plant from the same species is different enough to receive its own name. This usually happens with plants that are genetically enhanced to improve some attribute such as coloration or eliminate another aspect.

THE HYBRID

A hybrid exists when two genetically different plants interbreed and produce descendants. If the descendants can reproduce by themselves they are called hybrids regardless of whether this is a natural occurence or by human manipulation.

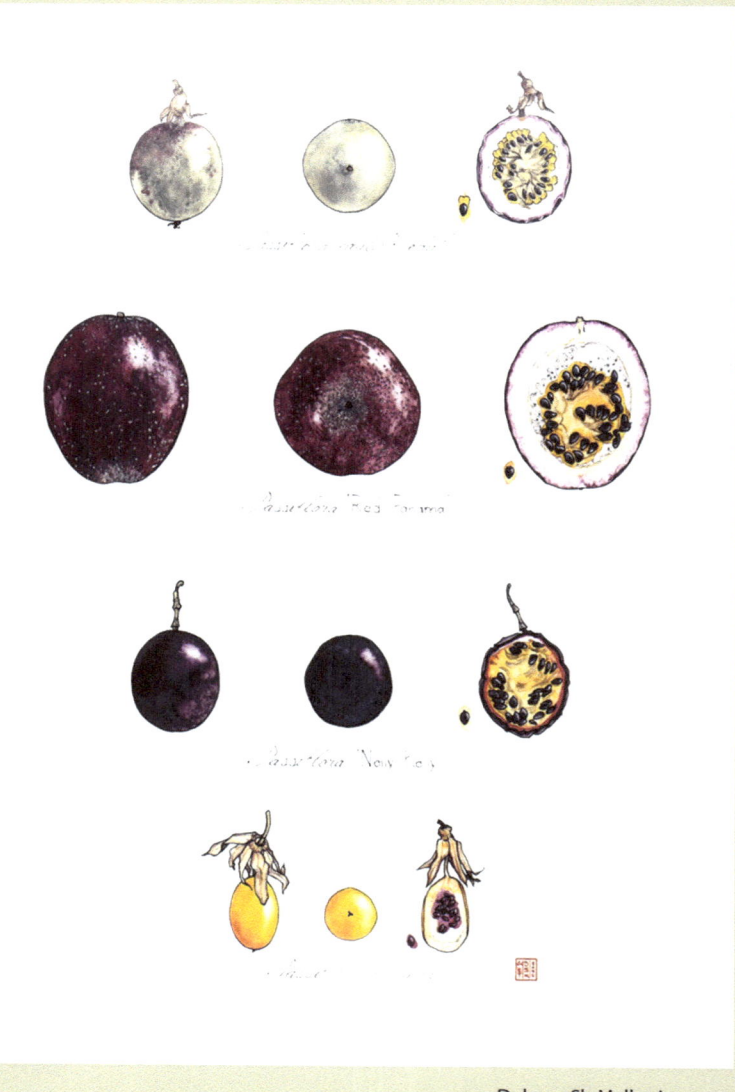

Dolores Sk-Malloni
Fruits of *Passiflora* species
Watercolour

PUBLICATIONS

The idea of portraying several versions of a plant, usually the flower, but sometimes other forms such as the fruits or leaves or cones, can make for some intriguing image making. The theme of illustrating a group of hybrids or cultivars has its own history bound up with publications, and the rise in popularity of horticulture as a hobby. The introduction of new species, developments in hybridization and most of all for fashions in ornamentals, gave a variety of plants a mass market. Many of these plants had their own heyday when they would be seen everywhere. Some we can still see today, but others are almost forgotten. This was the world of the plant catalogue, where you could browse at your leisure and make your choice, or buy horticultural journals to let you know what was new, interesting and fashionable.

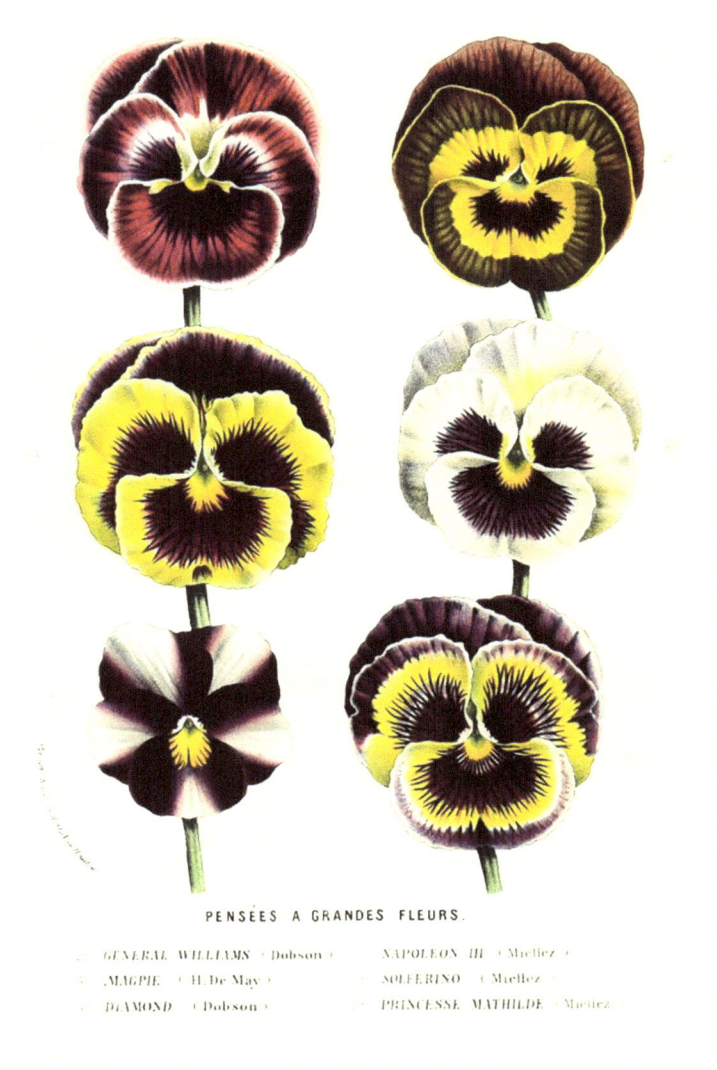

Image of Pansy varieties from the horticultural journal 'Flowers of the Greenhouses and Gardens of Europe.' 1845-1888

PENSÉES A GRANDES FLEURS.

GENERAL WILLIAMS (Dobson)   NAPOLEON III (Muellez)
MAGPIE (H. De May)   SOLFERINO (Muellez)
DIAMOND (Dobson)   PRINCESSE MATHILDE (Muellez)

THE HORTICULTURAL INDUSTRY

The horticultural industry constantly produces new versions of plants and as time goes by, preferences for specific plants change. A broad list of plants that had their heyday could include: Hyacinths, Anemonies, Petunias and Ranunculus, Chrysanthemums, Cyclamens, Pansies, Hollyhocks, Carnations and Polyanthus, Auriculars and Calceolarias. Very few gardens between the world wars were without their Dahlias and Sweet Peas. Roses of course, are a perennial favorite, but even they have had their own glory days from the floribundas to the hybrid teas.

FLORILEGIA

The publication of florilegia began in the early 1600's. Previously plants were valued primarily for their medicinal and culinary uses. But the Renaissance began an aesthetic revolution that included plants, and they began to be appreciated for their beauty and visual appeal. This happened with the rise of science and its need to classify and understand. It coincided with European countries establishing trade routes and expanding their empires. This made it possible for royal and wealthy patrons to import exotic plants. In time these beautiful species of plants, flowers, and fruits led to the development of a new concept in gardening - the "flower garden." These gardens were planted solely to display plants for their aesthetic value, instead of growing for practical purposes. For wealthy and influential people the garden gave pleasure as well as status. As printing techniques advanced, owners of such gardens and botanic gardens began to commission artists to record their plant collections in Florilegia or 'flower books'. They were generally books of the cultivated plants of these status gardens, designed to be beautiful books and usually had minimal text, emphasizing the name of the plant and of course the illustrations of flowers. They flourished further into the 17th century when more rare and exotic plants were arriving from new locations. Another type of Florilegia was created to record plants gathered on expeditions to far locations and a third kind that were published dedicated to plants from specific localities.

FAMOUS FLORILEGIA

GRAND GARDENS:

Hortus Eystettensis 1613. Basilius Besler

One of the most famous books dedicated to a garden is the Hortus Eytettensis, a florilegium that contains 367 engraved plates depicting more than 100 flowers from 'The Garden of Eichstätt'.

In 1611, the Prince Bishop of Eichstatt in Germany commissioned the florilegium to record hundreds of his favourite flowers, plants from around the world, from the spectacular garden he had created at his palace in Bavaria. A feature of this book is that the plants are presented according to the seasons.

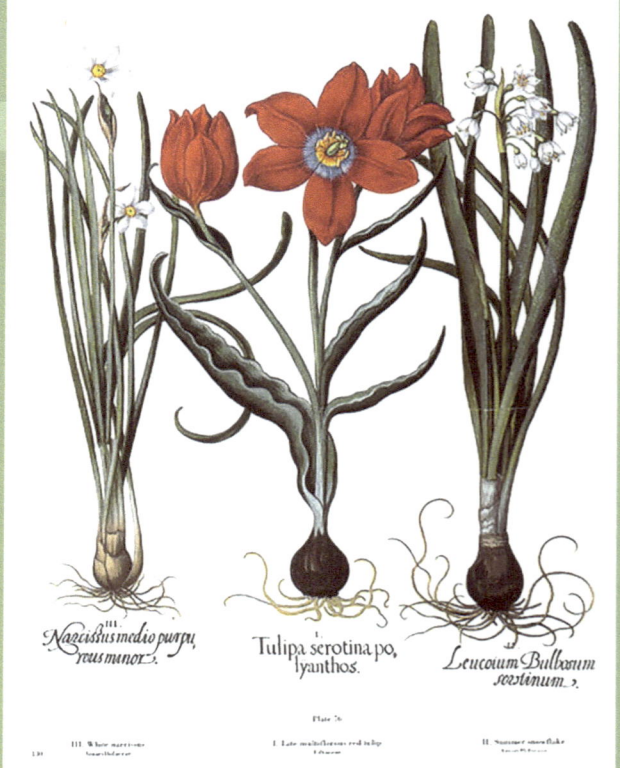

Hortus Eystenttensis. A page of flowering bulbs.

GEOGRAPHIC:

Flora Graeca Sibthorpiana. 1806 -1840
10 Volumes. John Sibthorp and Ferdinand Bauer.

The Flora Graeca was a result of a survey by John Sibthorp and Ferdinand Bauer, from March 1786 to December 1787. It was undertaken to identify medicinal plants used in Greece in the eastern Mediterranean. Sibthorp collected and described, while Bauer made dried specimens and produced colour-coded sketches. Bauer created around a thousand annotated sketches, which are now regarded as one of the finest examples of botanical illustration. The botanical descriptions and the finely crafted illustrated work was of both scientific and horticultural interest, and were to become highly regarded. Sibthorp had originally gone to Vienna, to study a copy of a classical botanical text by Dioscorides, and it was here that he first met Ferdinand Bauer.

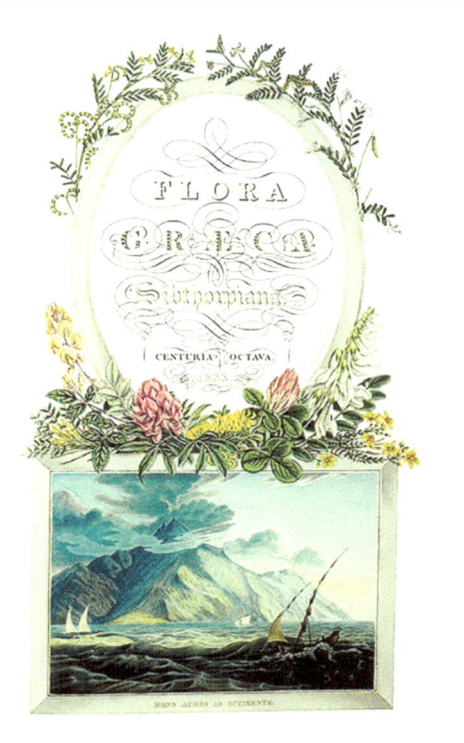

Front Cover. Volume 8. Flora Graeca

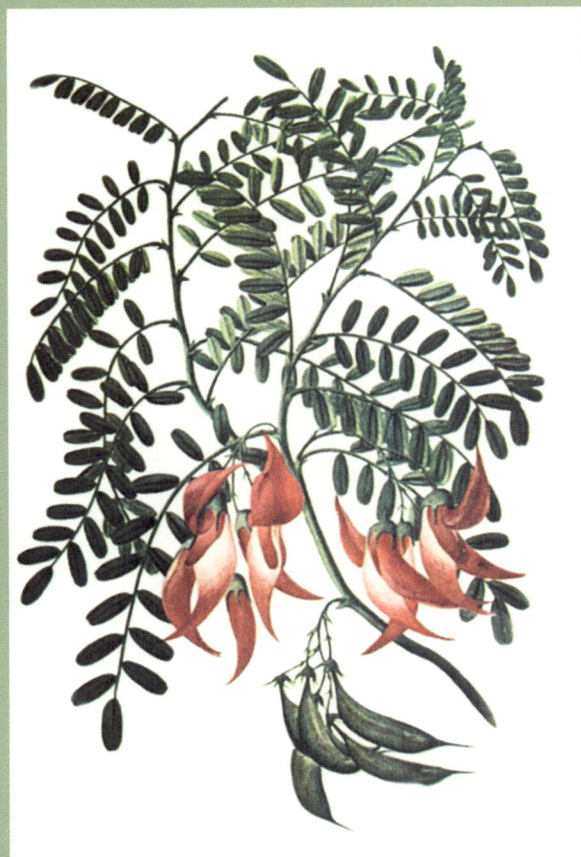

Clianthus puniceus. Engraving based on Sydney Parkinsons' work

VOYAGES OF DISCOVERY:

Banks Florilegium
Banks Florilegium records the plants collected by Sir Joseph Banks and Daniel Solander and painted by Sydney Parkinson, while they accompanied Captain James Cook on his voyage around the world between 1768 and 1771. They collected plants in Madeira, Brazil, Tierra del Fuego, the Society Islands, New Zealand, Australia and Java. Bank's and Solander's specimens were studied and drawn aboard the HM Endeavour by Sydney Parkinson. Unfortunately he died on the voyage and the finished watercolours were subsequently produced by a team of artists using Parkinson's work. It took 18 engravers to produce the copperplate line engravings from 743 completed watercolours. However the Florilegium was not actually printed until the 1980's when a complete colour edition was produced as 100 sets in 34 parts.

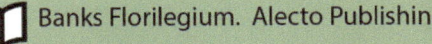 Banks Florilegium. Alecto Publishing 1980

CONTEMPORARY FLORILEGIA

Recent times have seen the development of modern versions of Florilegia. The idea of taking part in creating a modern Florilegium can be an attractive proposition. It can be a great antidote to the usual lonesome life of an artist. It is a totally different experience to take part in a group project, and you are bound to learn something along the way.

The reasons for developing a collection of specific plants can be varied. There could be ready access to a botanic garden or a heritage garden, or a desire to record the plants of a specific habitat or are endemic to a certain area.

Just as in the past some modern Florilegia are destined to be kept in institutions and only to be seen in special circumstances, such as specified exhibitions, or by special request. Many contemporary florllegia rely on the gifting of works and some even insist on giving up copyrights. This can be a lot to ask, from an illustrator of a work so long in the making, and taking advantage of a high level of expertise.

Many parts of the world have ecology issues of sustainability and endangerment and for several new florilegia in the making this is the central theme of their collection, and that has to be a good thing.

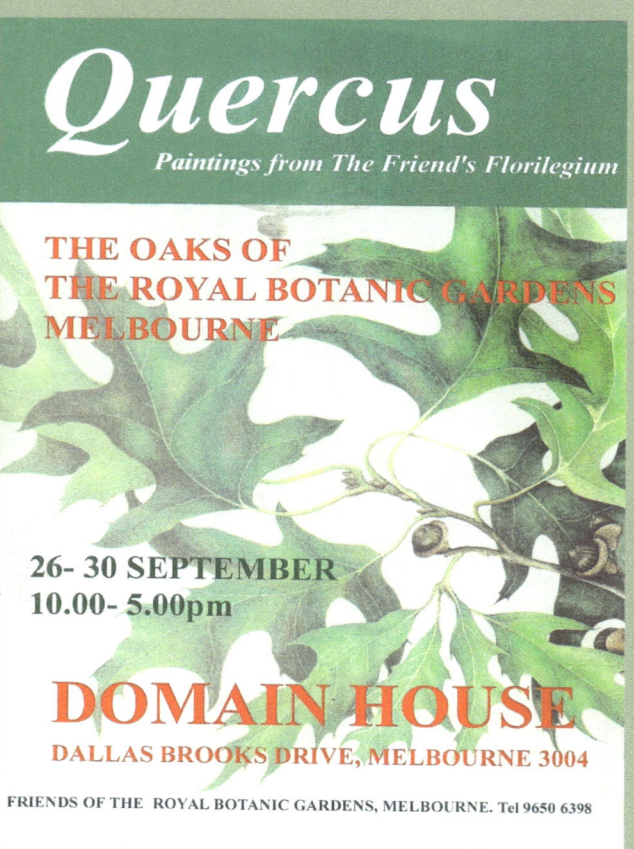

Poster for the 'Quercus' exhibition which featured works of mature oaks, from around the world in The Royal Botanic Gardens. Melbourne. Australia. Florilegium held at the Melbourne Herbarium.

Quercus palustris. Watercolour

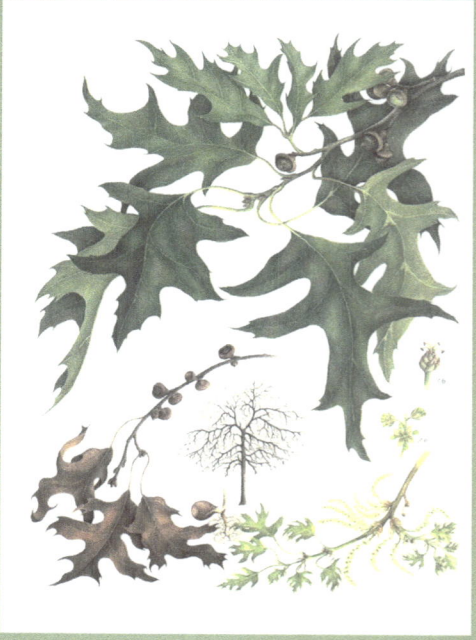

ACCESSIBILITY OF CONTEMPORARY FLORILEGIA

Sheffield Botanic Gardens Florilegium. United Kingdom
An archive of botanical illustrations of the plants of the
Sheffield Botanical Gardens.

Archived originals held at the
University of Sheffield Library.

*The Florilegium Society at the Royal Botanic Garden
Sydney.* Australia
A collection of paintings of significant plants growing in
the estates of the Royal Botanic Gardens & Domain Trust.

Originals art archived at Royal
Botanic Gardens and Domain Trust.

Chelsea Physic Gardens Florilegium. United Kingdom
The Florilegium Society records in paintings and drawings,
the plants growing in the Chelsea Physic Garden. London.

Artwork held at The Garden Archive.
Chelsea Physic Garden.

Highgrove Florilegium. United Kingdom
The Highgrove Florilegium of botanical illustrations is a
record of plants in the garden of Charles, Prince of Wales
at Highgrove House in Gloucestershire.

Florilegium published as a Two
Volume Ltd Edition Publication.
175 Numbered sets.

Sonoran Desert Florilegium. Arizona. U.S.A
A florilegium to document plants native to the Sonoran
Desert Region.

Online Collection of Digital images

The Friends Illustrated Garden. The Friends of the Royal
Botanic Gardens, Melbourne.
A collection of botanic illustrations kept as digital images
selected for inclusion from the bi- annual exhibitions.

Copies of images held and available
to the Friends of the Royal Botanic
Gardens. Melbourne.

The Eden Project Florilegium Society. Cornwall. UK
A record of the plants from The Eden Project and from
Cornwall, using traditional methods of botanical illustration.

Original artwork held in archive.

The digital world of today opens up extraordinary possibilities unheard of in the past. The images of a
florilegia can be seen by far more people as a digital file, available to many than work that is archived.
Of course this would depend on the ultimate purpose of the florilegium.
  The Sonoran Desert Florilegium is an online collection of digital images of botanical art that reaches
a far wider audience than a curated collection of physical artworks. With an online collection, visitors
can view the works of the Florilegium, zoom in to see intricate plant details, follow links to the artists' other
works, and read interpretive materials. All of which can have benefits for participating artists.

A FLORILEGIUM OF TREES

Taking part with a group to create a collection of works on a theme, can be a great way to extend your botanical illustration experience. It is enjoyable to part of a group of like minded people. The work may require a different approach to your usual way of working and there is always something to learn along the way. There can be many reasons to create a modern florilegium. It could be the access to a botanic garden or a heritage garden, or there could be an area of specific plant diversity nearby. There could be a wish to document a particular species, such as the Oaks illustrated on the preceding page.

People do find it difficult to gift an artwork to a collection that has taken such a long time to create to a specific standard. But the technology of the contemporary world can make it more useful to keep images as a digital file and then the artwork can be retained or sold in the normal way.

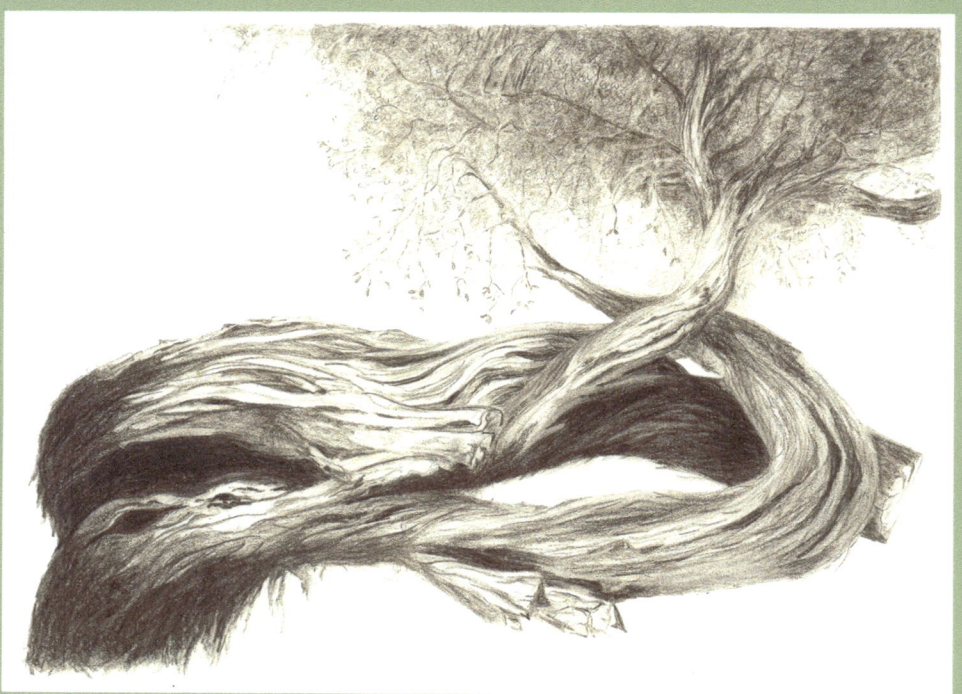

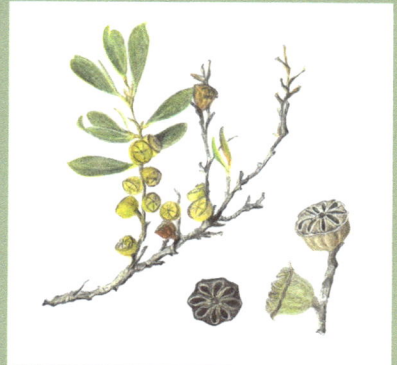

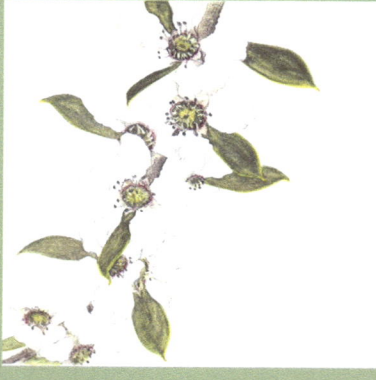

Above: Carole Barwick.
Leptospermum laevigatum
Monotone study. Burnt umbre conte crayon

Below: Carole Barwick.
Leptospermum laevigatum. Details
16 x 16cm. Watercolour.

Right Above: Pam Pryor.
Carica pubescens. Mountain Paw Paw. Linocut

Right Below: Dianne Kirk.
Sequoia gigantum. Giant Redwood
Monotone study. Charcoal

TREES OF THE
GEELONG BOTANIC GARDENS

The images from this page were created as part of a project to document some of the magnificent trees from the Geelong Botanic Gardens by students of School of Botanical Art. The approach taken was to emphasize the artist's viewpoint rather than the more usual Linnean approach. The finished works included full sized monotones of the whole tree, using a range of media from conte crayons, coloured wax pencils and charcoals. There were also small works which focused of details, done in a small square format. It included an exploration of other media such as the linocut and scratchboard.

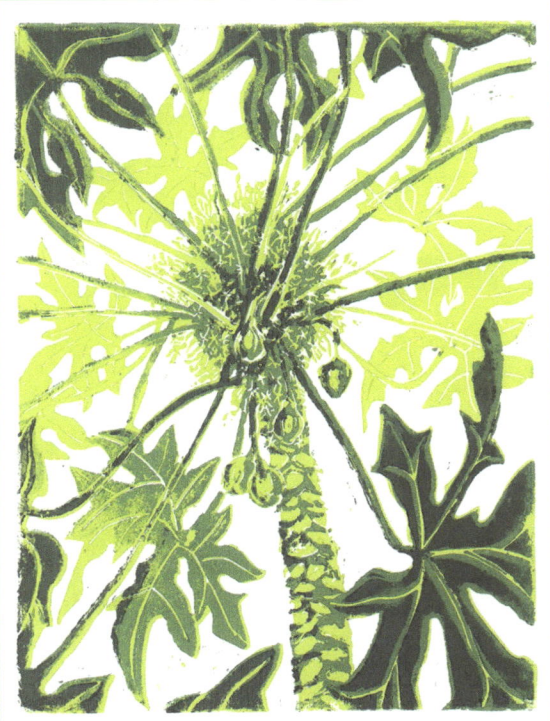

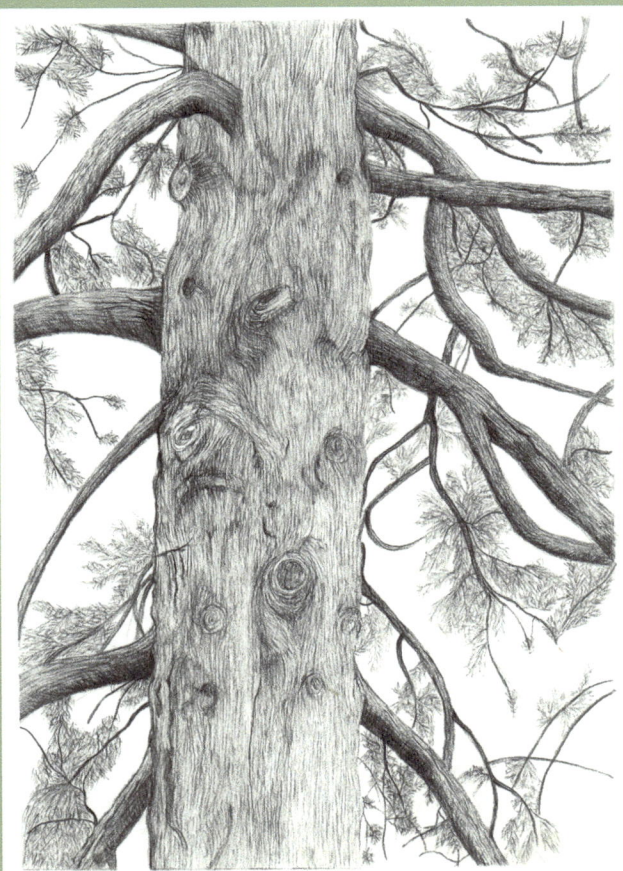

The works on these pages were designed to form part of a digital collection that could be used in many different ways for the benefit of the Geelong Botanic Gardens, now and in the future. The first use of these images was to form the basis of a book documenting the Gardens as a source of inspiration to artists. The book was published in 2016, presenting a unique artists view of a garden, well known to many local residents.

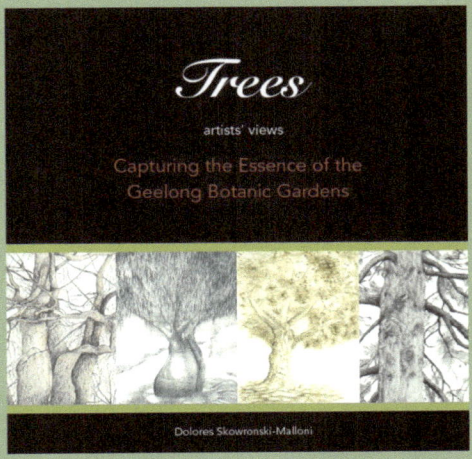

PASSIONS AND MANIAS   Pteridomania - Fern fever

We don't usually think of horticulture as a matter of fashion, but it most certainly is. The history of horticulture is full of fashions and crazes, as new plants came to be known and became popular to a wide public. But there have been times when a mere trend transformed into something quite different and became a 'craze'. Nothing illustrates this so much as the Victorian obsession for cultivating ferns. This 'fern madness' was christened 'Pteridomania'.

Incredibly this craze lasted for over 30 years. Ferns had been rare in England, until the nineteenth century, when they began to be imported by botanists who travelled to places such as Jamaica or Australia. But it was difficult to successfully mass reproduce these tender ferns in these colder climes. That is until the amateur naturalist Nathaniel Ward devised a method of raising the plants in 'closely glazed cases.' The discovery that plants could survive very well if provided with a moist substrate and enclosed in glass, set the craze on its course. In time this gave rise to fern houses, conservatories and glass cases. The fern became fashionable and popular amongst all classes of society. The low light in many European houses made them well suited to the typical Victorian home. In time most botanic gardens developed their own ferneries.

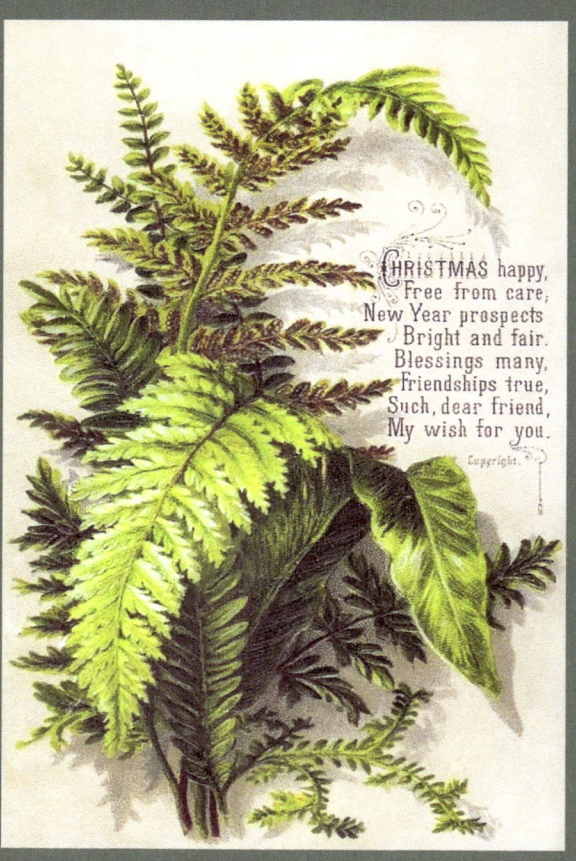

CHRISTMAS happy,
Free from care,
New Year prospects
Bright and fair.
Blessings many,
Friendships true,
Such, dear friend,
My wish for you.

Copyright.

THE FERN MOTIF

The beauty of the feathery foliage of ferns influenced the decor of many a private home. Victorian decorative arts presented the fern motif in architectural design, in carpets and textiles in pottery, glass, metal, textiles, wood, printed paper, and sculpture, china and glass ware, and dresses – not to mention the design of greetings cards to send to fellow fern admirers. Of all the many passions and vogues in nineteenth century gardening and natural history, none was as long lasting or as wide reaching as the fern fever of Victorian times.

IN PURSUIT

The interest in ferns had begun in the late 1830s but the main period of popularity of ferns extended from the 1850s until the 1890s. when it began to attract increasing numbers of amateur and professional botanists.The outdoor pursuit of 'fern hunting', was considered a healthy pastime and also educational and moral. It was of course coincidental that this provided an opportunity of fraternizing with the opposite sex in the idyll of the verdant countryside. Books on ferns were in constant demand, along with specialist periodicals which encouraged collectors to join fern societies and visit botanical gardens. New discoveries were published in popular botanical periodicals.

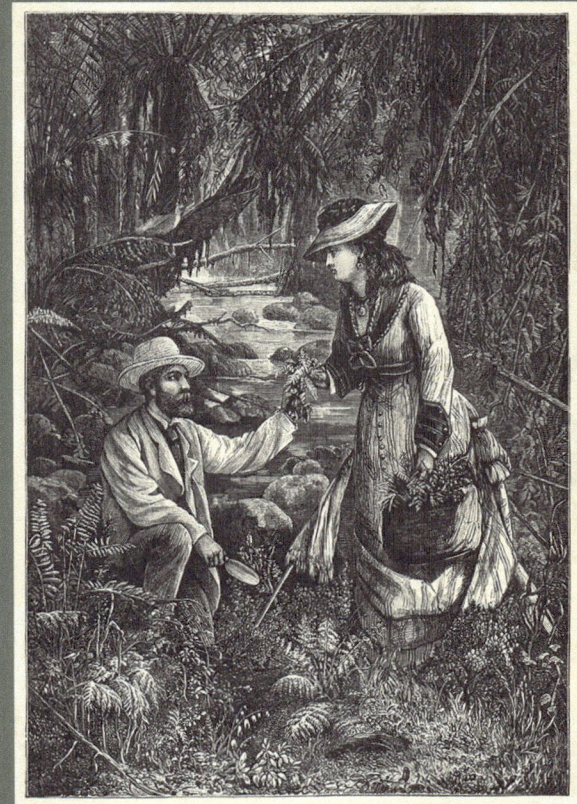

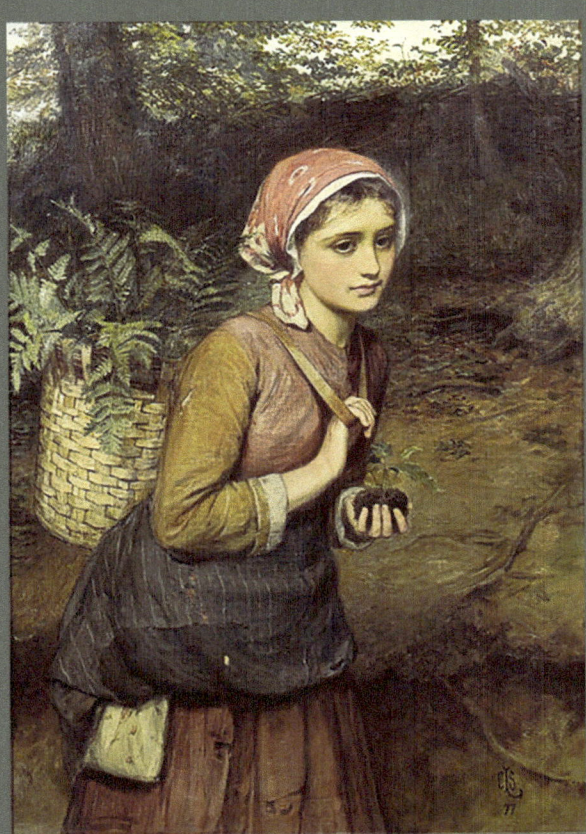

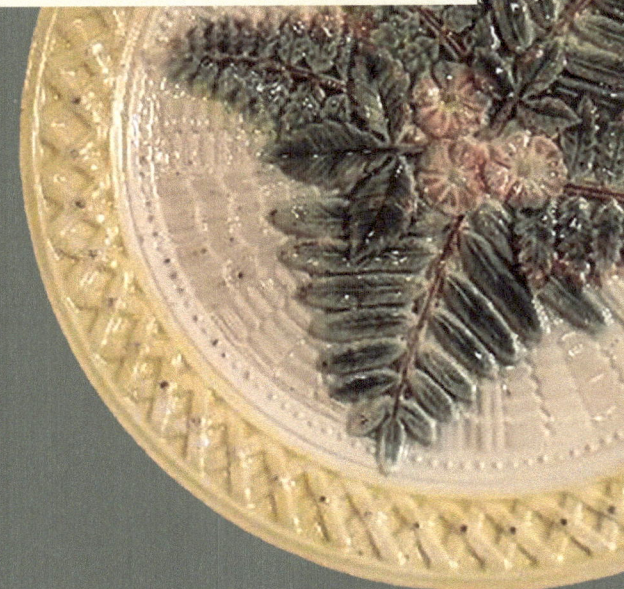

Right: Majolica plate. 1880
Abovet: The Fern Gatherers in Australia. Engraving
Left: The Fern Gatherer. Charles Sillem Lidderdale. 1877
Left opposite: Fern Christmas Card. 1875

FERNS

The frenzied fashion for ferns has long faded away. That's a good thing as you don't have to battle crowds to get close to them. But once you have experienced their charm you can understand what a wonderful subject they can be. There is something about their feathery daintiness and the beauty of their unfurling fronds and their fresh greenness that makes them an interesting subject to explore. Ferns can be huge and woody such as the tree ferns - Cyathea, Dicksonia - or medium sized, fleshy and clumping such as the Pteris and Blechnum ferns or fine and delicate such as the Maiden-hair ferns.

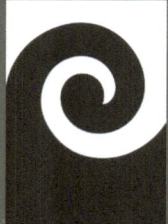

THE CROZIER

The coiled frond of a fern is called a crozier or fiddlehead. It can be a very potent image and has become iconic in certain fields. This is never more so than in New Zealand where it is a very important symbol In Māori culture, where it is called a Koru. The word 'Koru' is the Maori word for "bight" or "loop" and refers to the unfolding new shoots of a silver fern frond. The circular movements towards an inner coil refers to 'going back to the beginning'. The unfurling frond itself is symbolic of new life, rebirth or awakening, the very spirit of rejuvenation. It forms the basis of design for tattoo carving and the painted rafters called Kowhaihai.

Kowhaihai are the traditional painted patterns that appear on the inside rafters of Maori meeting houses in New Zealand. They are always elaborate curvilinear designs, often based on the looping "koru". The simple basis of this motif can be worked into a wide range of pattern variation, usually painted in natural pigments of black, red and white. So significant is the image of the Koru that it has come to represent New Zealand itself.

Kowhaiwhai
Rafter design.

Rita Parkinson. Crozier form. *Asplenium bulbiferum.* Hen and Chicken fern.

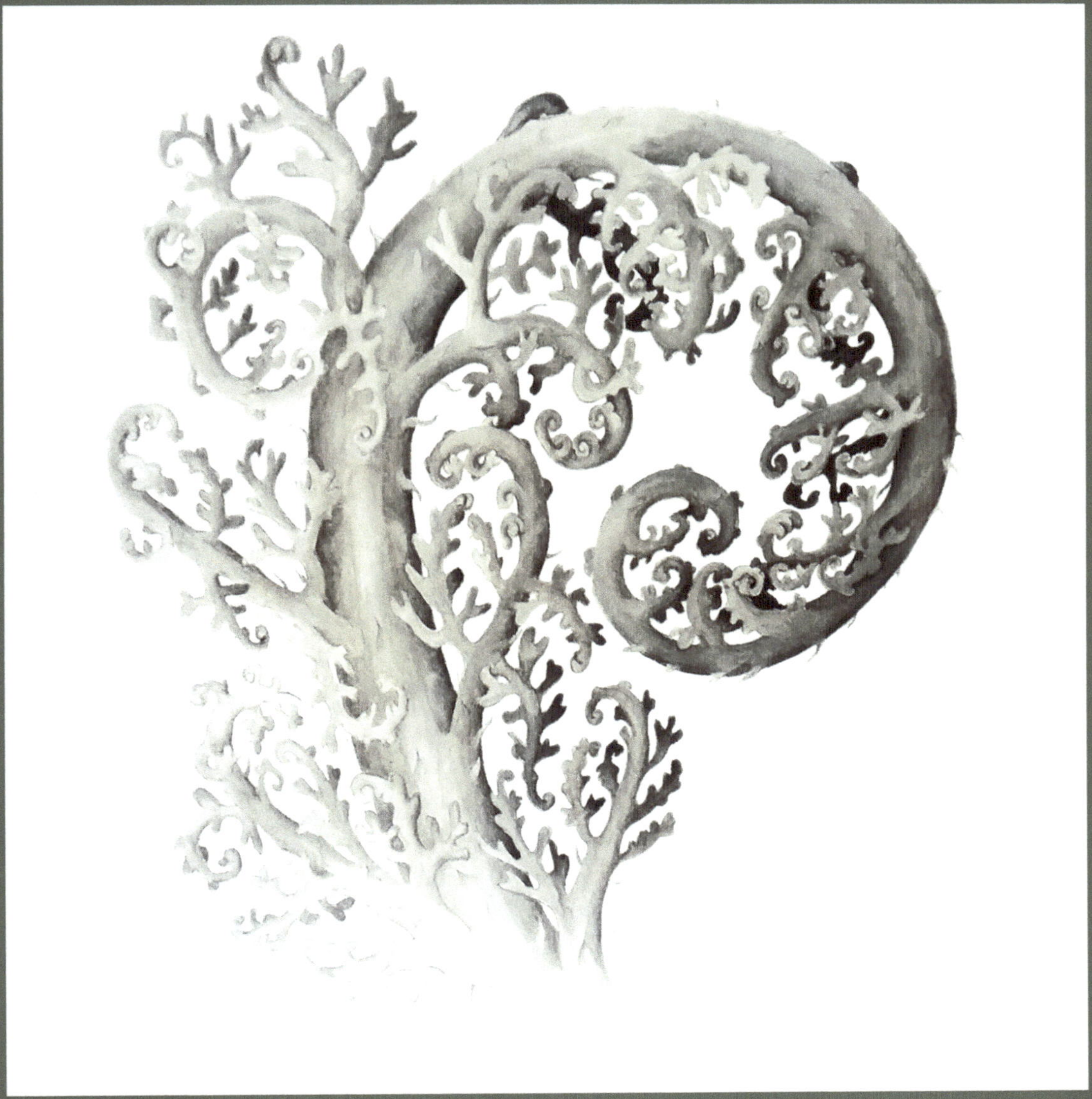

Ferns are an ancient type of plant. The first examples are found in rocks of the Paleozoic period. There are over 10,000 species of ferns worldwide. They do not flower, but instead reproduce by means of spores that can be observed on the under-surface of the fertile fronds as brown or yellow patches. These patches may be lines, dots or markings spread in a specific pattern or they may be found as a continuous line around the margin of the frond. The patches are groups of spore sacs which contain spores. These shapes and patterns are important as they may be used to identify different families of ferns.

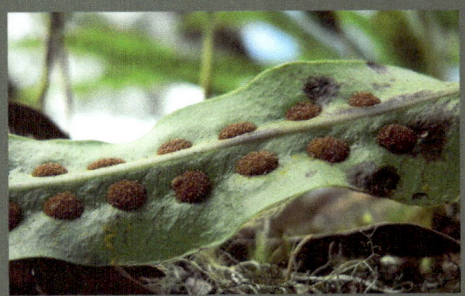

PASSIONS AND MANIAS Tulipomania

The Great Dutch trading obsession with tulips began in Holland when tulips were introduced to the Netherlands from the Ottoman Empire in the mid-1500s. The mania for tulips which lasted from 1633-37, evolved in a very different way to the later 'Pteridomania'. The Victorian fern obsession remained essentially a horticultural interest, with a further influence on design. It never entered the rarified world of high finance, in the way that the tulip mania did.

AN OBSESSION

The interest in tulips began as a garden enthusiasm, until a rare phenomenom occured that caused freakish breakouts of patterns such as stripes, streaks, feathering and flame-like effects all in a variety colours. These fantastic tulips could then be propegated. This caused an unusual level of excitement and expectation. It was not long before speculators noticed that demand for the most beautiful flowers was pushing up their price and a trade in tulips soon evolved where they were traded for ever increasing sums. At the height of the craze, for almost a year, rare bulbs changed hands many times for incredible prices. Single flowers were being sold for more than the cost of a house. Thus began the Dutch love affair with tulips that between 1633-37 caused a tulip bubble or "Tulip Mania". Fortunes were made overnight, but eventually were lost when, without warning, the market collapsed with disastrous consequences for those directly involved but also for others as it affected the whole economy.

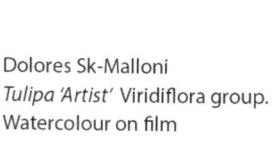

Dolores Sk-Malloni
Tulipa 'Artist' Viridiflora group.
Watercolour on film

THE SEMPER AUGUSTUS

The famous tulip named the Semper Augustus became the most expensive bulb sold during tulipomania. Described as a Rosen, with blood-red flames vividly streaked on a white ground, and flakes and flashes of the same color at the edge of the pedals, Semper Augustus was recognized as an extraordinary flower, and one renowned at the time for its superlative decorations and rarity. Because Semper Augustus was scarce, it was very desirable and so it was expensive. This rarity was reflected in the price. In 1633, one Semper Augustus was said to have sold for 5,500 guilders, and in 1637, just before the crash, a price of 10,000 guilders was asked - an exorbitant amount that would have purchased a grand house on the most fashionable canal in Amsterdam, or clothed and fed an entire Dutch family for half a lifetime.

Tulips have remained a perennial favorite subject for botanical artists. Perhaps it is something about their basically minimal form, allied with their appealing colours and patterns that still has the power to fascinates us.

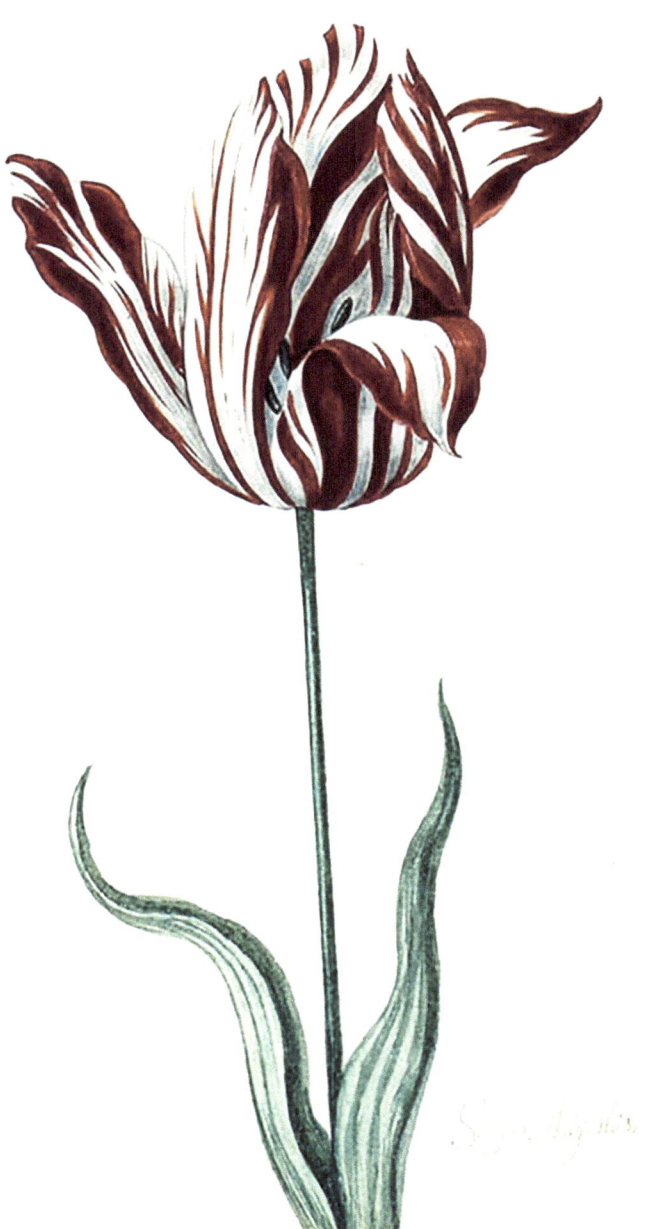

Tulipa semper augustus Anonomous

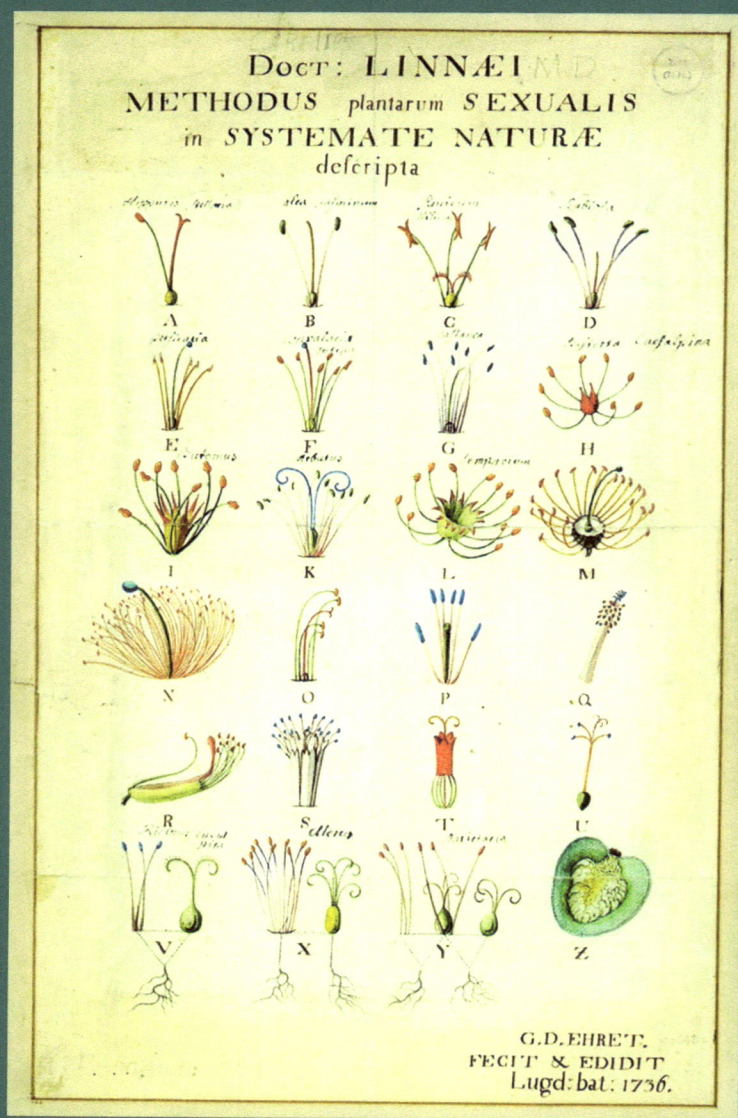

Georg Ehret 1708-1770

Systema Naturae . The Sexual System of Plants. Carl Linneas. Published in 1756

TAXONOMIC ILLUSTRATION

A painting that depicts a plant with an emphas on the features of identification, through the small parts of flowers is the cornerstone of botanical illustration.

  The classic style, commonly used has a long history, but essentially began with Georg Dionysius Ehret 1708 -1770, the German-born artist. He became one of the most influential botanical artists of all time through his development of the Linnaean style of botanical illustration. Ehret worked closely with Carl Linnaeus, the founder of modern taxonomy, and the style of botanical art that he developed is still in use today.

THE CONVENTIONS OF THE LINNEAN STYLE

A painting in the classic Linnean style will depict the plant with an emphasis on the visual differences of the small parts of flowers necessary for identification. These parts are usually small, so he devised the method of using expanded views of these minute parts. The convention developed to present these elements lined up at the bottom of the plate. This method only became possible through the development of the lens and consequently the microscope.
To produce this kind of illustration today will depend upon good microscope and dissection skills. It is interesting to note that in the early works of this style, the conventions, so strongly insisted upon today that insist on the use of either italics or regular text, and lower and uppercase, was by no means a standard principle at this time.

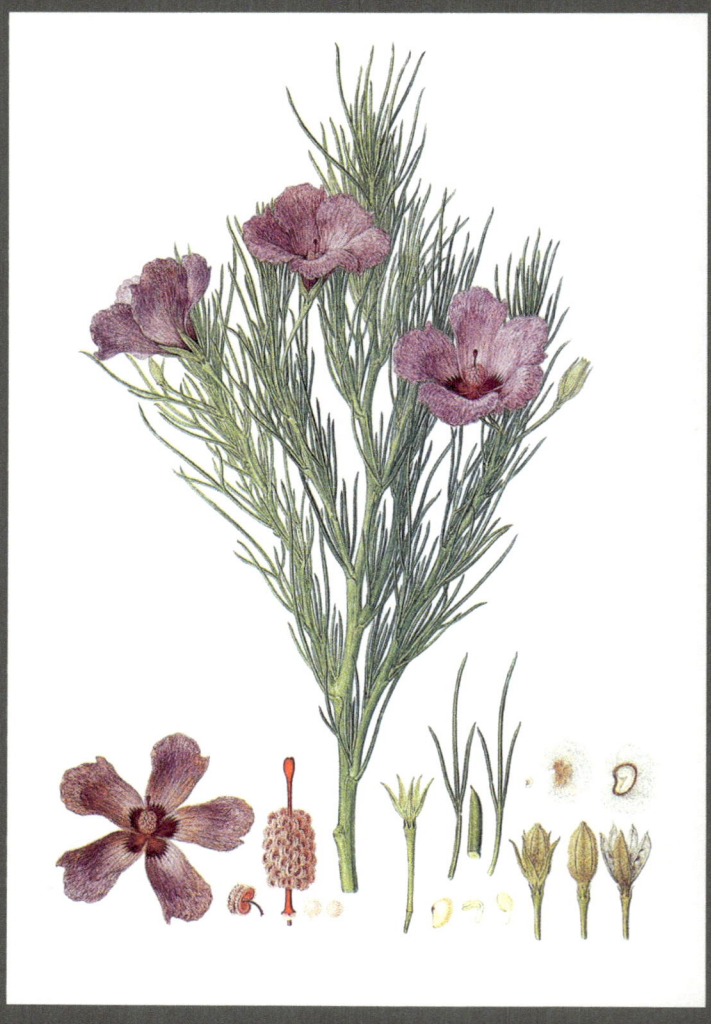

Ferdinand Bauer. *Alyogne hakeifolia*

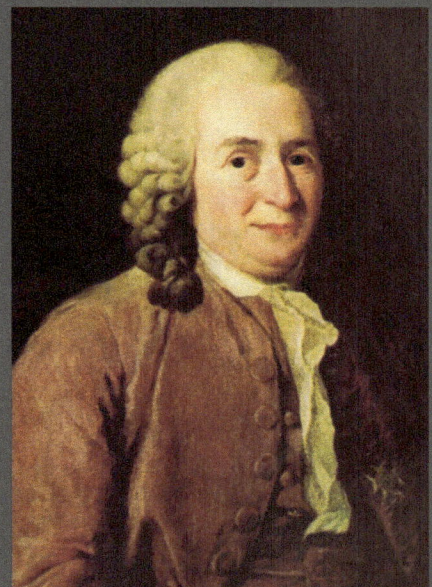

Carl Linnaeus 1707 -1778
The Father of Taxonomy

Carl Linnaeus, born in Sweden, developed the system of a hierarchy of nested groups, based on the structural differences in the smaller parts of flowers. In time this developed into the binomal latin name that we are so familiar with today. This is the descriptive form of the genus followed by a single-difference description. Eg. *Erica taxifolio*. Later adjustments needed to accommodate Darwin's theory of shared descent. This notation system is still in use today.

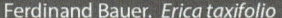

Ferdinand Bauer. *Erica taxifolio*

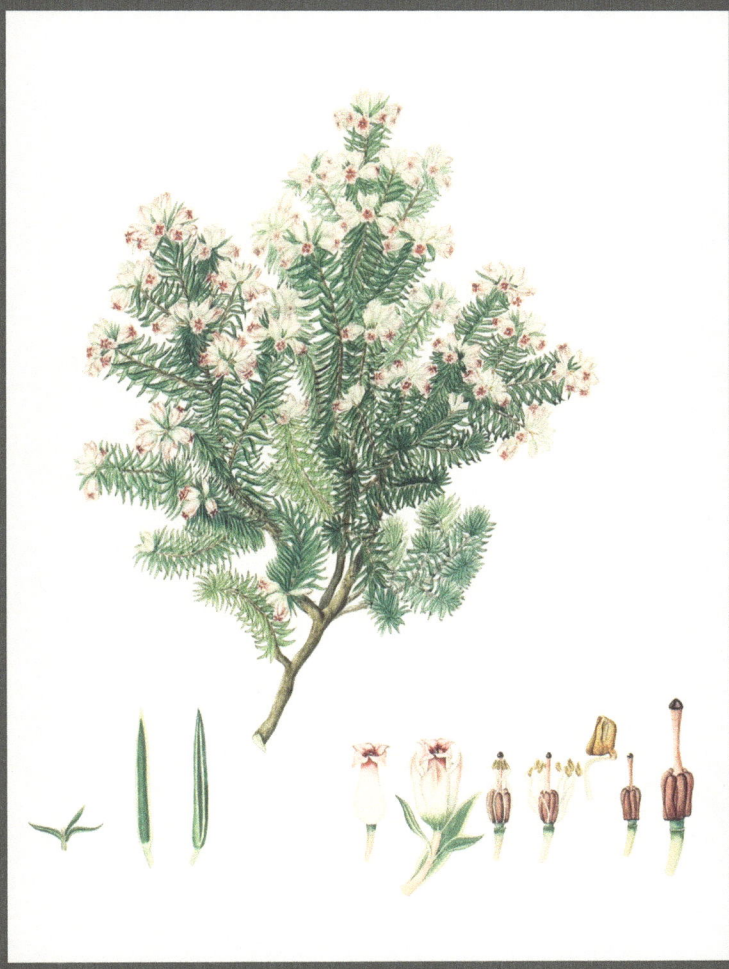

Modern biology tends to view the Linnean system of plant classification as a vestige of the past. The new field of molecular phylogenetics, the study of hereditary molecular differences mainly in DNA sequencing, that can trace a plants evolutionary trail, can essentially tell us more than the visual differences that we have relied on in the past.

FEATURES OF THE LINNEAN STYLE

The classic style of botanical illustration developed in a period when several conditions came together. Advances in printing techniques and the publishing industry were aligned to the ongoing push of science and classification, and the interests of an expanding, educated middle class. It was a time when a rush for the wealth developed from newly opened up far continents and created great empires based on commerce. The main engine of change was the development of printing technologies. The simple forms of intaglio engraving gave way to the more subtle form of the mezzotint and then to the sensitive tonality that lithography could provide. It's important here to remember that it is the engraver that was the producer of the end product, not the illustrator. All of the illustrators were well aware of this and when they created their work they had this in mind. They knew they needed to create a template that an engraver could transfer successfully.

AN AESTHETIC IDEAL COMBINED WITH SCIENCE

THE TEMPLATE

The painting was often done as a template for the engraver, essentially to be a single page in a publication. Many people would see the print but very few would see the actual painting. How it would print was vitally important. Some illustrators, such as Redouté learnt the skills of engraving, but he was an exception.

A WHITE BACKGROUND

Printing was a relatively crude process in the early part of this period and the engraved image was usually hand coloured. The subject showed up crisply when set against a white background.

A CLOSED FORMAT

The closed format would have been an automatic choice in this period. The pictorial devise of running the image out of the frame did not come into use until the 20th century.

NO THROWN SHADOWS

In most instances there were no thrown shadows. This would have been difficult to achieve effectivly in the earlier part of this period with only basic engaving techniques available. Not until the mezzotint could subtle graded shadows be produced, and later still the development of lithography delivered the most effective technique for creating subtle graduations of tone.

EYE LEVEL VIEWPOINT

The eye level viewpoint was probably a cultural attribute evolved from the old herbals.

EXPANDED VIEWS

The developments in lenses and thus microscopes made the expanded view possible. It was designed to get the important small identifying details onto a single plate. But whatever size the original painting, the engraver needed to make the expanded view details correct and understandable at the size of the final printed page.

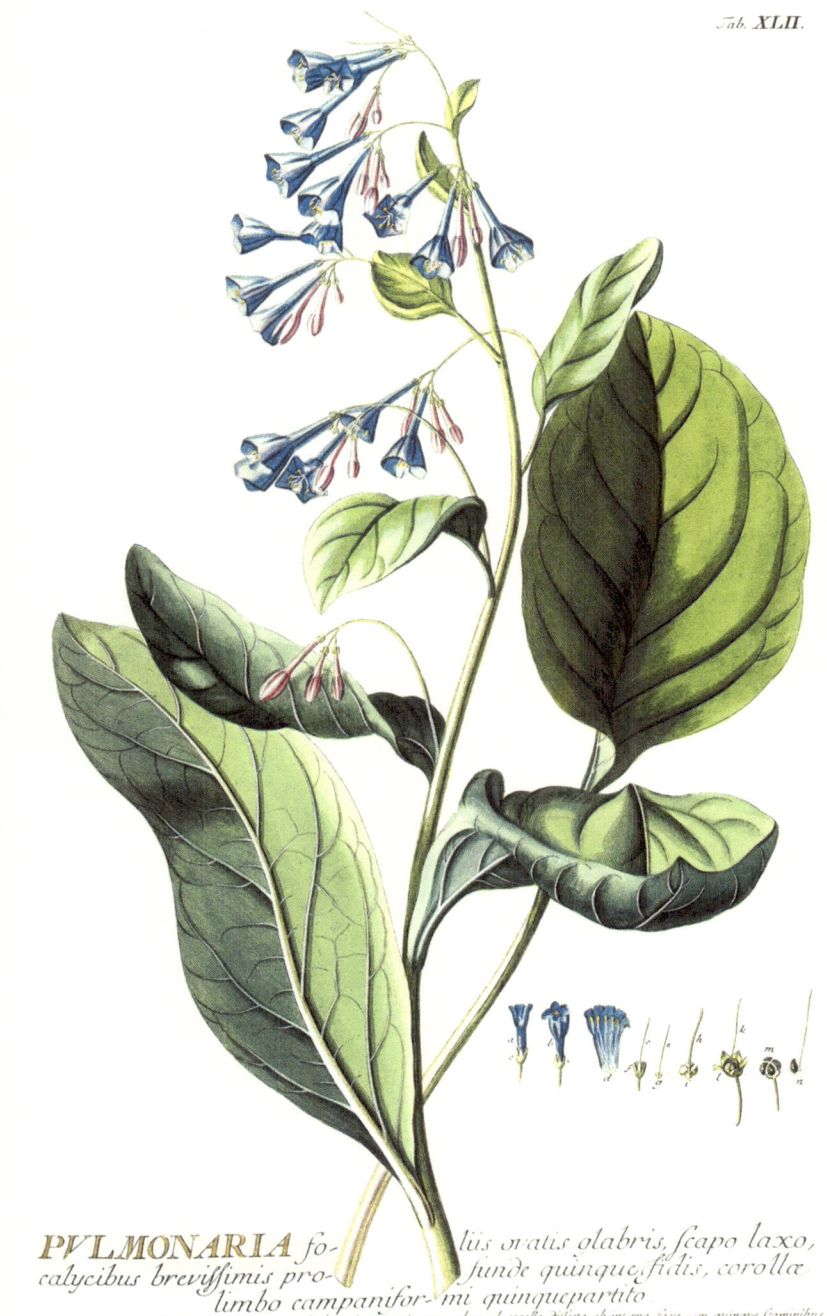

Georg Dionysis Ehret. *Pulmonaria foliis ovatis glabris*

INFLUENCES

Aesthetic ideals developed from Renaissance times were at the heart of a general approach to pictorial balance. The genesis of this attitude reached further back to the classical world and its ongoing influence running on through many art movements and cultures. The idea that beauty itself is an important component of art finds a deep resonance with many people today and perhaps partly explains the popularity of botanical illustration. The illustrators quest for beautifully rendered natural forms is an element that most people understand and appreciate today.

The basic tenets of this style were developed in the 18 Century. Printing was an expensive process and it was necessary to get all the necessary details for identification onto a compact single plate.

The traditional elements of the style, emanating from this long tradition are still the customary form of botanical illustration that we often see at exhibitions today. They employ the general precepts of this formal study, but the style has evolved into a general description of the plant. It could be intended for serious identification, but is sometimes intended more as a decorative element.

THE LINNEAN STYLE TODAY

Works done in the Linnean style or an adaptation of it, still form the greater part of works seen in botanical illustration exhibitions. And for good reasons. The style evolved in the Golden Age of Botanical Illustration and produced some of the iconic works of Botanical art. The origins of the style lie in the necessityof arranging a vast amount of very specific information onto a single copper plate. Since those times we have come to love the best examples of these formats where the necessary features were magically worked into compositions of great beauty and painterly skill.

  The Linnean style developed as a response to the expensive reproduction techniques of the times. Today the conditions are very different and the impetus isn't there to get so much information into such a compact form. Today the choice is a matter of a preference for these traditional style formats. It is often adapted for a contemporary artwork, where many of the works are intended to be mounted and framed rather than created for publication.

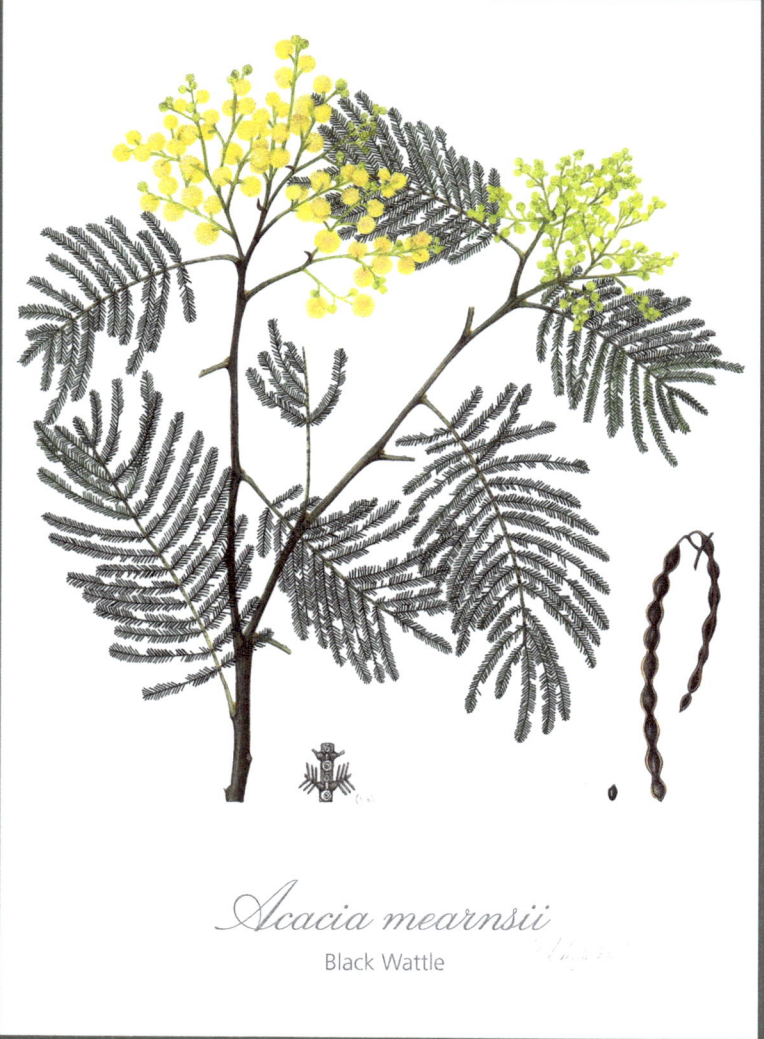

Acacia mearnsii
Black Wattle

The style evolved to be pictorially functional and just as in the past, if you want to reference this format, the crucial skill is to make good use of the format, 'the imaginary plate' to the best advantage in compositional terms.

  For many paintings created for exhibition it is not really necessary to include all the small identifying features in expanded forms, and many choose instead to focus on just some of the interesting features. The basic style taught in many botanical art courses will be an adaptation of this style, and is something to work towards. To be able to complete a plate in this manner requires the ability to do effective working drawings and some degree of skill in pre- planning and composition. A work in this format is something that most botanical illustrators will realize at some time in their career.

  At heart this is essentially a formal style and because of this, it is often seen as the most appropriate form for formal Florilegia.

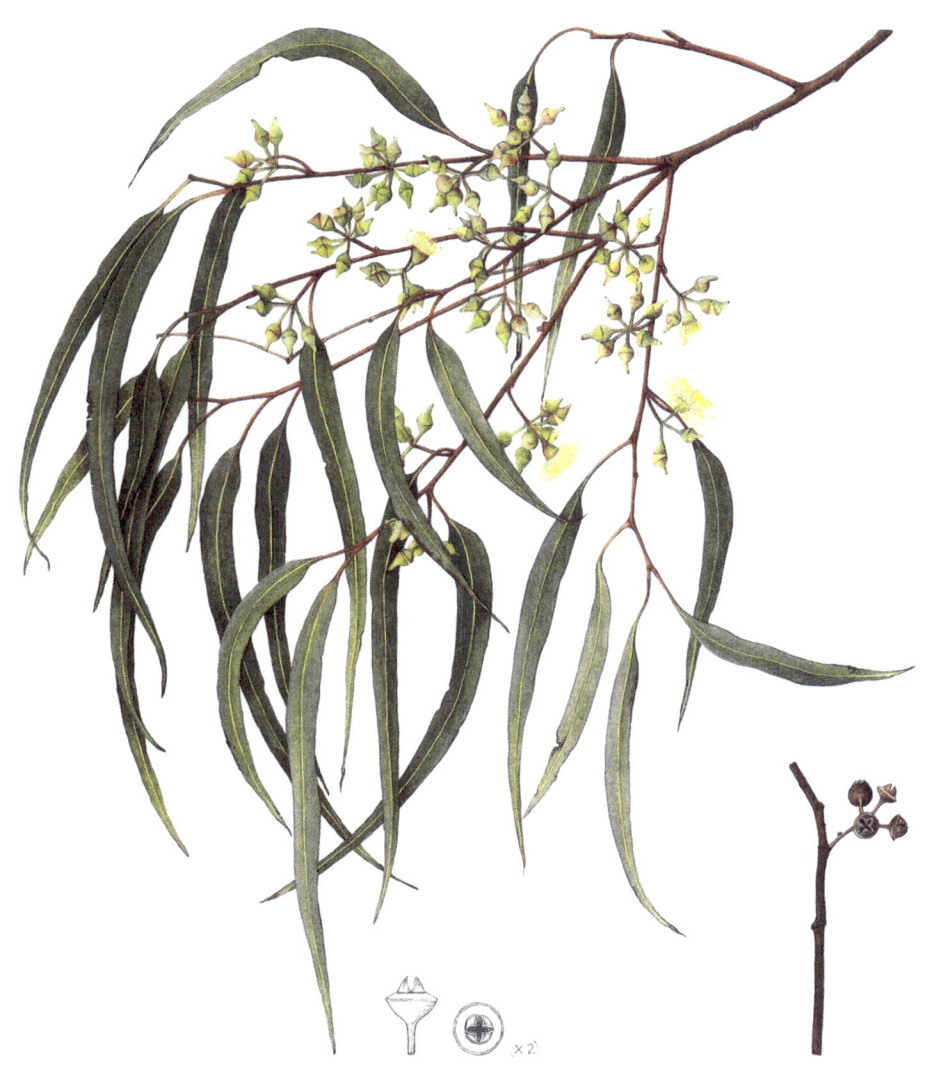

Eucalyptus camaldulensis

River Red Gum

Far left: Dolores Sk-Malloni
Acacia mearnsii
Watercolour
Left: Dolores Sk-Malloni
*Eucalyptus camaldule*nsis
Watercolour

EXPANDED VIEWS

The use of the expanded view is a part of the lexicon of botanical illustration. The origins of this technique lies in the work of illustrators such as Ferdinand Bauer and their early work with microscopes. Essentially it was a logical pictorial device invented to get all the required information onto one plate, to be printed as a single page. All of this, meant that an illustration needed to be succinct. The convention developed to line up the expanded views along the bottom of the page. Printing and publishing was a slow and expensive business in those times. The making of a plate was a laborious enterprise that would entail an engraver working from the key watercolour painting supplied by the illustrator. In the earlier period this would result in a black line engraving and others would be employed to add colour by hand. With the invention of lithography colour would be supplied by using multiple plates. Essentially using any of these techniques meant that an edition could take many years to complete.

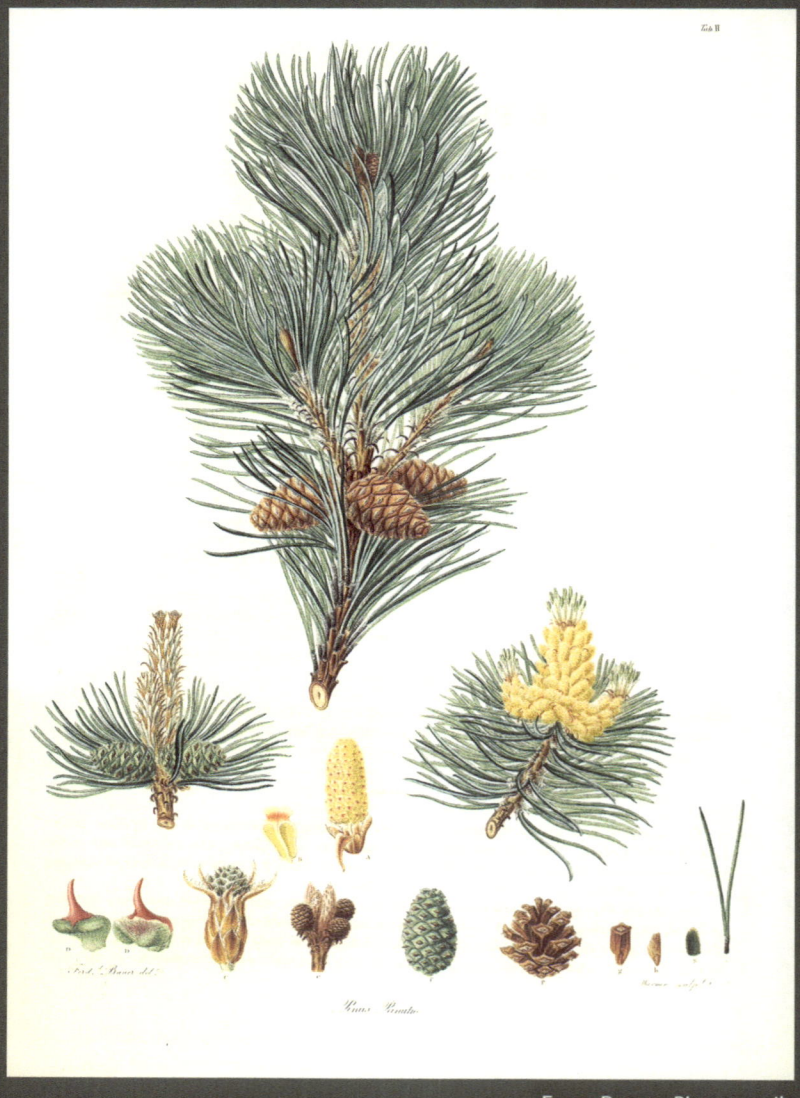

Franz Bauer. *Pinus pumilo*

Dolores Sk-Malloni *Corymbia ficifolia*. Flowering gum. Watercolour
Eucalyptus caesia. Silver Princess. Watercolour

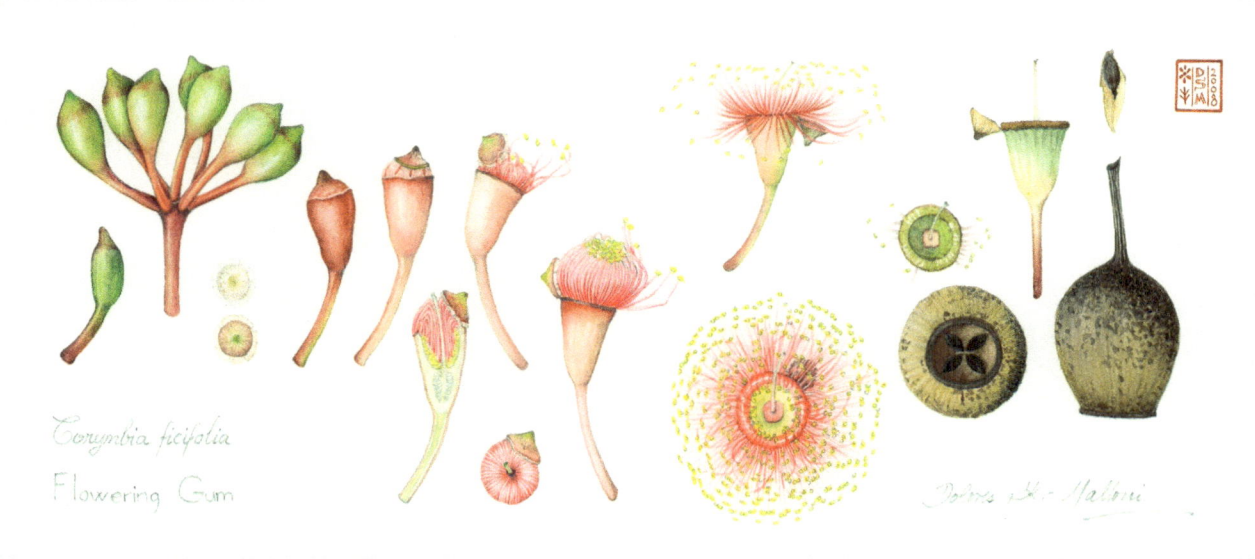

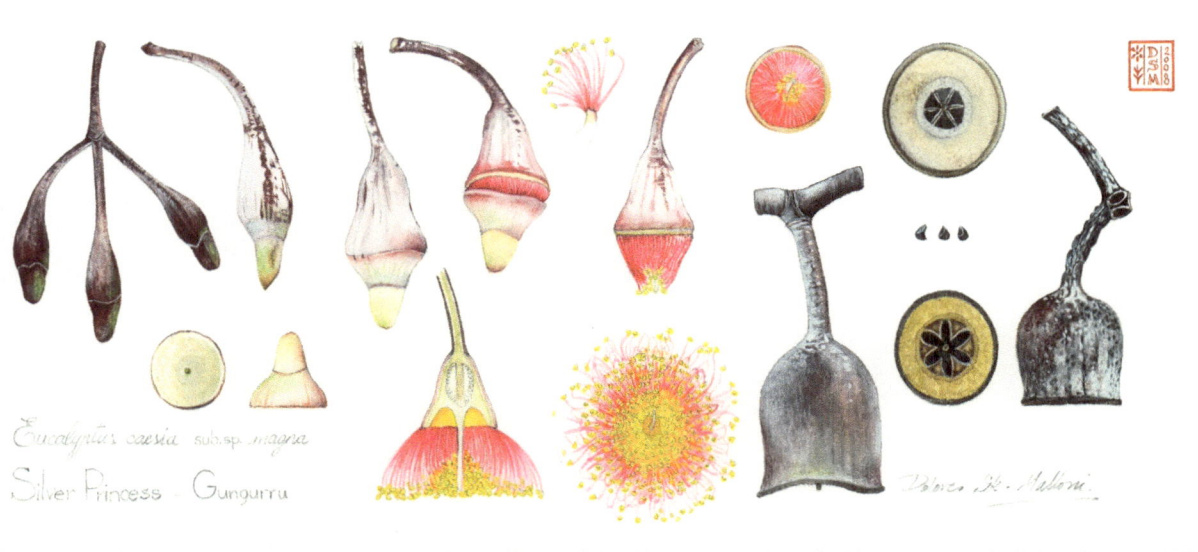

The devise of the expanded view in these two paintings is not used as an adjunct to a larger painting but as the work itself. Both works focus on a detailed description of the process of the development of eucalyptus flowers.

EXPANDED VIEWS

Enlargements of particular plant details which, in ordinary circumstances, would remain unseen by the naked eye become quite be fascinating when they are revealed to us. Plant structures, processes, forms and shapes that we don't usually perceive, are revealed and made known to us. For example an illustration of a lichen, algae and some fungi, that is rendered to size, can only tell us so much. Only when the subject is enlarged can some of the subjects specific characteristics be viewed. Given that you might choose to increase the natural size anyway, magnification could as well be X 2, X 8, or even X 20.

SEEING MORE

The conventions of Botanical illustration state that it is prefer-able render a subject to its actual size. But most plants, even those not necessarily small to begin with, can reveal many more details when they are magnified, details that cannot be properly observed when the subject is drawn to size. En-larged images have the ability to change our perceptions, even of plants we thought we knew well. It shows us that size really is relative.

 If the artist is free to choose and a much larger enlargement is possible, it's a simple fact that the greater the enlargement the more can be revealed to the human eye. And in some cases the larger the better.

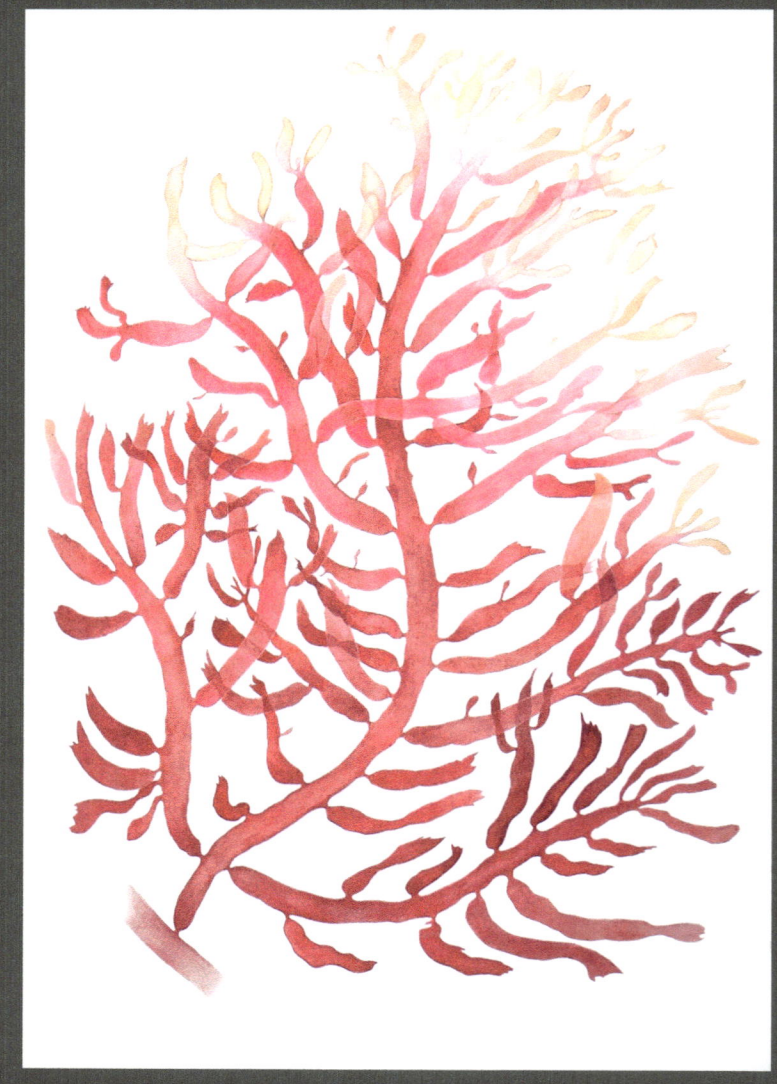

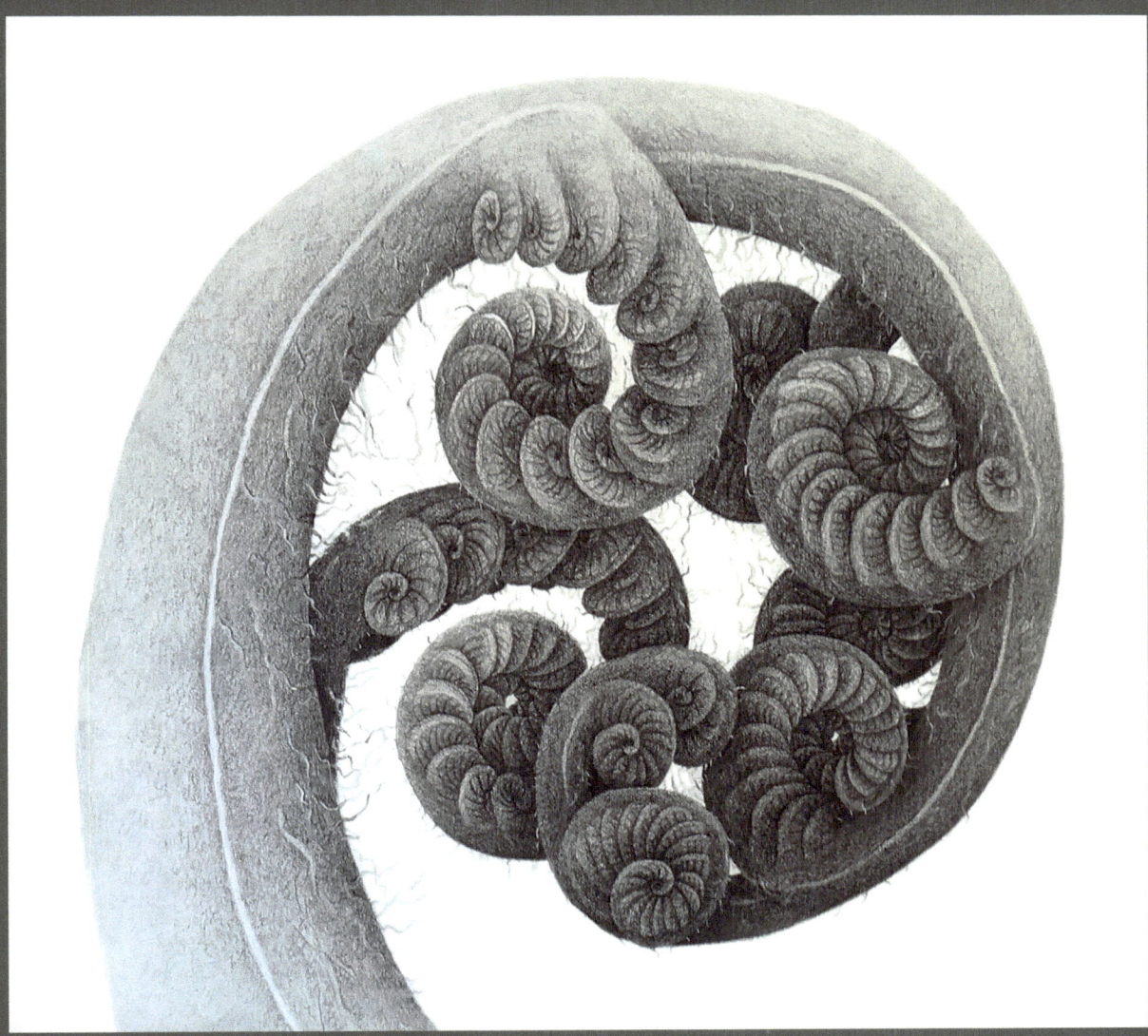

Rita Parkinson
Above: *Cyathea australis.* Fern crozier form. Black conte crayon   X 6
Left: *Nyzemenia australis.* Australian algae. Watercolour *X 5*

ECOLOGY A Question of Balance

Ecology is defined as the science of relationships between organisms and their environment. An increase of interest in ecology has meant environmental issues are now a theme in many exhibitions of contemporary botanical art. The problems of bio-diversity are best understood by appreciating the various categories of plants as they are evaluated in the ecological sense.

ENDANGERED

A plant species is classed as endangered if it exists in such small numbers that it is in danger of becoming extinct. One of the principal factors in the endangerment of a species is the destruction or pollution of its native habitat. Other factors include intentional extermination, and the accidental or intentional introduction of alien species that outcompete the native species for environmental resources.

NATIVES

Native plants are generally held to be plants that have occurred naturally, over many years in a defined area, that have become established without direct human influence. They would include trees, flowers, grasses and other plants. The word "native" should always be used with a geographic qualifier, for example "native to Australia".

ENDEMIC

An endemic plant differs from "native" species in that the latter, although they occur naturally in an area, can also be found in other areas. The term "endemic" is also relative, in that a species may be said to be endemic to one very small area or to a very large land mass, for example "endemic to Brazil".

EXOTICS

An exotic is an introduced species, usually by means of human activity. It is a plant that is living outside its native distributional range. The huge interest in horticulture means there is a high rate of exotic introductions in the modern world. This places a burden on native plants that are often unable to compete with these uncontrolled intruders.

NATURALIZED

Naturalization is the process by which non-native plants spread into the wild and their reproduction is sufficient to maintain its population. Well established exotics are sometimes said to be naturalized, but that does not make them native, no matter how long ago they were introduced.

BIO-DIVERSITY

A reduction of bio-diversity world wide is a major concern today. It is a paradox that at the same time, we are still discovering new plants, as the newly identified are added to the number of known plant species of the world. Today the known species are estimated at 250,000 and the predicted final total is estimated to be over 300,000. So the story about newly identified plants goes on concurently with the the story of loss. At the present time the estimated loss is of 30% of plant bio-diversity by 2050.

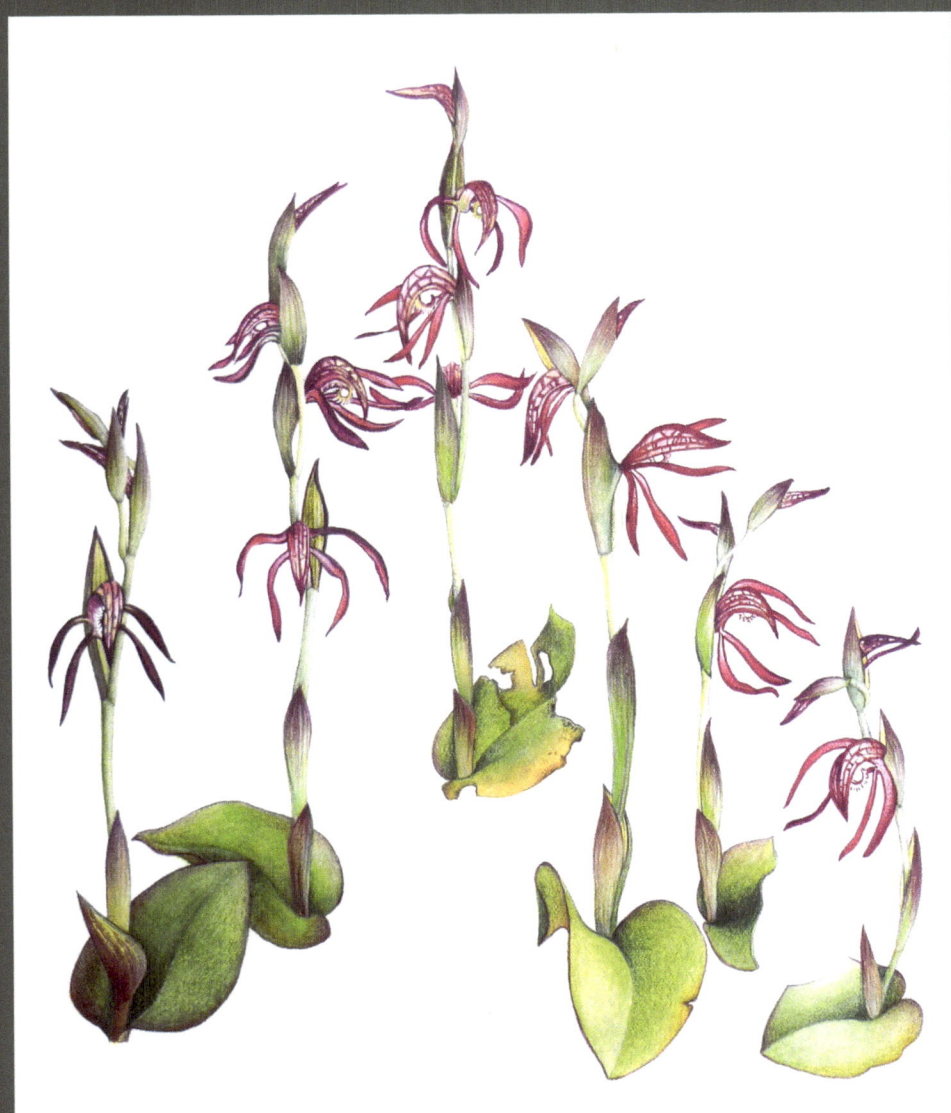

Dolores Sk-Malloni
Lyperanthus nigri
Watercolour

Lyperanthus nigrica
is endemic to the
Grampians region of
N.W. Victoria. Australia

HABITAT

The majority of botanical illustrations are of individual specimens, depicted in isolation against a white background. Essentially this is a close-up of the subject with the attention on individual features, sometimes specifically to aid identification. This works best when the subject is spatially detached and the focus is all on the subject and all its relevant features. A different purpose altogether can be an 'ecological illustration', the depiction of a plant in its habitat. This idea of portraying a plant within its surroundings, is a question of context, the natural environment. It can mean portraying the subject with a background of endemic plants of the surrounding area and can sometimes include the surrounding landscape. There are very good reasons today to do habitat studies, but inexplicitly we don't often see these types of compositions very often today.

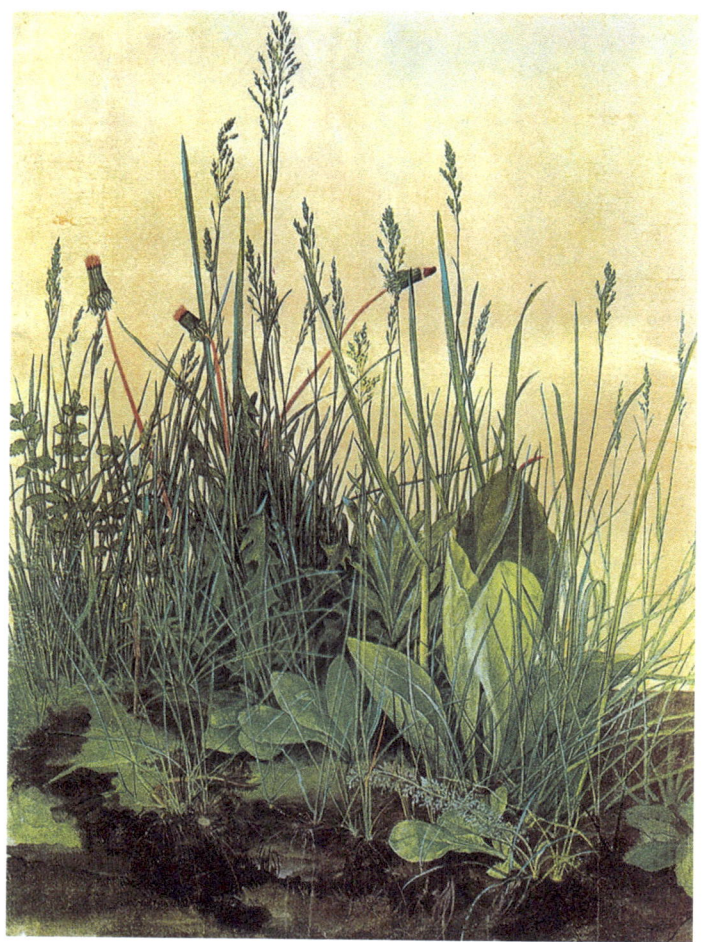

The Great Piece of Turf. Watercolour and gouache. Albrecht Durer. 1503.

ALBRECHT DURER 1471- 1528

The famous painting known as 'The Great Piece of Turf' was created by Albrecht Durer in Nuremberg in 1503. It details a group of plants of the typical local meadow vegetation, ostensibly a random group of plants. The painting shows a superb level of realism in its portrayal of these natural subjects. Even some of the roots are depicted exposed, to be displayed more clearly. The various plants are painted so specifically that they can be identified. They are cock's-foot, creeping bent, smooth meadow grass, daisy, dandelion, germander, speedwell, greater plantain, hound's-tongue, and yarrow. Of the individual plants none are more important than another. There is no subject here in isolation from the other plants. The subject is entirely about habitat. Although this picture is so famous, surprisingly it did not set any long term trends.

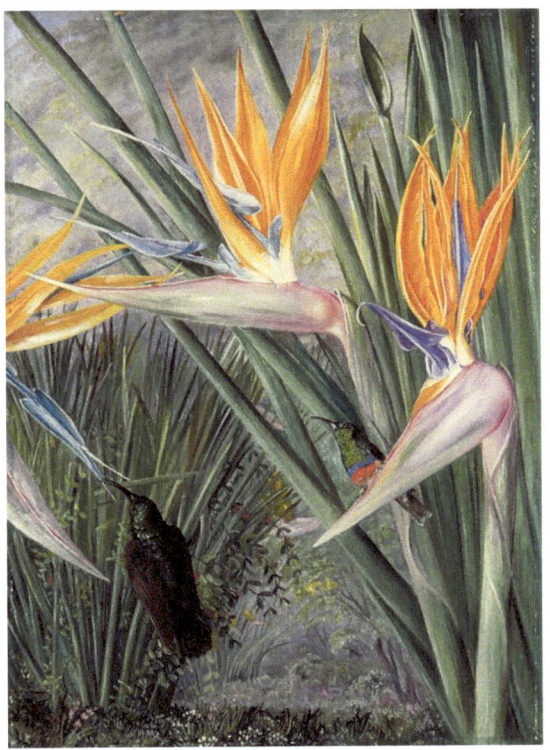

MARIANNE NORTH 1830 -1890

Marianne North made a major contribution to habitat illustration. Coming from a wealthy English family, she had the ability to travel the world looking for her subjects. Strictly speaking she wasn't a botanical illustrator. She had no intention of painting uprooted, specimen types against a white background, in the traditionally approach. She preferred to treat the plants and environments she chose as individuals set within distinctive settings, all of which she wanted to portray with the vibrancy and immediacy of the original encounter.

She worked in oils and her output was an amazing 833 paintings of over 900 species, most of which included habitats and often some landscapes was included. Today this collection is housed in the Marianne North Gallery at Kew Gardens. London. UK.

ALEXANDER VON HUMBOLDT 1769 -1859

The writings of Alexander von Humboldt had a profoundly significant effect on habitat illustration. Importantly, they included the observation that a climate had a characteristic group of plants, and that the same sequence could be observed when descending a mountain range, as you would observe when passing through a different climatic, or geographical zones. The illustration featured here is by the German illustrator Albert Berg from a series of illustrations 'Physiognomy of Tropical Vegetation in South America'. Because of Humboldt's influence, ecological illustration remained a largely German interest for a long time.

Above: Marianne North. 1887
　　　Strelitzia reginae and Sugar birds. Oil on paper ground.
Left: Albert Berg. 1854.
　　　Andes of Quindfo. Oil on canvas

📖 *The Invention of Nature. Alexander von Humboldt's New World.*
Andrea Wulf. 2015

PAINTERS OF HABITAT

ELLIS ROWAN 1848 -1922

Ellis Rowan was one of Australia's most adventurous and talented natural history artists, specializing in flowers and birds, and occasionally insects. She grew up in Victoria in a family familiar with natural history and art. Living in New Zealand with her husband Frederic Charles Rowan, she began to develop skills as a 'wild flower' painter. She was untrained, but she rapidly emerged as a talented artist and began to win important art prizes in Australia and overseas.

ENVIRONMENTS

Ellis Rowan was obsessive about her work and this led her to seek subjects in difficult environments at the time, such as Western Australia, North Queensland and Papua New Guinea. Conditions in these environments were challenging and sometimes dangerous. She also spent time in North American where she illustrated a text-book on the flora of the USA. Her work crossed the boundaries between art and natural history illustration. Much of her work is of a very high standard in both of these disciplines. Her style differs from a traditional botanical study approach. Her works on flowers, insects and birds were usually set in context, sometimes with the background environment being completed in an impressionist style. She always worked on various neutral coloured backgrounds.

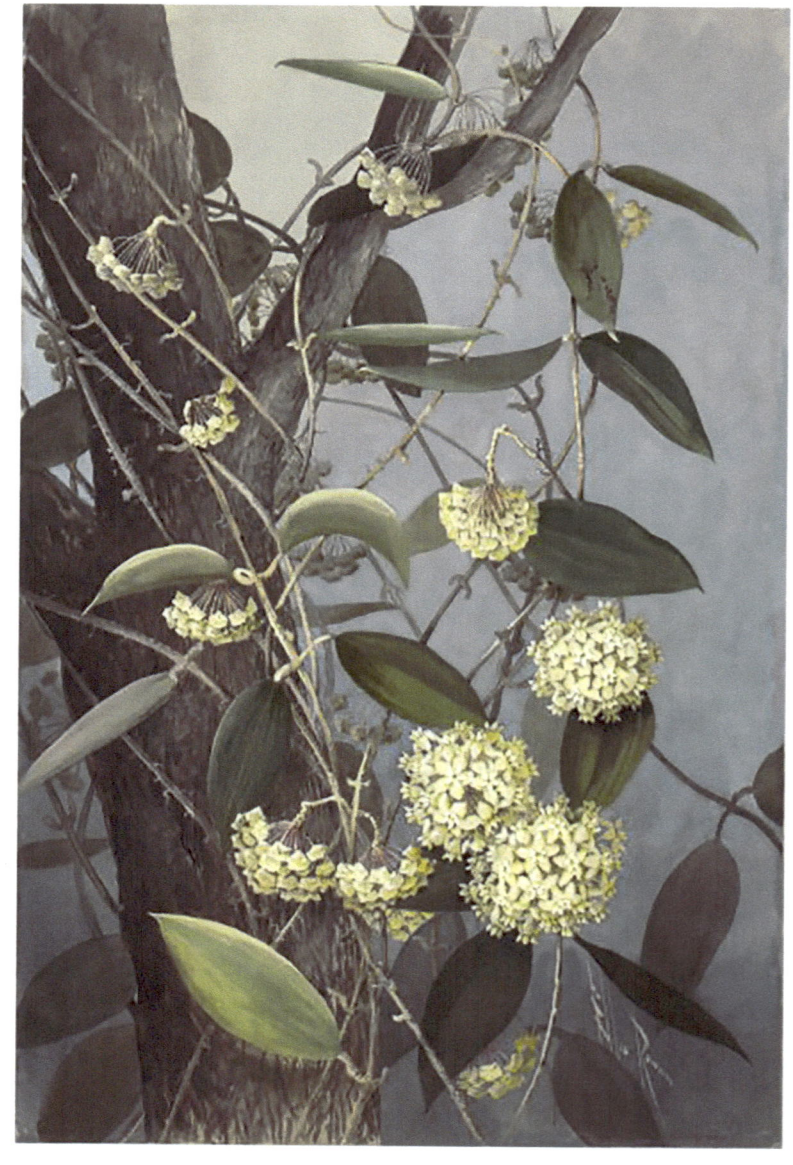

A UNIQUE STYLE

Her studies of flowers were developed into a unique style. In the work portrayed here, the foreground and background are very clearly defined. The background environment is very loosely depicted in an impressionistic manner. She worked on neutral coloured paper, possibly a pale grey in this work. In contrast the plants in the foreground are painted in a much more defined way. There are three plants depicted here, and cumulatively they evoke a scene in the Australian bush. The banksia cones are shown at different stages and are entwined with two other plants, both of yellow hues. The coloration is wonderful, as the contrast of the yellow with the main subject gives enough isolation and focus to the main subject the Banksias.

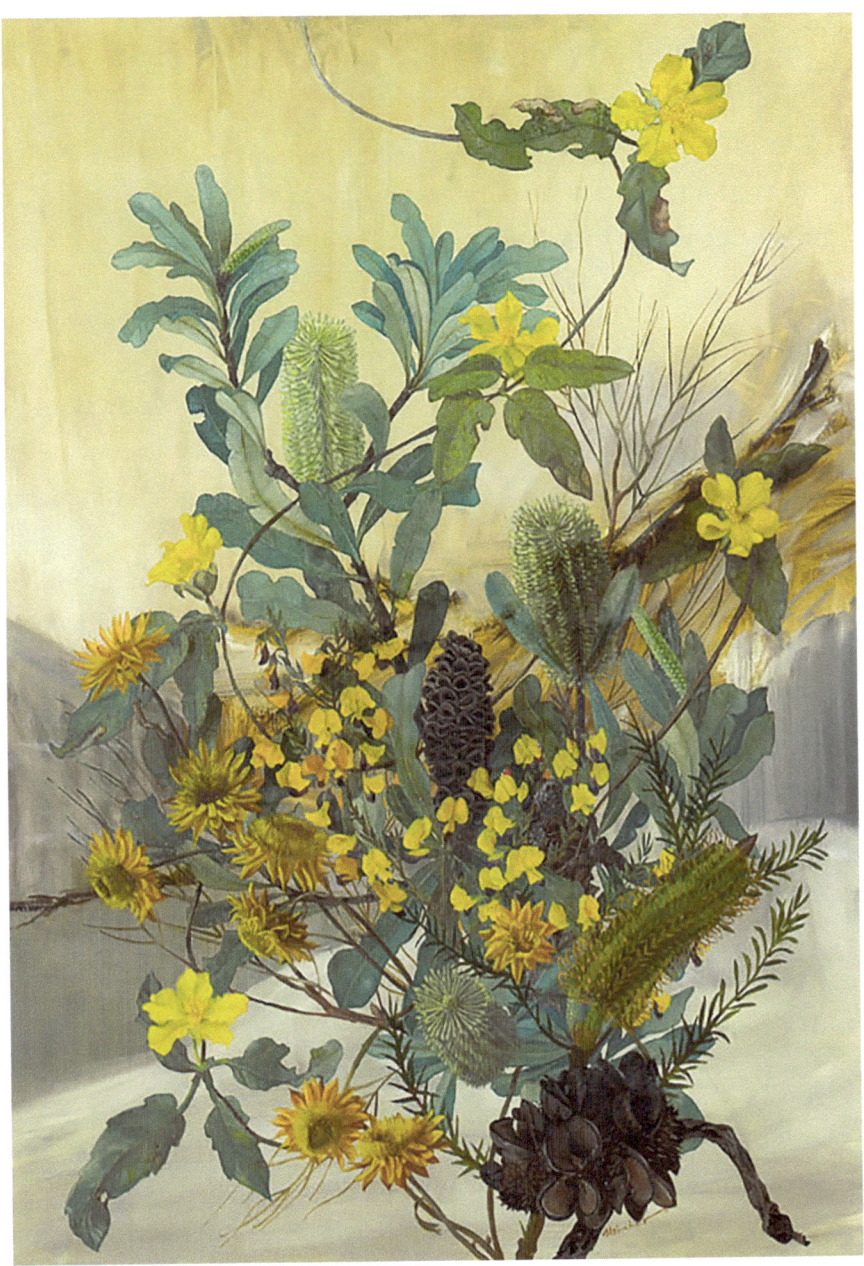

Above: *Banksia integrifolia*.
Gouache and watercolour

Left: *Hoya nicholsoniae*. Wax flower.
Gouache and watercolour

ENDANGERED

The biggest story in the plant world today is about the huge loss of diversity world-wide, that endangers all areas of life. This situation is mostly caused through a loss of habitat and degradation. The problem needs active support and publicity to achieve the robust eco systems we need for a healthy level of bio-diversity.

The Red List specifies species of flora and fauna which have been categorized by the International Union for Conservation of Nature (IUCN) as likely to become extinct. There are four ranks of endangerment. They are:

VULNERABLE. ENDANGERED. CRITICALLY ENDANGERED. EXTINCT IN THE WILD

The IUCN Red List featured 3079 animal and 2655 plant species as endangered worldwide. The IUCN Red List is intended to be an easily and widely understood system for classifying species at high risk of global extinction. The general aim of the system is to provide an objective framework for the classification of the range of species according to their extinction risk.

ONE STORY

There are many stories of plant endangerment and extinction, and this is just one. The pictured image is of *Rafflesia arnoldii,* painted by Franz Bauer in 1822. The plants common name is the Corpse plant, evidently because of its unmistakable pungent smell. On a more positive note, it is the largest known flower on earth and can reach 3ft in diameter. But is it really a flower? The Rafflesia family challenges the traditional definitions of what a plant is, because it lacks chlorophyll and is therefore incapable of photosynthesis. It has no roots or leaves. It is likened to fungi, but is not classified as such.

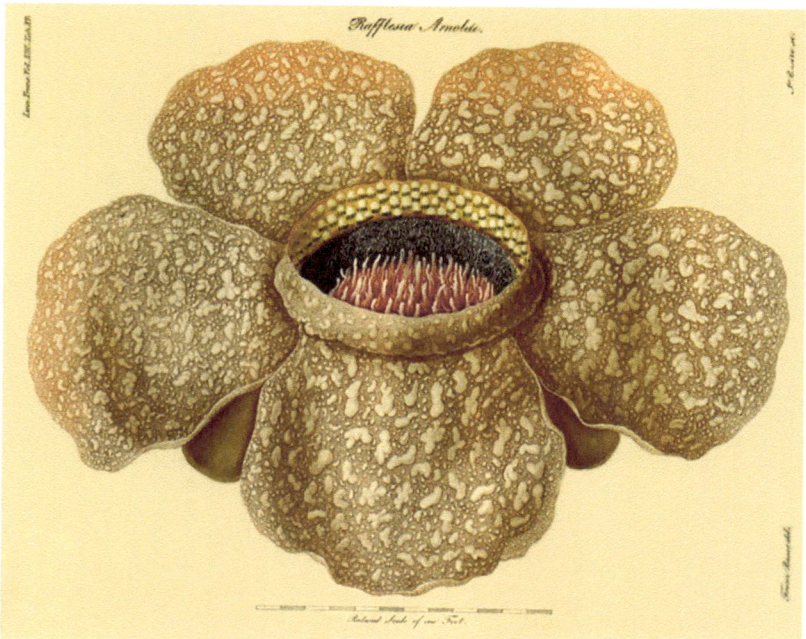

These spectacular plants are found only in the tropical rainforests of Indonesia, Malaysia, Thailand, Borneo and the Southern Philippines. *Rafflesia arnoldii* is parasitic and is totally dependent upon a vine called *Tetrastigma*. It is endangered for the usual reasons of habitat loss, but also because of a high collection rate because for its rarity value.

It is not a plant you are going to have in your backyard. But if this strange, unique plant was lost to us, it would be like losing the Dodo or New Zealand's Moa.

All known species of Rafflesia are classed as threatened.

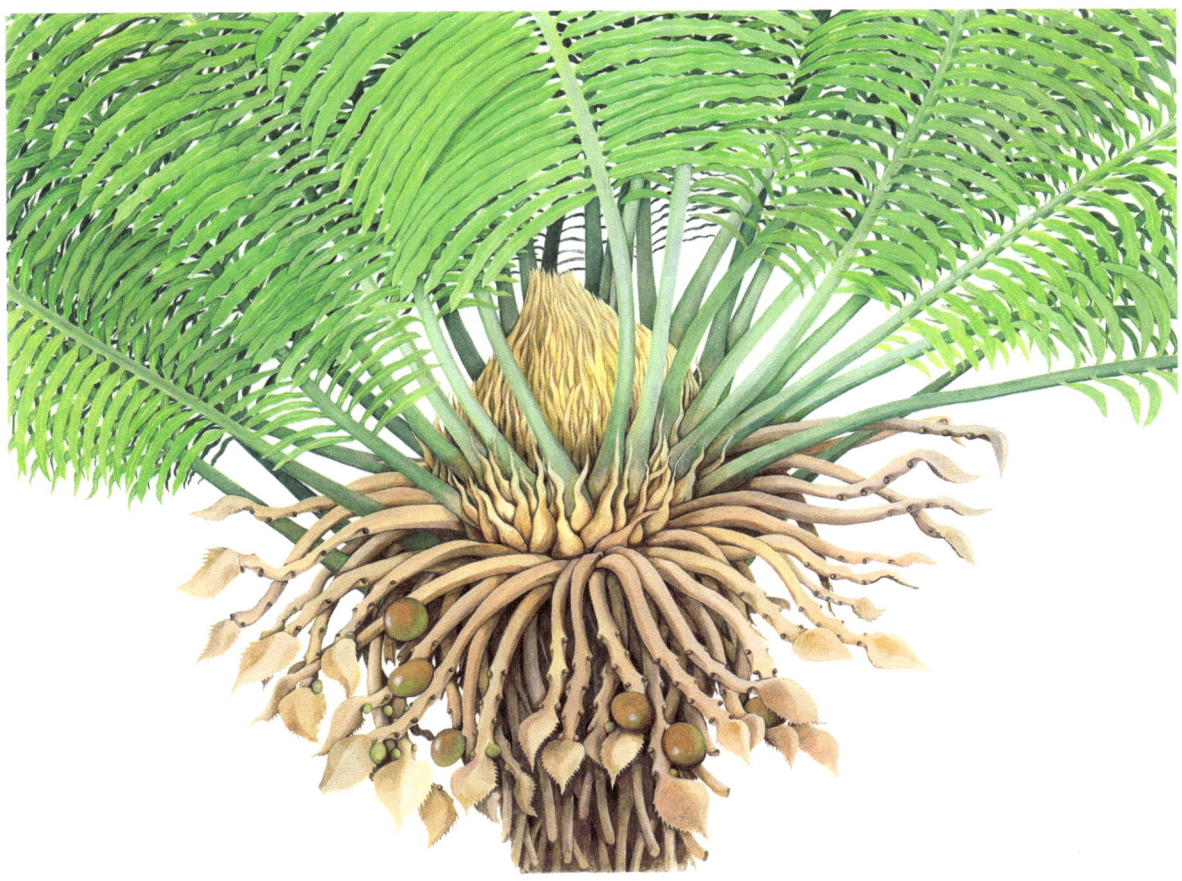

A LOST PARADISE?

'Losing Paradise? Endangered Plants Here and Around The World', was a traveling exhibition curated by the American Society of Botanical Artists (ASBA), that explored the conservation efforts of scientists and illustrators around the globe. The exhibition focused on the planet's rich diversity of plant life currently at risk. At the present time more than 20% of the world's flora is threatened with extinction, and it is a race against time to gather information on known plants and to document the estimated 50,000 plant species that have never been scientifically described. For this exhibition Botanical artists worked to capture plant diversity for future generations and to give a focus to our vanishing botanical wealth.

 The *Cycas seemannii* featured in the exhibition was found in the Fiji islands. The cycads are amongst the earliest plants found on earth. There have been fossils found from 270-280 million years ago. They are mostly found in tropical and sub-tropical areas around the world. At the present time about half are considered threatened.

Above: Rita Parkinson. *Cycas Seemannii*
Left: Franz Bauer. *Rafflesia arnodii* 1822

HARD TO FIND

A plant doesn't have to be remote to be 'hard to find'. There could be many unique plants to be seen almost under your feet. But at the same time, they may take some time and effort to find and identify. So, surprisingly Illustrating the local flora or the rare, in today's world can be far more difficult than the exotics that exist all around us.

But many botanical artists have a strong affinity to their local native species and appreciate the specifics of habitat and species loss in their own areas, and for them the idea of bringing these situations into focus with detailed and specific images is a major objective.

I live in an area on the outskirts of Melbourne, in the State of Victoria, Australia where much of the surrounding bio- region is classed as native grasslands. The flora of the region has suffered because of urban development and farming, resulting in loss of habitat. Consequently, the remnant indigenous plant population can be hard to locate. But if you take the trouble, wonderful examples of native lilies, orchids, daisies, peas and others are there to be found.

Many of us live in populated areas, and you may have to look for these remnant populations in various small public areas or road and rail reserves, or perhaps in cemeteries or sometimes on private land. But it is quite possible to live in an area for some time and not be aware of the really unique plants that can be an important part of the local bio-diversity.

NATIVE GRASSLANDS

Natural grasslands are types of native vegetation where the grasses are the dominant or common feature on the ground. But they are usually rich in other plants that grow between the grass tussocks and often appear as wildflowers in Spring. In Victoria, Australia, the natural temperate grassland of the Victorian volcanic plain hold many critically endangered ecological communities.

PLANTS CAN BE CLASSED AS ENDANGERED BECAUSE:

- There is a severe decline in their numbers.
- They have a very restricted distribution.
- They are under continuous threats.
- They suffer from a severe reduction in their habitat integrity.

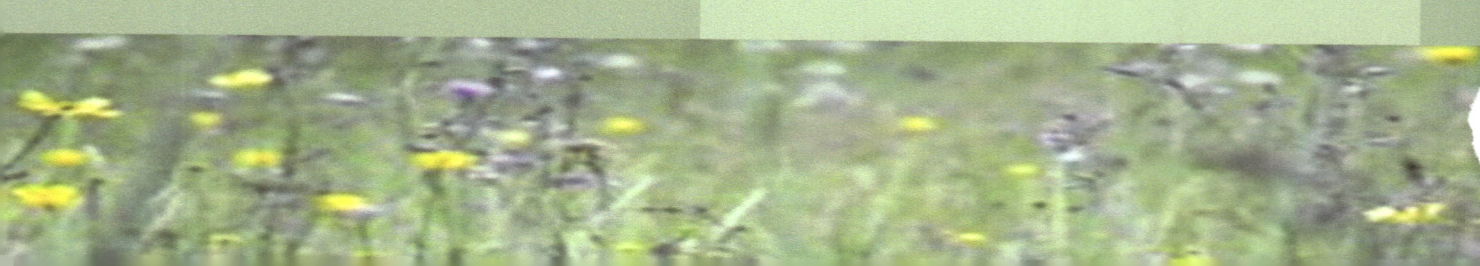

A LOCAL STORY.
Victoria. Australia

Native grassland ecological communities were formerly extensive on the Victorian volcanic plains, but now comprise mostly small, highly fragmented remnants resulting from land clearance, largely due to agriculture or urbanization. There are remnants that still occur, but are still subject to clearance and other threats from urbanization. Less than five per cent of the original extent of these communities remains, and patches considered to be in good condition probably constitute less than one per cent.

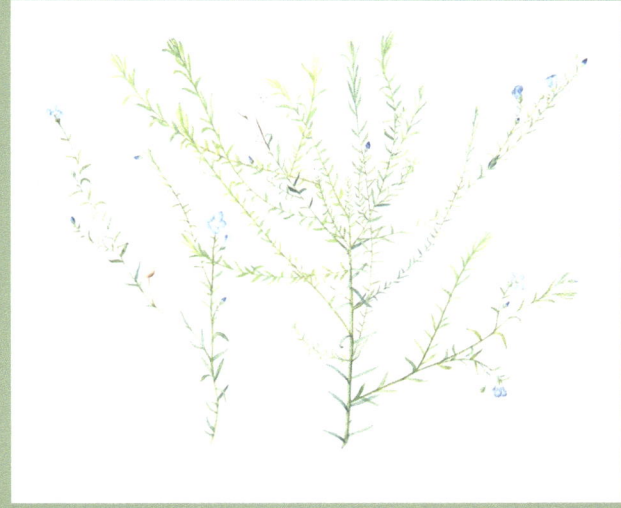

Most of the known remnants in Victoria are small – under 10 hectares in size. Many patches of these communities are so degraded, due to weed and feral animal invasion and loss of native bio - diversity, that their capacity to maintain ecosystem function is so impaired that they will need serious efforts to recover. These ecological communities provide habitat to several nationally and state-listed threatened species. Although these conditions are local to our community, they would be replicated in many populated areas worldwide.

Above: *Linum marginale*. Wild flax
Right: *Poa morrisii*. Velvet Tussock Grass

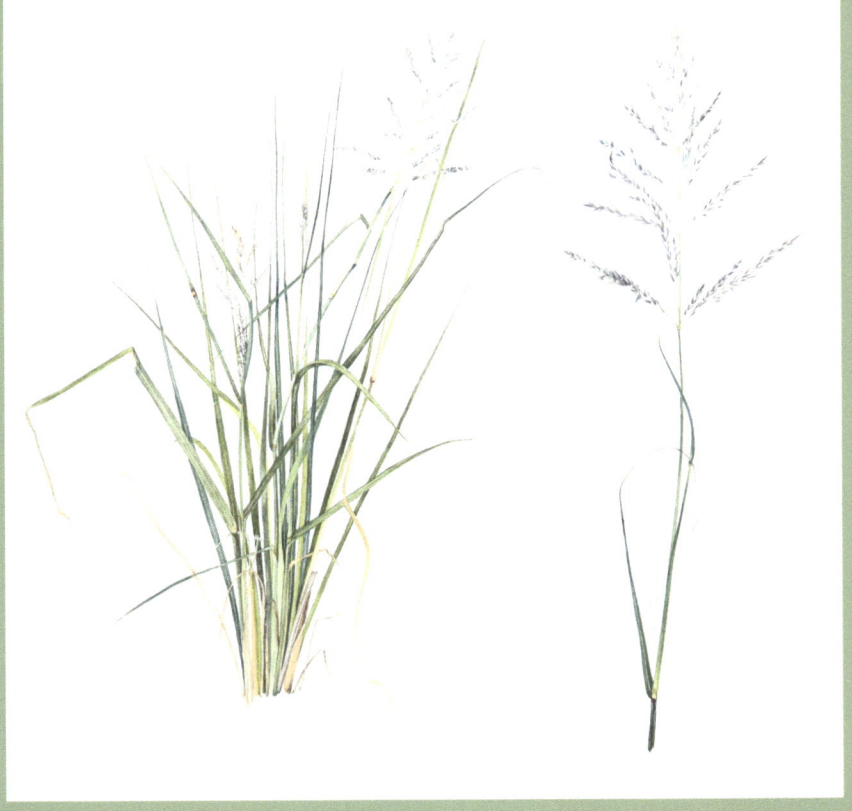

FIELD TRIPS

Taking part in a field trip is a great way to get to work with some really interesting subjects. You may get to illustrate some unique flora, and it's possible that it has not been illustrated before. It's a good way to get some serious concentration over a short period, and in the process produce some really exciting work. It's an opportunity for illustrators to focus on their subjects without the distractions of everyday life. Australia is a special place in the plant world. It is home to some 20,000 species, 91% of which are endemic, and amazingly, although it is home to many talented botanical artists, a great many Australian species have never been illustrated.
  Every year we take a group of students on a field trip to the Grampians, a mountain region in Victoria, Australia that has its own distinctive ecological footprint. Here you can find a third of Victoria's species, including heaths, native grasses, orchids and many more. The wildlife is also abundant and readily seen. That could be kangaroos, emus and wedge- tailed eagles among many others. There are rock formations and native forests and aboriginal rock art, all of which helps to get you in the zone. This area has become well known for its wild flowers, but surprisingly there is not a lot of information for the public. We spend a week here annually, in the Spring when the flora is abundant. Over several years, we have built up a serious collection of images of the flora of this very special place.

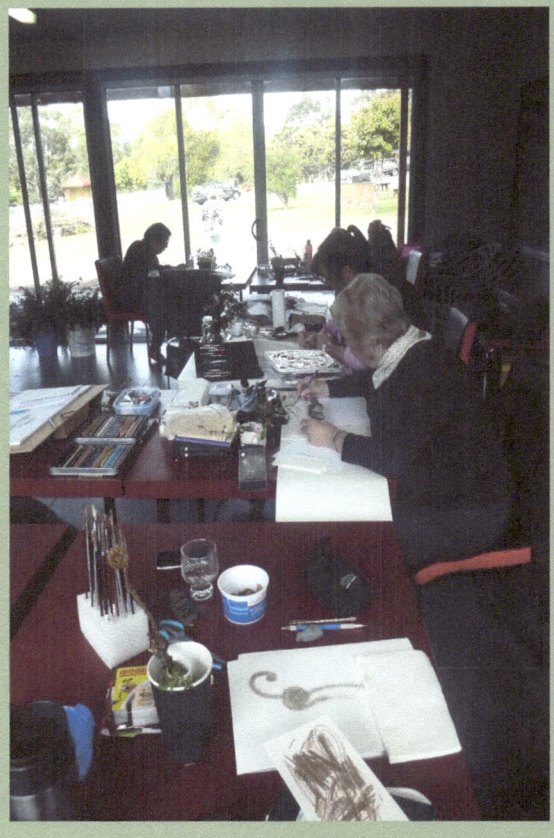

THE NEW AGE OF DISCOVERY

The facts about our huge loss of bio-diversity, can be disheartening. But we need to remember that at the same time we find ourselves still in the Age of Discovery. The known plant species of the world are estimated today at about 250,000 and the predicted total is estimated at over 300,000, as newly identified plants are added to this number every year. The full number of species cannot be estimated. But it's important to remember that new discoveries and new classifications go on concurrently with the sad story of loss.

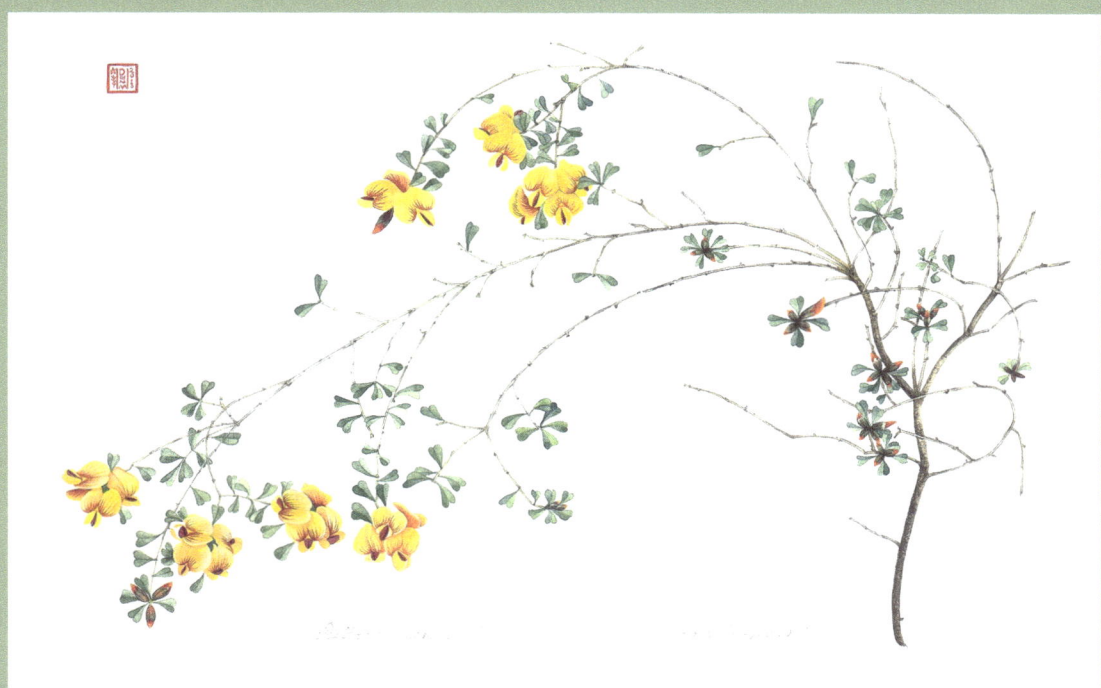

THE LOSS OF BIO- DIVERSITY

The plant world's huge loss of bio-diversity today isn't new, but does seem to be accelerating. The real worry is that the loss is estimated to be 30% of plant bio-diversity by 2050. The cause is mostly through the effects of loss of habitat and degradation, brought about by the growth of agricultural interests and an increase in the built environment. This loss ultimately endangers all areas of life. It could be worth getting to know if this loss is part of the situation near to where you live. We need to get involved in supporting the robust eco systems needed to sustain bio-diversity.

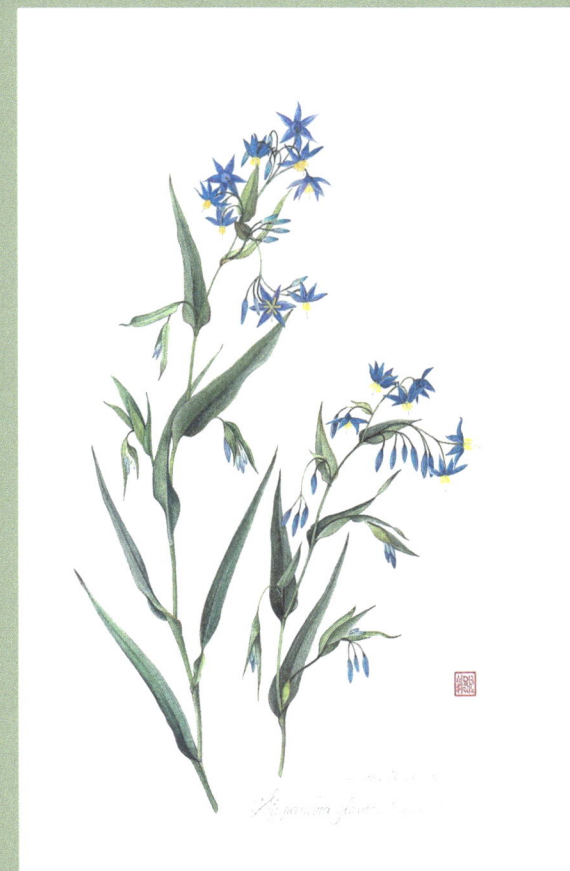

Above: Dolores Sk-Malloni
Pultanea scabra. Rough Bush Pea. Watercolour
Right: *Stypandra glauca*. Nodding blue Orchid. Watercolour
Left : Studio time. Grampians Field trip.

NATIVES

NEW AND UNILLUSTRATED

Newly discovered species of flora are being found and classified all the time. The fact is that the vast majority of the mass of plant life has not as yet been illustrated. Many plants that are indigenous and quite widely found, can remain relatively unknown, even in their own areas.

  The plant illustrated below was one of the first plants discovered by Europeans in Australia. In 1699, a ship called the Roebuck sailed into Western Australian waters under Captain William Dampier. He immediately set about recording its flora and fauna, which he had recorded by his clerk, James Brand. One of those plants was the *Pittosporum angustifolium*, a beautiful, small to large tree with an elegant weeping habit.

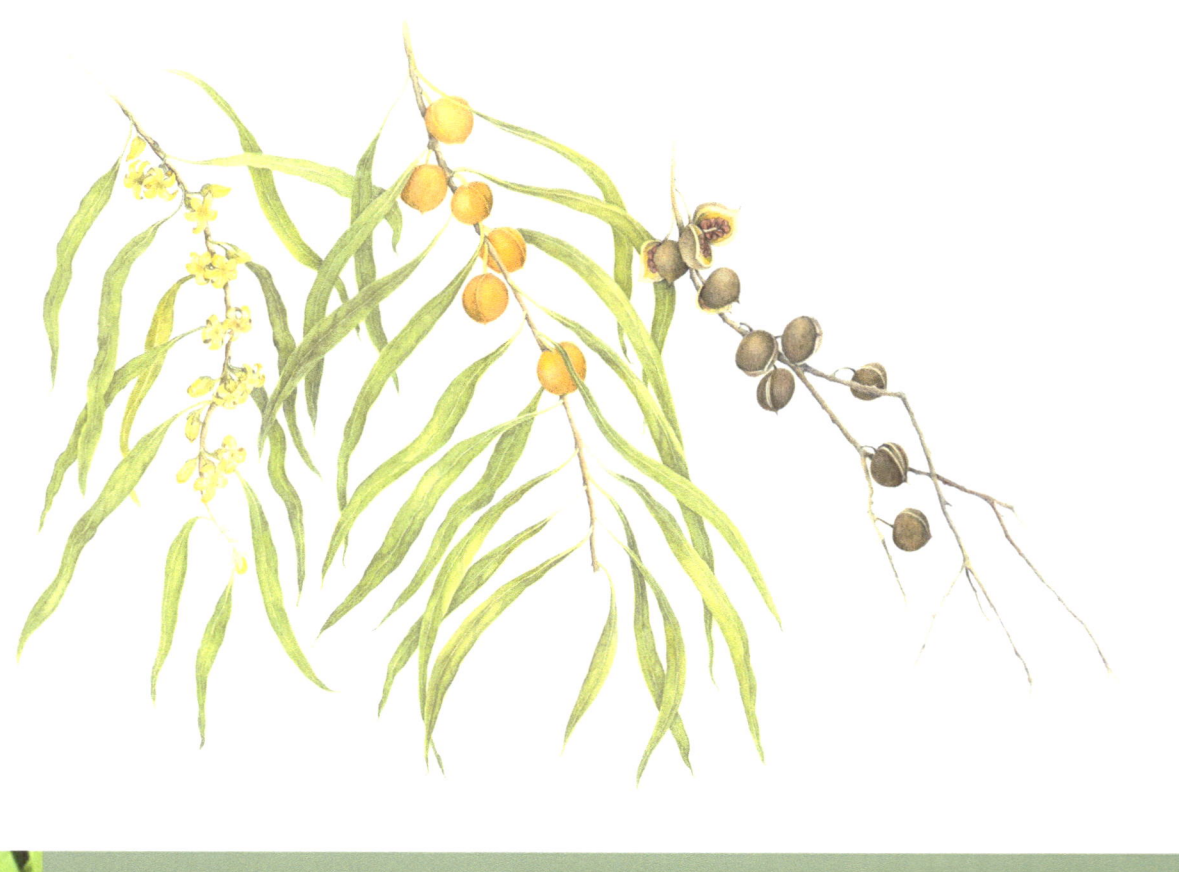

Rita Parkinson. *Pittosporum angustifolium* . Western Australia. Watercolour

AN HISTORICAL QUEST

Illustrating indigenous plants is not the first choice for many botanical artists. It can sometimes be the case that endemic plants are more subdued in coloration and form than the exotics, which are often more visually intense, because the horticultural world has an interest in developing them commercially. But illustrating indigenous plants has its own rewards as many illustrators know. There are many reasons to paint endemic species. Perhaps the most rewarding would be to promote an interest in the problems of maintaining bio-diversity. The pictures here were done for a very different reasons, an historical quest.

A RARE COLLECTION

The Geelong Botanic Gardens is home to a unique, specialized Pelargonium collection. It includes the original source plants, type specimens, early hybrids and representatives of all the modern varieties. You might associate these plants with Mediterranean window boxes, but the actual history is very different. The majority of Pelargoniums come from a challenging environment, the Cape Province of South Africa. This is an area with soil of a high clay content. It was just this hardy quality of the Pelagoniums that led to the multiple hybrids, that in time developed into the modern Zonals, Royals and Ivy-leafed varieties.

The *Pelargonium leipoldtii* is one of the wild ancestors of the more showy modern Pelargoniums. The flowers are relatively inconspicuous, as most of the flowers of the originals were.

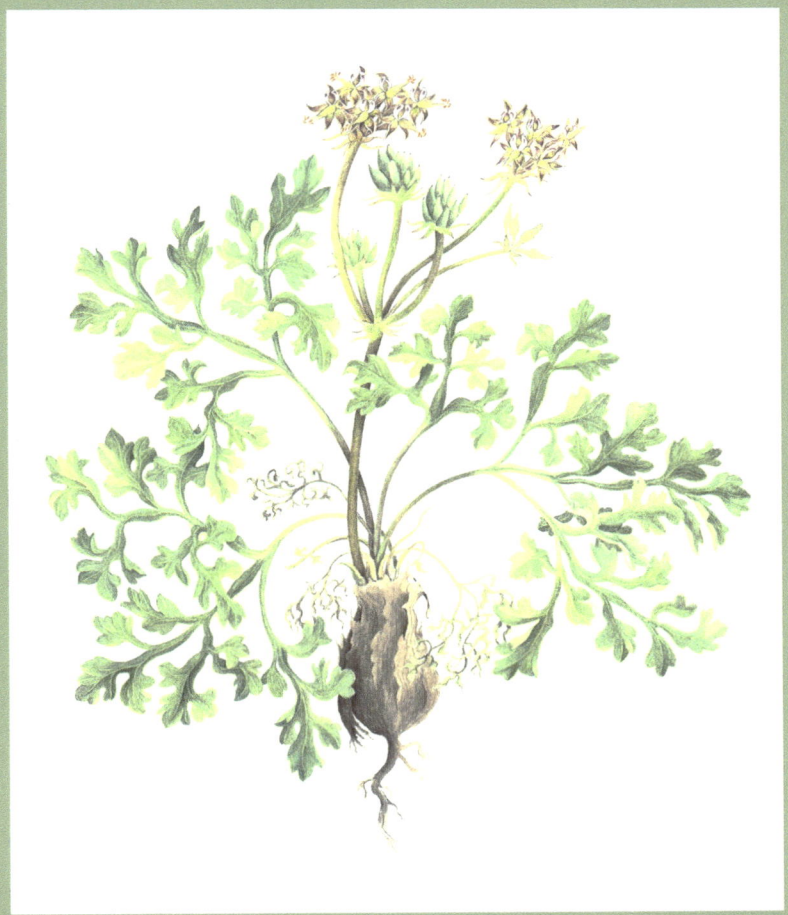

Rita Parkinson. *Pelargonium leipoldtii*. Cape Province. South Africa. Watercolour

POLLINATION

Appreciation about the processes of pollination is an important message for botanical illustration to promote. The success of the pollination process is so critical to the world of plants, whether this is to the production of food or the balance of eco-systems. It's crucial to appreciate just how essential the health of the process is, and how dangerous the situation can be when it is endangered, often as a result of reductions in bio- diversity. At the present time there is a worrying decline in the health of bees, and that poses a threat to so much of the global food industry.

When animals such as bees, moths, butterflies, flies, and birds pollinate plants, it's accidental. They are not trying to pollinate the plant. Usually they are there to get food, the sticky pollen or a sweet nectar made at the base of the petals. When feeding, the animals accidentally rub against the stamens and get pollen stuck all over themselves. When they move to another flower to feed, some of the pollen can rub off onto the new plant's stigma.

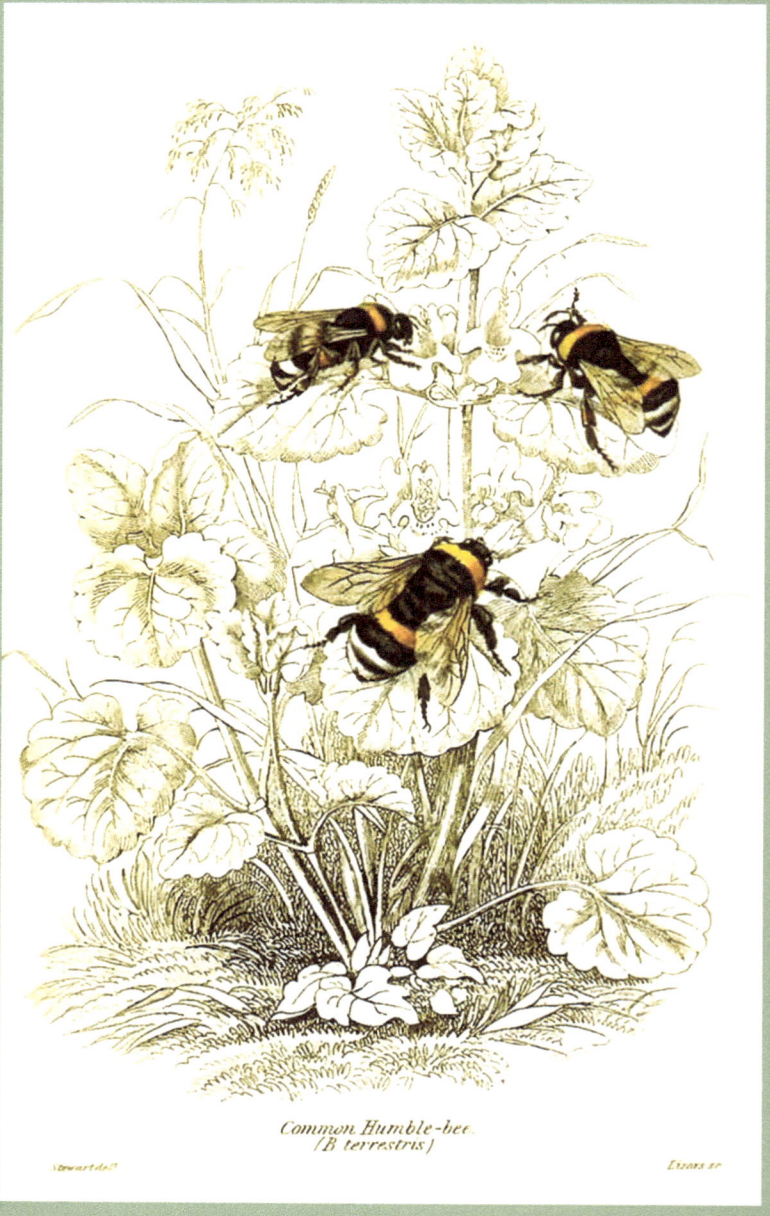

Common Humble-bee
(B terrestris)

Bombus terrestris Bumble Bee
The Naturalist's Library. Vol 3. Entomology. William Jardine 1840

THE BIRDS, THE BEES, INSECTS AND THE WIND

Pollination is the process by which plant pollen is transferred from the male reproductive organs to the female reproductive organs. In flowering plants, pollen is transported from the anther to the stigma by insects or birds or the wind. The male parts the stamens, produce a sticky powder called pollen. Flowers also have a female part called the pistil. Pollination is needed to start the production of seeds, which are made at the base of the pistil, in the ovule. The plants must be of the same species. Only pollen from a daisy can pollinate another daisy. Pollen from a rose to an apple tree would not work.
 The cone bearing plants, such as pines or spruce trees reproduce by means of pollen that is produced by a male cone and travels by wind to a female cone of the same species. The seeds will then develop in the female cones.

   Plants such as mosses and ferns don't have flowers, but reproduce by spores.

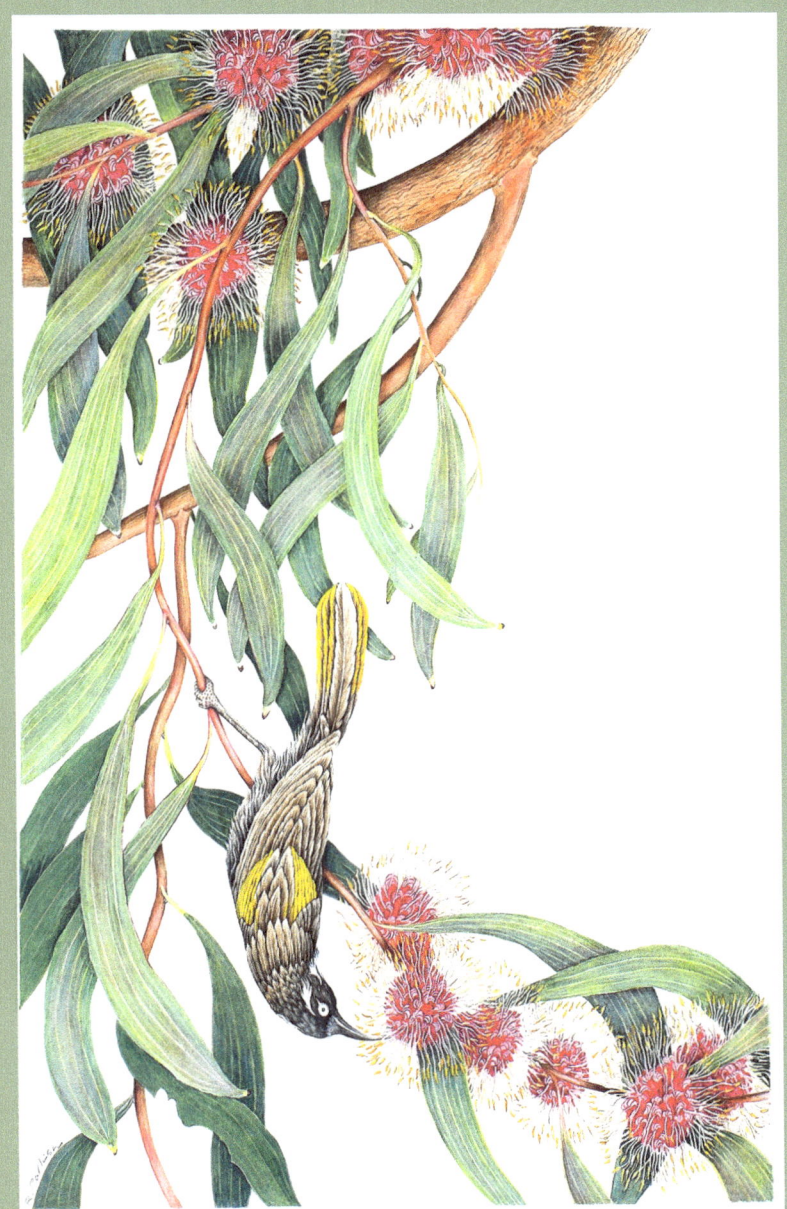

Rita Parkinson. *Hakea laurina.* Pin Cushion Hakea
   Phylidonysis novaehollandiae. New Holland Honeyeater
   Watercolour

SPOTLIGHT ON FLOWERS

The illustrations pictured here come from a publication called 'Paxton's Flower Garden'. Joseph Paxton was the landscape gardener at Chatsworth, the Duke of Devonshire estate in Derbyshire. UK. He would have been very familiar with working on the large scale. Here it could be a matter of removing inconvenient villages that got in the way of a picturesque view, or creating large vistas of mature trees and lakes, all in the fashionable style of Claude Lorraine. But Paxton was also interested in botany on the small scale. Between 1850 and 1853, his book 'Paxton's Flower Garden' was published, following a series of plant-collecting expeditions. With hand-colored plates and over 500 woodcuts, the work was copious. At Chatsworth, he was at the forefront of horticulture, growing and propagating the most interesting plants arriving from exotic places. With his book, Paxton was taking advantage of the growing interest in gardening in Victorian society.

The text and illustrations are aimed at amateur gardeners and botanists, encouraging them to try their hand at growing these marvelous new flowers. The flower book is just that, the illustrations and text are all about the flower, anything else illustrated is really just to provide the context. The foliage and stems when pictured, usually take second place. The flowers are placed centrally to focus mainly on the flower and its detailed structures. The composition is essentially simple, but the need for visual balance within the format is high. Illustrating flowers is a priority for many botanical illustrators and this could be an interesting format to try.

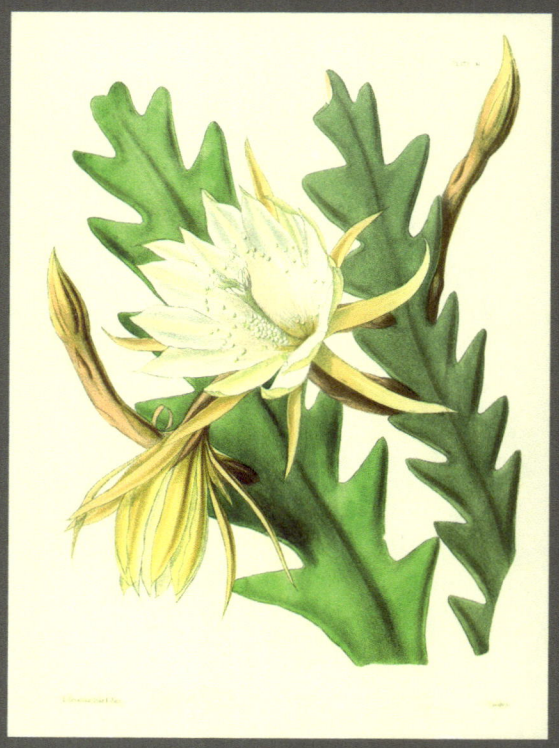

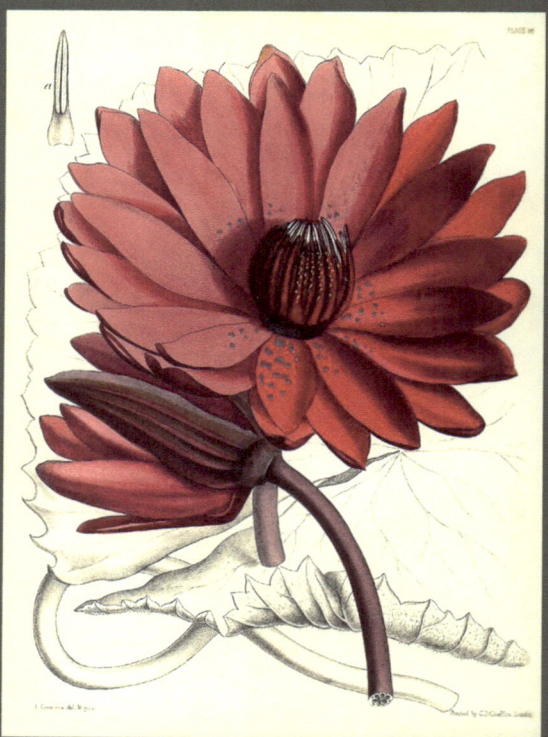

Images from 'Paxtons Flower Book'
Top: *Epiphyllum anguliger* L.Constans
Below: *Nymphaea rubra* L.Constans

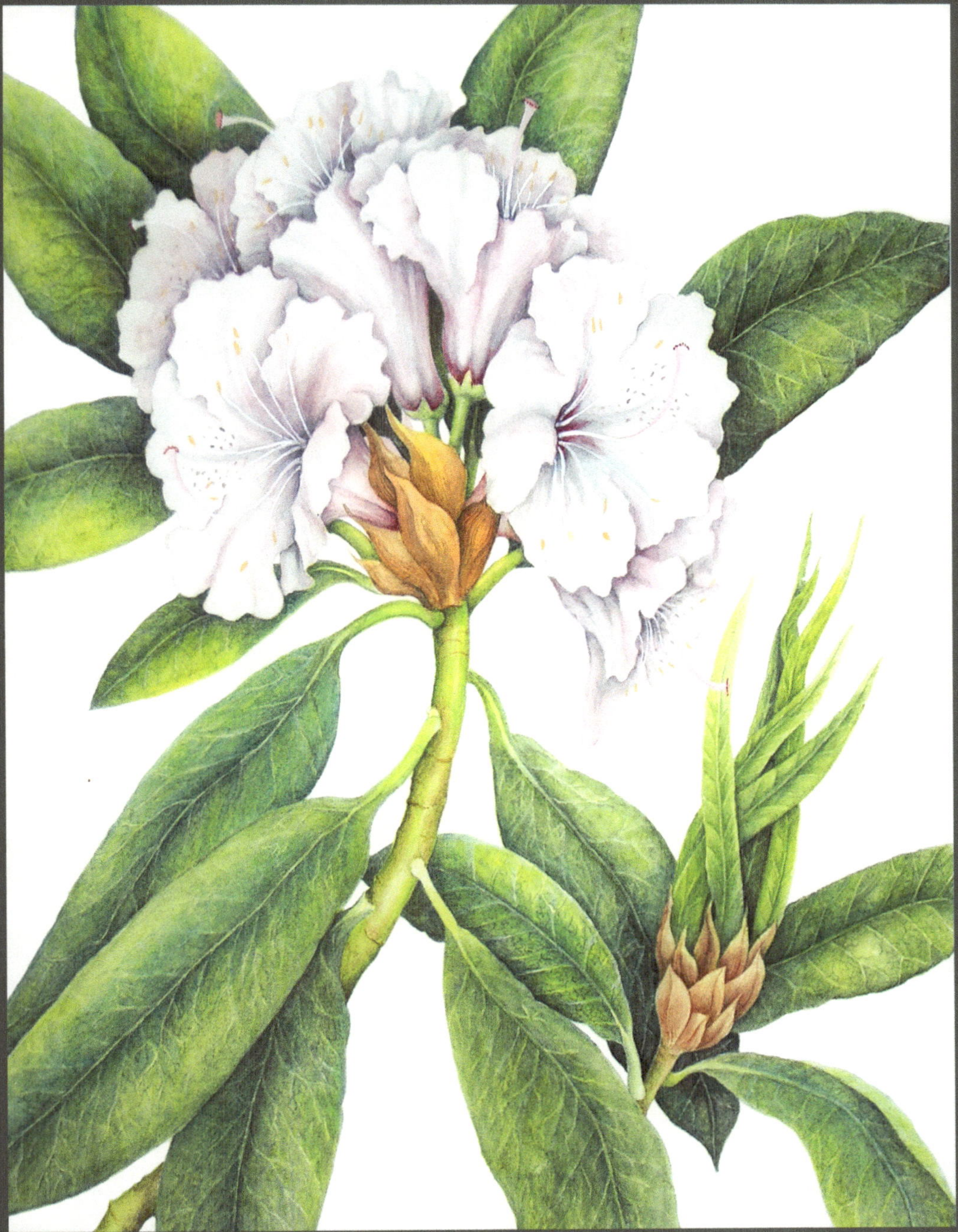

Rita Parkinson *Rhododenrum* cv. White Pearl . Watercolour

Paxton's Flower Garden, 3 vols., Bradbury and Evans, 1850-53,
John Lindley. Sir Joseph Paxton. Various illustrators

SNAPSHOTS

A SMALL SQUARE FORMAT

The images on this page were done as examples for a project undertaken at the Geelong School of Botanic Art to create works on a small scale. The purpose was twofold. In the first instance this small square format of 16 x 16cms means the effective use of the negative spaces is especially important to the final outcome. The principle of negative space is prominent here because the format is a square and that means the usual vertical or horizontal bias is absent. In this way it frees the artist to interpret the subject in many more ways, as there isn't a definitive axis. Because the proportions are pr-set, the most successful will take full advantage of this consideration.

The second advantage has to do with size. Because the finished work will be small the students were encouraged to give the project their full concentration at every stage right up to the final stage, where a good deal of dry brush work can make a real difference with a finish of fine detailing. All botanical works are time consuming and it can be difficult to maintain the enthusiasm through to a well finished artwork. A small work can emphasize the quality of fine detail not quantity.

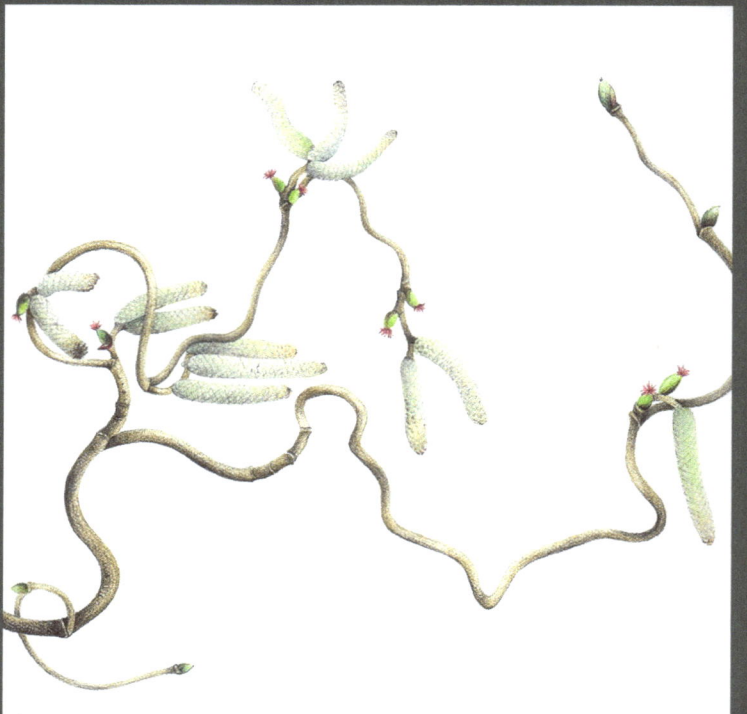

Corylus avella. Contorted variety

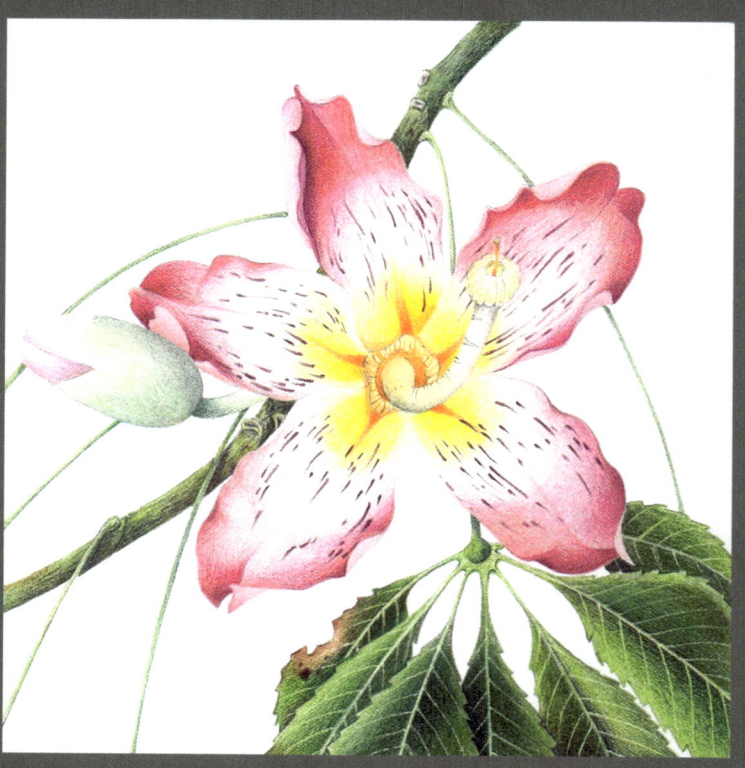

Chorisia speciosa

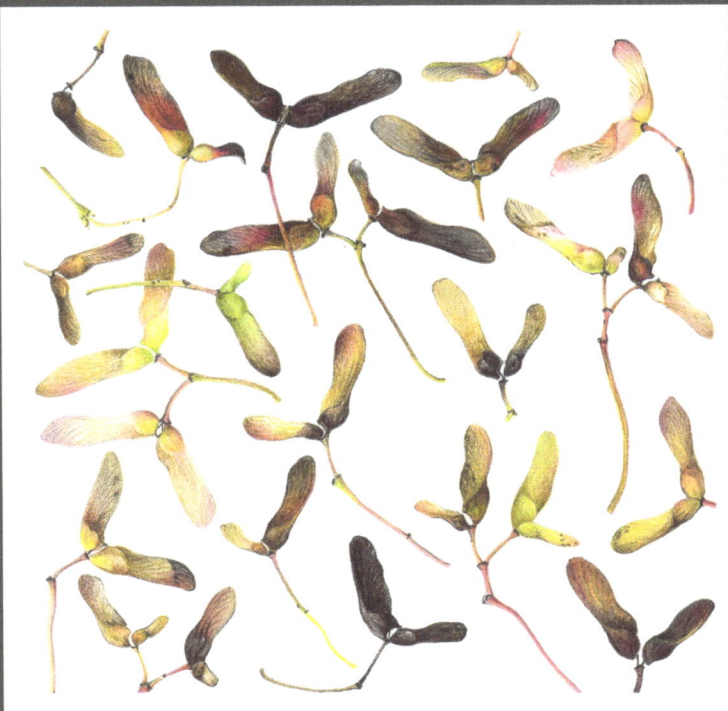

Acer pseudoplatanus. Pods

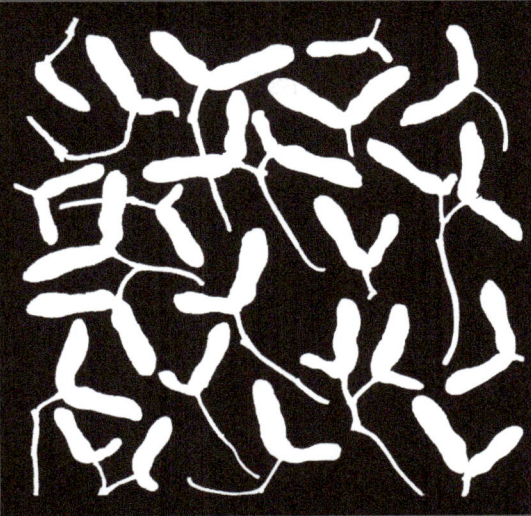

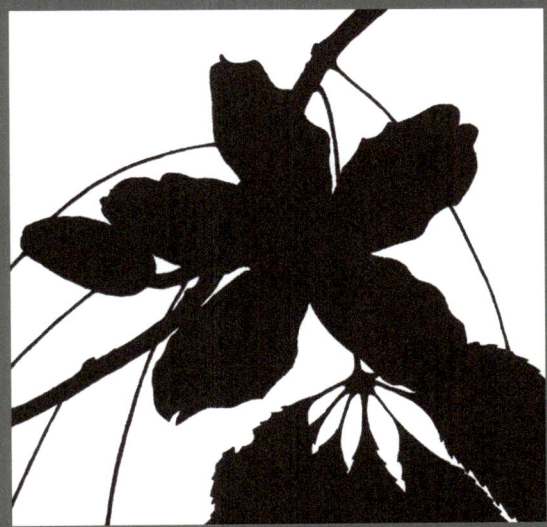

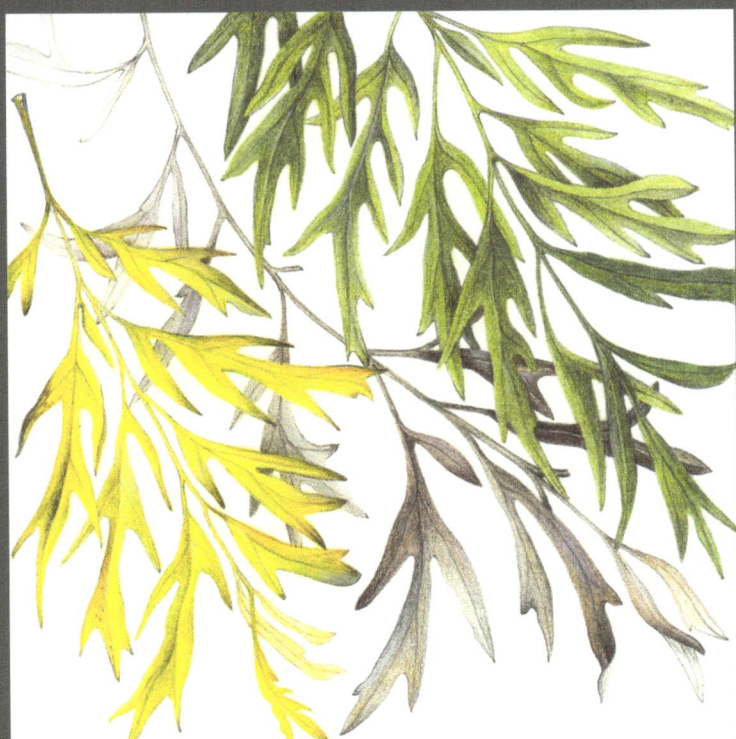

Grevillea robusta. Leaves

The diagrammatic black and white illustrations emphasize the importance that the principles of negative space and visual balance play within a square format. It also illustrates that with the abandonment of the usual portrait or landscape formats, a new way of looking at your subject can come to mind and free up some other interpretations of your subject.

All Illustrations: Dolores Sk-Malloni. Watercolour

LEAVES AS THE SUBJECT

The centre of interest for most flowering plants would naturally be the flower itself. The eye is automatically drawn to them, the colours and patterns and the particular structures for identification. This is no accident as flowers evolve their colorations and patterning to attract their specific pollinators. So it is logical that the foliage takes a secondary position.

ADAPTION

But leaves can be an interesting subject in themselves. They have evolved to support very different functions to flower. They are designed to function as a solar panel that has the capacity to convert the energy of sunlight into a carbon, and to hydrate and feed the tree for growth and nutrition. They are usually constructed as flat planes. If they are broad their large surface maximizes light exposure. They are mostly fairly thin in depth so that there is a short distance for the carbon dioxide to diffuse in, and for oxygen to diffuse out easily. This is the process of photosynthesis.

LEAVES SUPPORT A VARIETY OF FUNCTIONS

In hot climates, plants such as cacti have succulent leaves that help to conserve water. Many aquatic plants have leaves with wide lamina that can float on the surface of the water and a thick waxy cuticle on the leaf surface that repels water. These are just a few examples of the many ways leaves have adapted to circumstances. There are many fascinating aspects of leaves to explore in illustrations as the primary focus of an illustration.

THE COLOUR CHANGES OF AUTUMN

THE COLOUR CHANGES OF VARIAGATIONS

THE PATTERNS AND STRUCTURES OF VENATION

STRUCTURES AND DETAILS:
THE MARGINS, APICES, STEMS. ETC

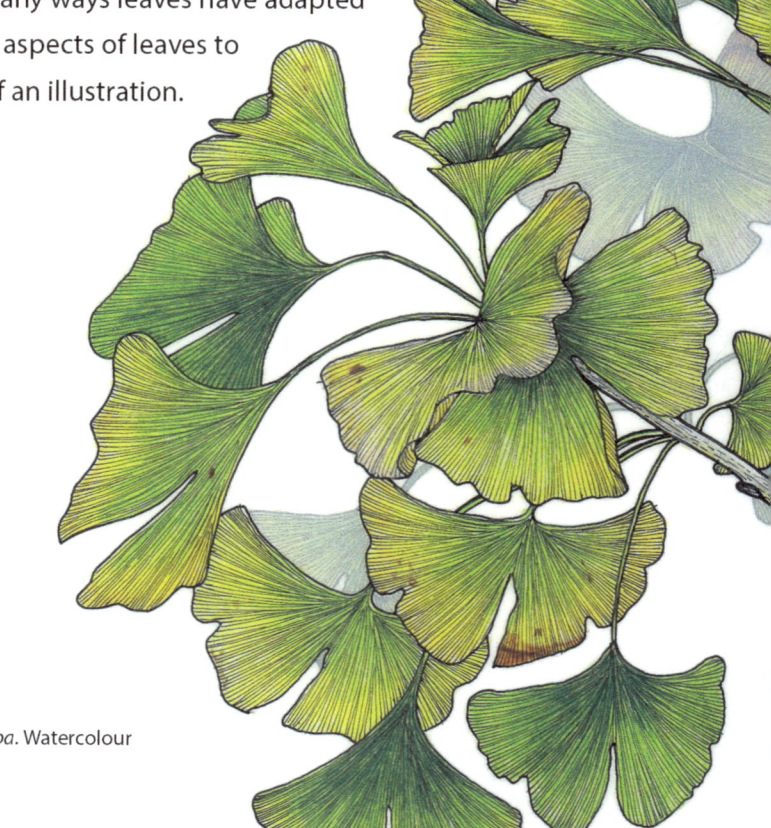

Dolores Sk-Malloni. *Detail from Ginkgo biloba.* Watercolour

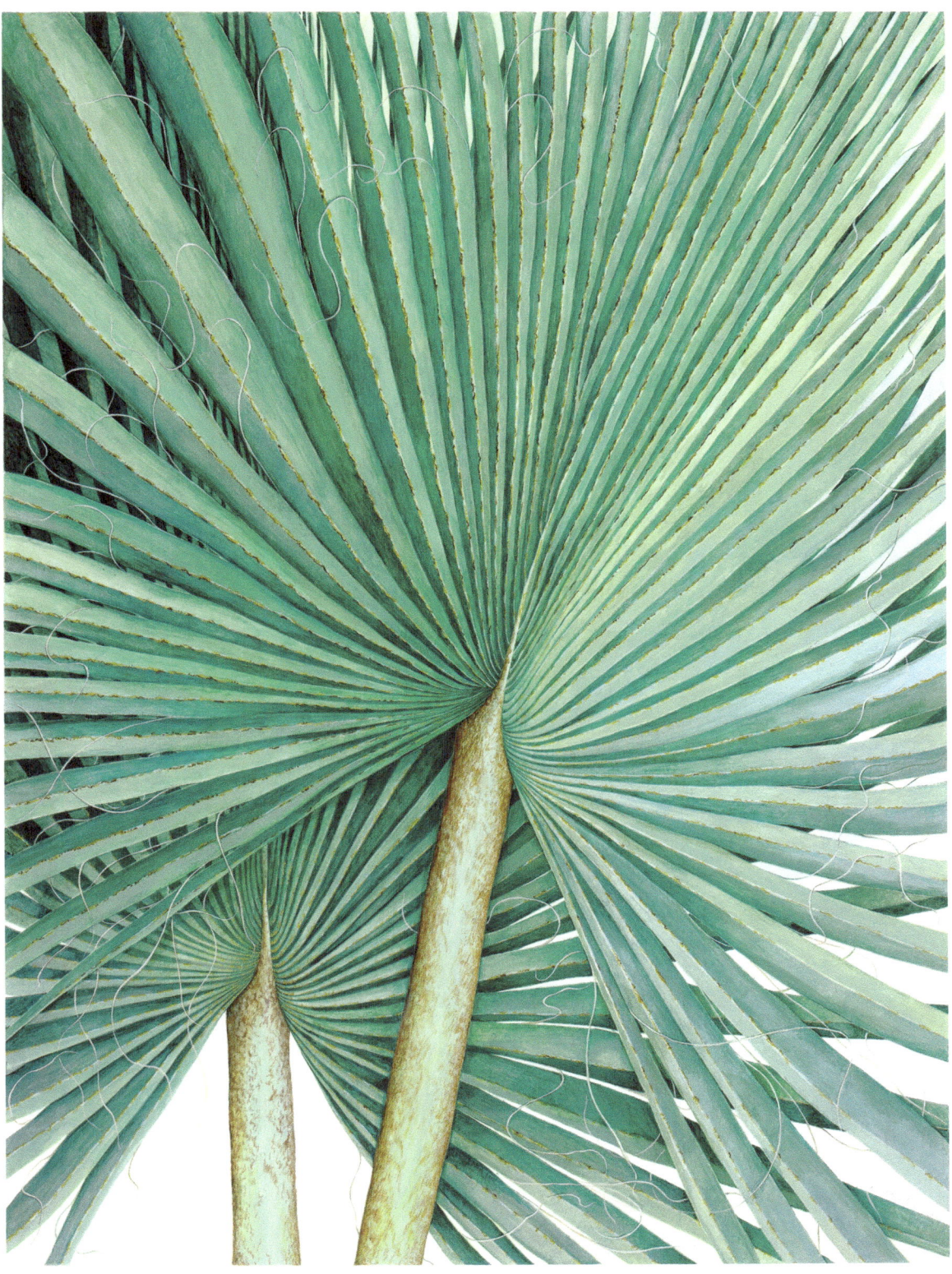

Rita Parkinson. *Pritchardia hillebrandii.* Gouache

COLOUR VARIATION IN LEAVES

Leaves are green because they contain
Chlorophyll, the molecule that causes
the light energy from sunlight to turn
water and carbon dioxide into sugar
and oxygen in the process we call
photosynthesis. It's the magnesium
base in plants that gives plants their
green colour. But plants do have addi-
tional pigments such as the xanthophylls (yellows) and carotenoids (yellows and oranges and reds). These
are also used in photosynthesis, but
occur in lesser quantities. The combinations of these different pigments are
responsible for the great variation in
greens that we see in nature.

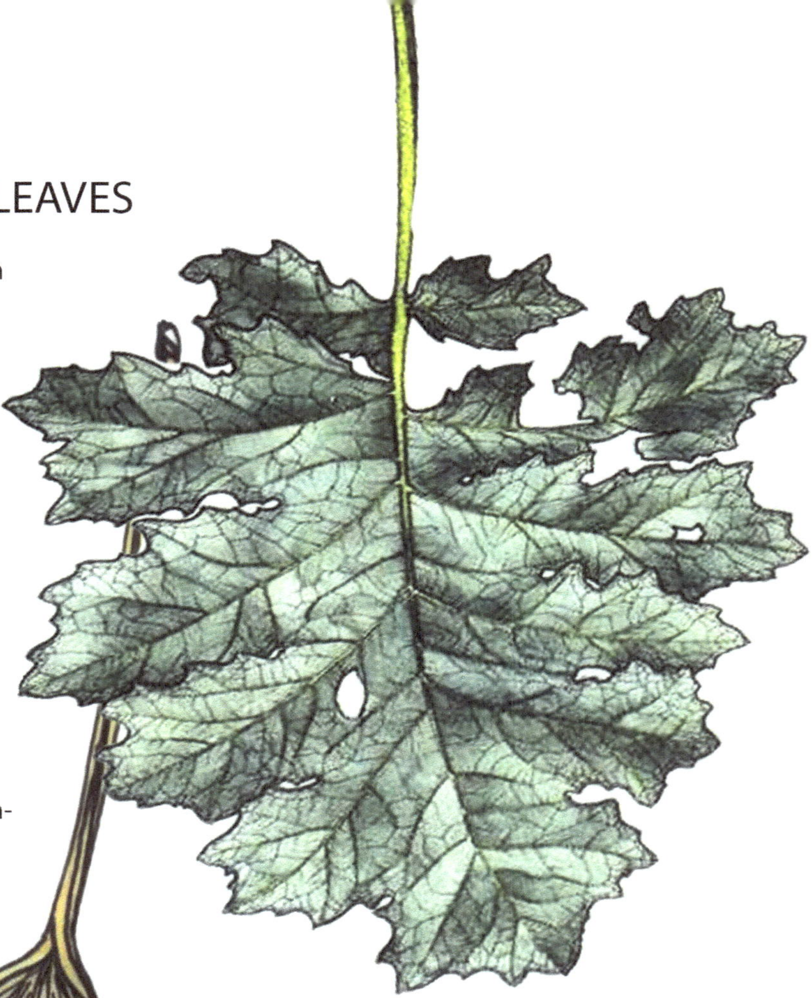

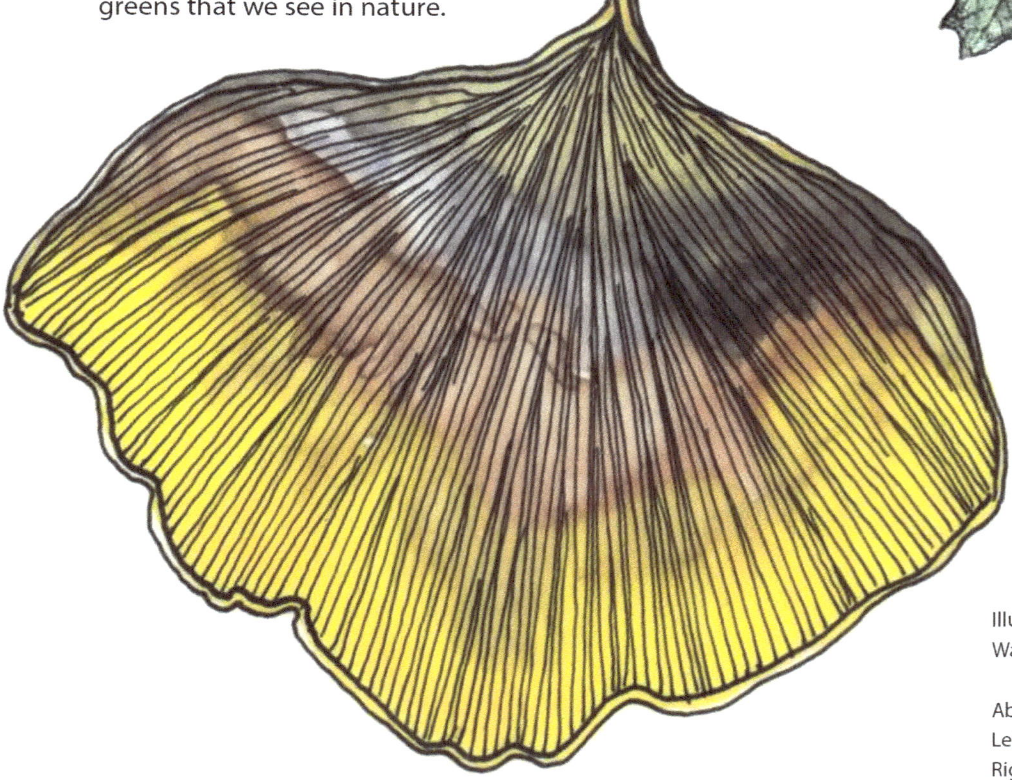

Illustrations: Dolores Sk-Malloni
Watercolour on film

Above: *Acanthus mollis*
Left: *Ginko biloba*
Right: *Codiaeum variagatum*

THE COLOURS OF AUTUMN

In Autumn as daylight hours shorten and the temperatures begin to cool, the chlorophyll begins to decrease. As the chlorophyll degrades, the other pigments present through the year, the yellow xanthophylls and orange beta-carotenes begin to show. Unlike the xanthophylls and carotenoids, there are other pigments, not present in the leaf through the growing season that are produced towards the end of summer. These colours come from the group of pigments called anthocyanins. These are the beautiful reds, purples, and their blended combinations that we see in autumn foliage.

VARIEGATION

Of course some leaves are variegated all the time. The pictorial qualities of these wonders of nature can provide for interesting pictorial effects to illustrate.

  Variegation of differently coloured zones in the leaves can be due to a number of causes. The simplest, and most common are:

Pigment variegation. This happens when the non-green parts of the leaf lack chlorophyll. Sometimes these parts have no pigments at all and look white, but more often there are other pigments present, so appear as cream or yellow, such as the variegated ivy.

Masking. Another cause is the masking of green pigment by other pigments, such as the anthocyanins. This can extends to the whole leaf, causing it to have red or purple tinges.

Zonal. But on some plants masking occurs as consistent zonal markings occur; such as on some Begonias, Bromeliads, certain Pelargoniums and Oxalis species and forms of Coleus. Variegation in plants is attractive and ornamental and the horticultural industry always has an interest in encouraging new forms.

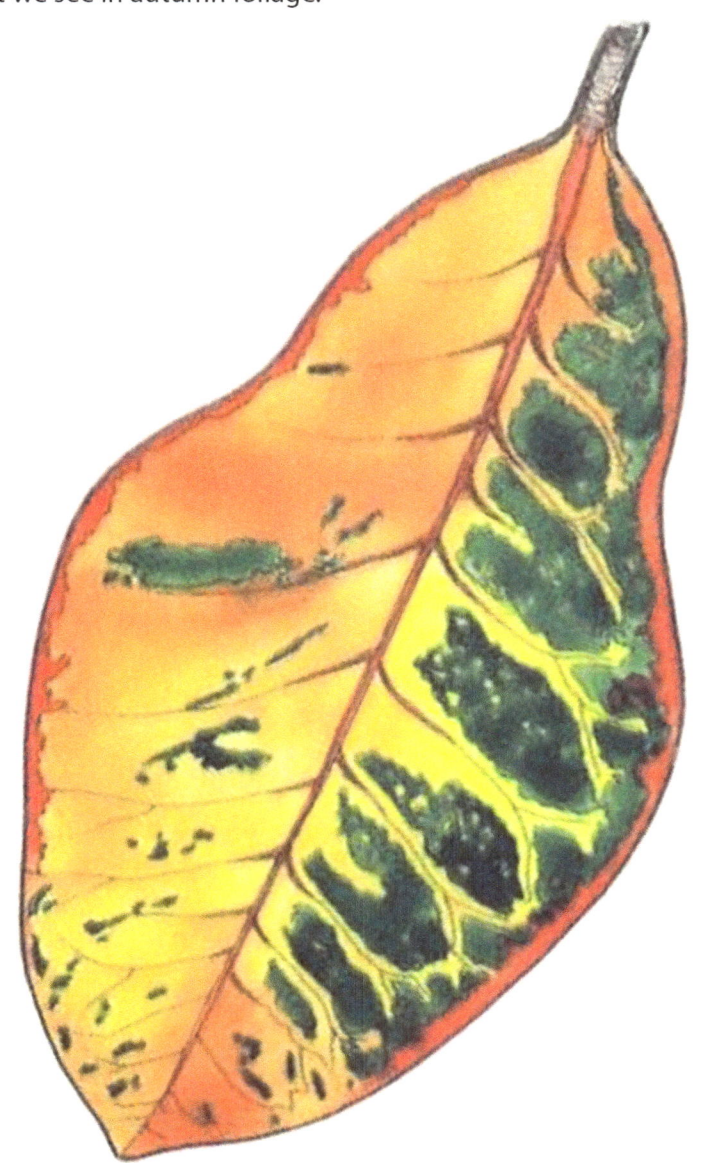

VENATION

The pattern of leaf venation is an important characteristic for the identification of plants. The veins consists of vascular bundles that help in the transport of water from the roots to the leaf, and the materials produced in the leaf to the rest of the plant. This networks of veins are also the vessels that transport vital mineral nutrients. They also support the structure of the leaf.

A composition that emphasizes the venation of leaves is one that focuses on these vital processes going on within the leaf, emphasizing the complex variety of web patterns that exist to do this. The main forms are:

PALMATE

A palmate leaf is one in which the veins, and lobes, all radiate from a single point, like a Maple leaf.

PINNATE

A pinnate venation is a vein arrangement in a leaf which has one main vein extending from the base to the tip of the leaf and smaller veins branching off the main vein

RETICULATE VENATION

Reticulated venation occurs when the veins branch repeatedly and unite forming a complicated network where all the veins are interconnected.

PARALLEL VENATION

A leaf with parallel venation has veins that run parallel or nearly parallel to each other and are connected by a network of smaller veins. This is consistent with the highly elongated leaf shape and wide leaf base, typical for most monocotyledons, such as grasses and irises.

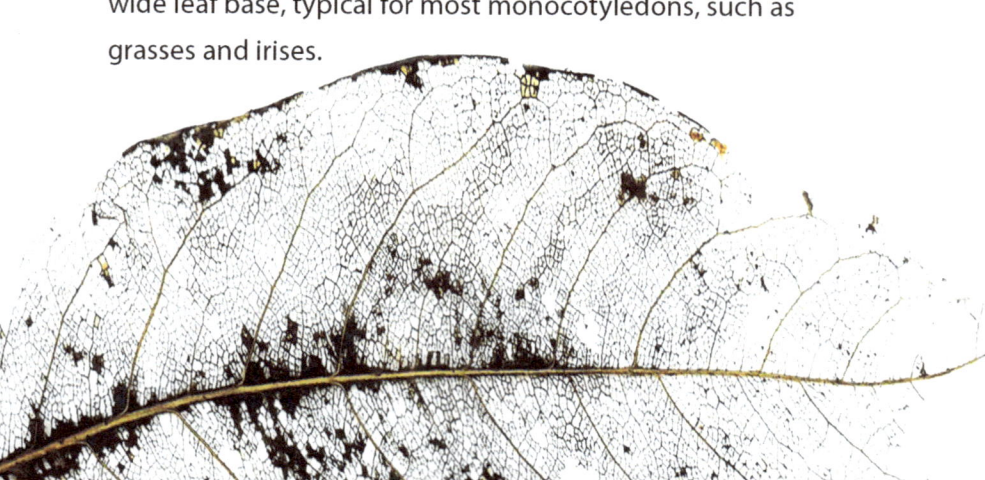

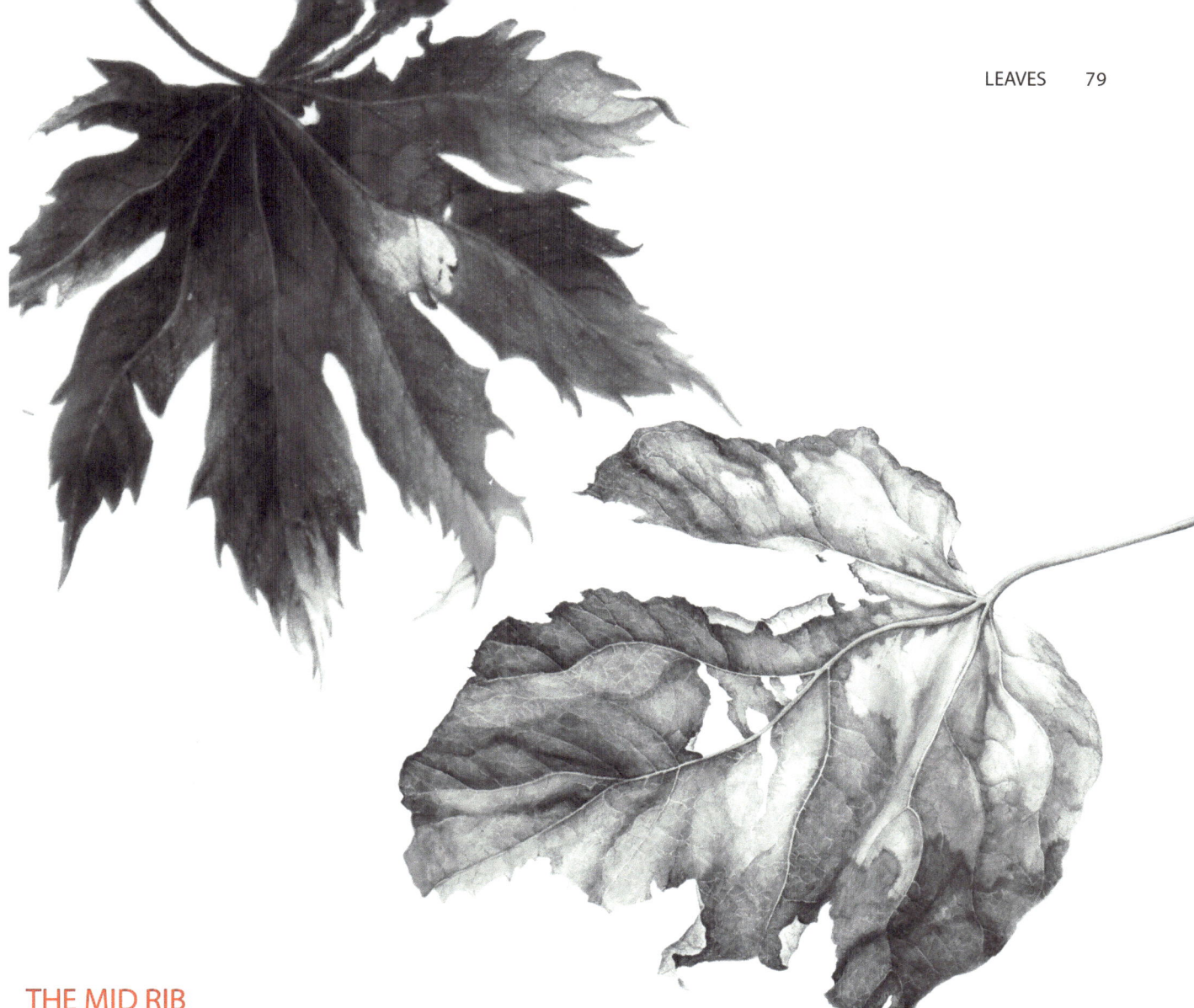

THE MID RIB

The middle prominent vein is the key vein known as the 'mid rib'. This primary vein supports a sequence of secondary veins, which may branch further into tertiary veins. The primary vein can be considered a support like a tree trunk and the secondary and tertiaries veins as the branches of the tree.

Painting venation well has its difficulties. If the veins are 'positive', they can be painted in with a darker hue. The more difficult situation is where the veins are 'negative', that is lighter than their surroundings. A skilled use of resist techniques is called for here. This gets progressively more difficult as the venation passes from the secondary to the finer tertiary veins. There is really no easy way to do this well, beyond a lot of practice, and of course a high degree of patience.

Far Left : Photocopy of unknown leaf with pinnate venation.
Near Left: *Iris germanicus*. Leaves with parallel venation.
Above: *Acer palmatum*. Japanese maple leaf with palmate venation.
Right: *Solanum betacum*. Tamarillo leaf with reticulate venation.

THE ARCHITECTURE OF PLANTS

Karl Blossfeldt 1865 – 1932

The father of the architectural approach to botanical illustration would have to be Karl Blossfeldt, the German photographer, sculptor and teacher. He was inspired by nature and the way in which plants grow. He is best known for his close-up photographs of plants and living things. He believed that 'the plant must be valued as a totally artistic and archi-tectural structure'. He was appointed for a teaching post at the Institute of Royal Arts Museum. Berlin, and worked there from 1898 -1932. Blossfeldt never received formal train-ing in photography. But he developed a series of home-made cameras, that allowed him to photograph his subject up to thirty times its size, revealing extraordinary details within a plant's natural structure. This reflected his enduring interest in the abstract shapes and repetitive patterns and textures, found in nature's structures.

   In Berlin, Blossfeldt's works were primarily used as teaching tools and were only brought to public attention by the publication in 1928 of 'Art Forms in Nature', published when Blossfeldt was 63 and a Professor of Applied Art at the Berlin Academy of Art. The book quickly became an international bestseller and in turn, made Blossfeldt famous almost overnight. The images fulfill their primary purpose, to educate and clarify, and they do this magnificently in the most sublime way.

His approach was to focus on the small parts, to enlarge them and to emphasize their form by the most artful use of tonality. He did all this with black and white photography. Of course he wouldn't have access to colour at the time, but none the less no one could doubt that here was an artist who could focus on his goal clearly with a very high level of visual acuity.

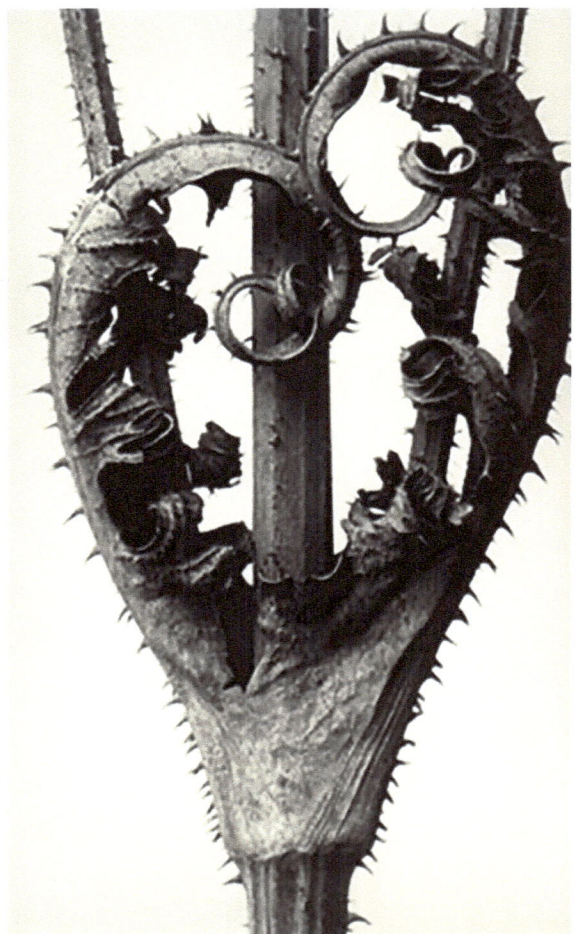

Karl Blossfeldt *Dipsacus laciniatus*
Cut-leaved teasal. Dried on stem

Rita Parkinson *Pritchardia pacifica* Fiji fan palm. Gouache on board.

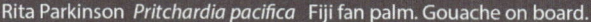

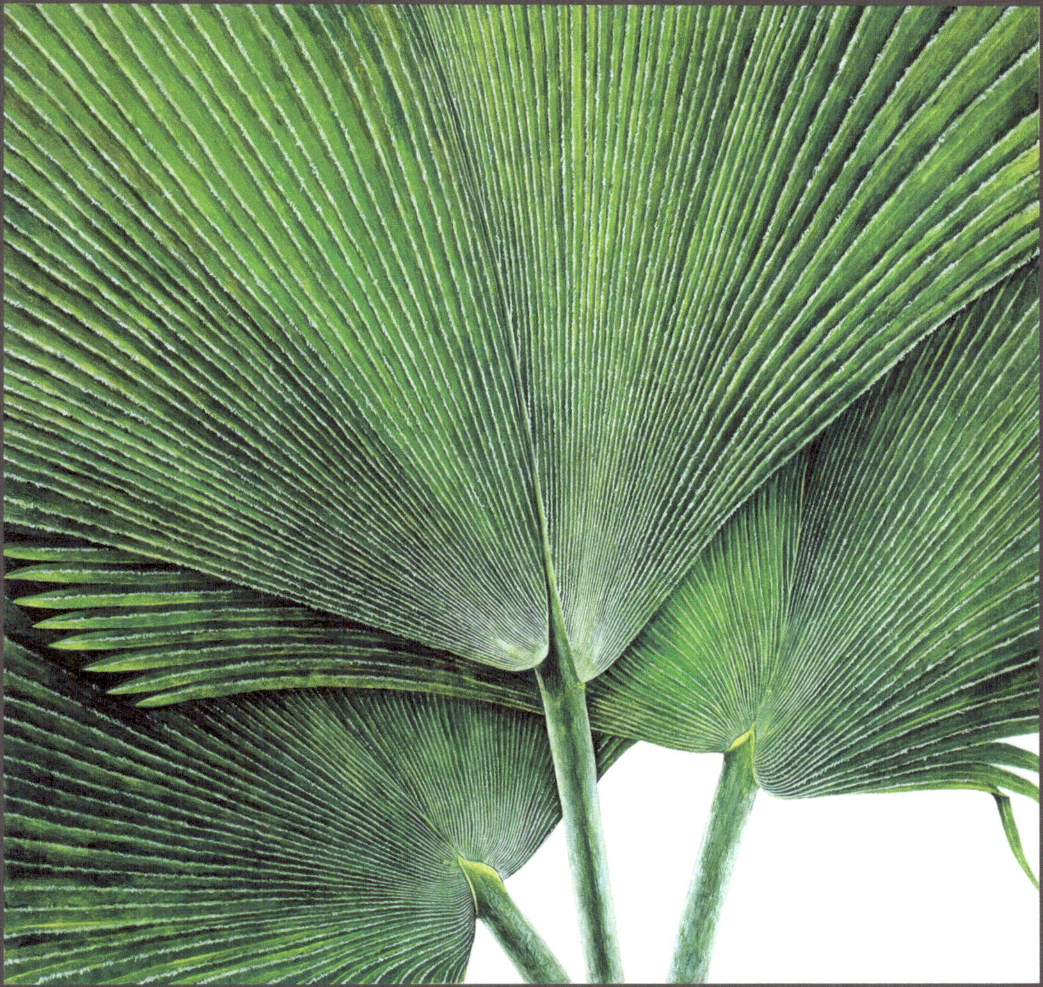

To choose to portray a plant for its architectural characteristics is to put the emphasis on structure. You could of course take this approach with any plant, but some subjects suit the approach better than others.

For me, the Agaves, Yuccas, Cacti and Grasses are all strong candidates for this approach. In many of these plants neither colour nor floral forms are their strongest characteristics in the pictorial sense. The more muted colorations, and simplified forms, are all factors that will enhance the structural approach.

The slowly evolved structures of plants have often been an inspiration for architects and engineers. But in the final analysis, as Blossfeldt proved, ultimately it is another revealing and useful way of looking at nature.

Urformen der Kunst (Art Forms in Nature).
Karl Blossfeldt. Published 1928.

THE ART OF NATURE

Ernst Haeckel. 1834-1919

People have always been inspired by observing the patterns inherent in nature. Anyone whose interests lie in this direction will sooner or later come across the work of Ernst Haeckel.

HAECKEL THE SCIENTIST

Ernst Haeckel was a German physician and Professor of Comparative Anatomy at the University of Jena in Germany. He was highly influenced by Darwin's revolutionary publication in 1859 of 'Origin of the Species by Means of Natural Selection'. He was convinced by the idea of evolution, but was less supportive of natural selection as the mechanism by which evolution occurred.

THE THEORY OF RECAPITULATION

So Ernst Haeckel set about creating his own philosophy which he called 'The Theory of Recapitulation', and then set about illustrating it. Unfortunately for posterity his theories turned out to be less than correct. The science of his theory was simply wrong.

But this wasn't his only field of study. Haeckel's literary output was extensive, and we can also remember him as the one who coined the words ecology, phylum and stem cell.

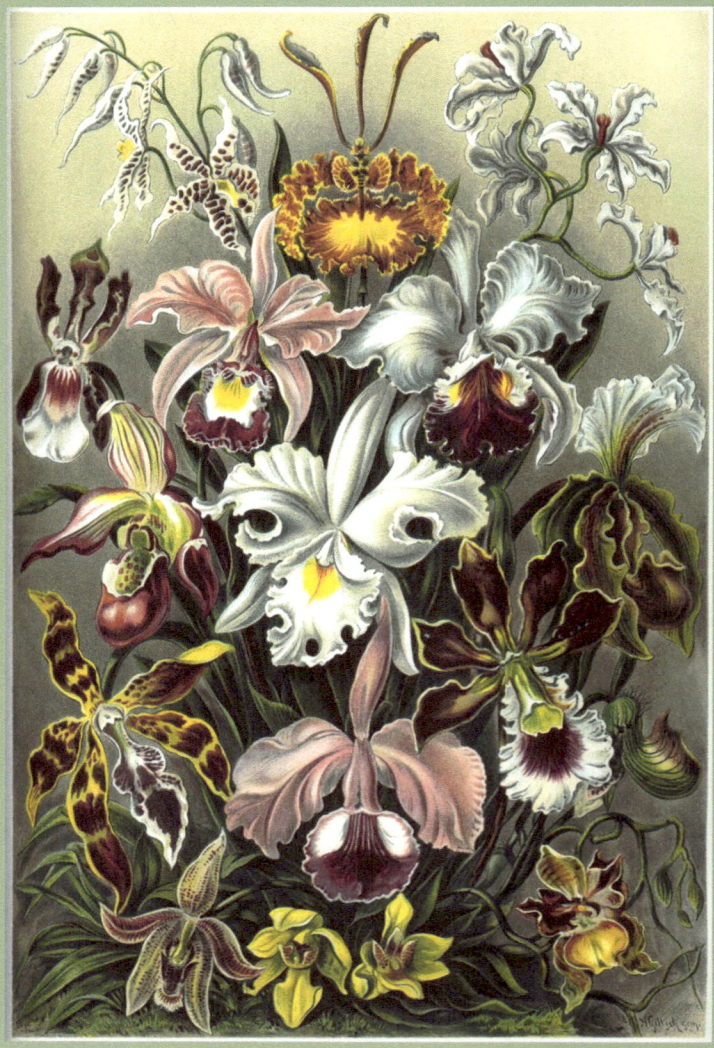

Plates from 'Art Forms in Nature'. Ernst Haeckel
Right: *Orchidae*
Far right: *Nepenthaceae*

HAECKEL THE ILLUSTRATOR

As it turned out Haeckel was a highly gifted illustrator, albeit of a theory that wasn't correct. But in the process he did create a series of brilliant, engaging diagrammatic illustrations of natural forms that have fascinated many ever since. He produced his famous treatise 'Art Forms in Nature' in 1904 and it is here that his name lives on.

ART FORMS IN NATURE

'Art Forms in Nature' contains over a hundred detailed multi-coloured plates of animals, sea creatures and plants. His illustrations have entranced generations, and life being essentially chaotic, they paradoxically proved to be very influential in the illustrative arts. The uniqueness of his sinuous style that combined symmetry and organic forms, was a major influence on the style that came to be known as 'Art Nouveau'.

His best known plates are those he made of jelly fish and other sea forms. But he did create some wonderful plant illustrations.

Haeckel's illustrations can't be a direct influence on botanical illustration. They break too many of the conventions. None the less, they are a tour de force of illustrative imagination and an engaging view of natural subjects.

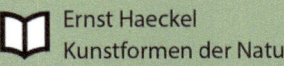

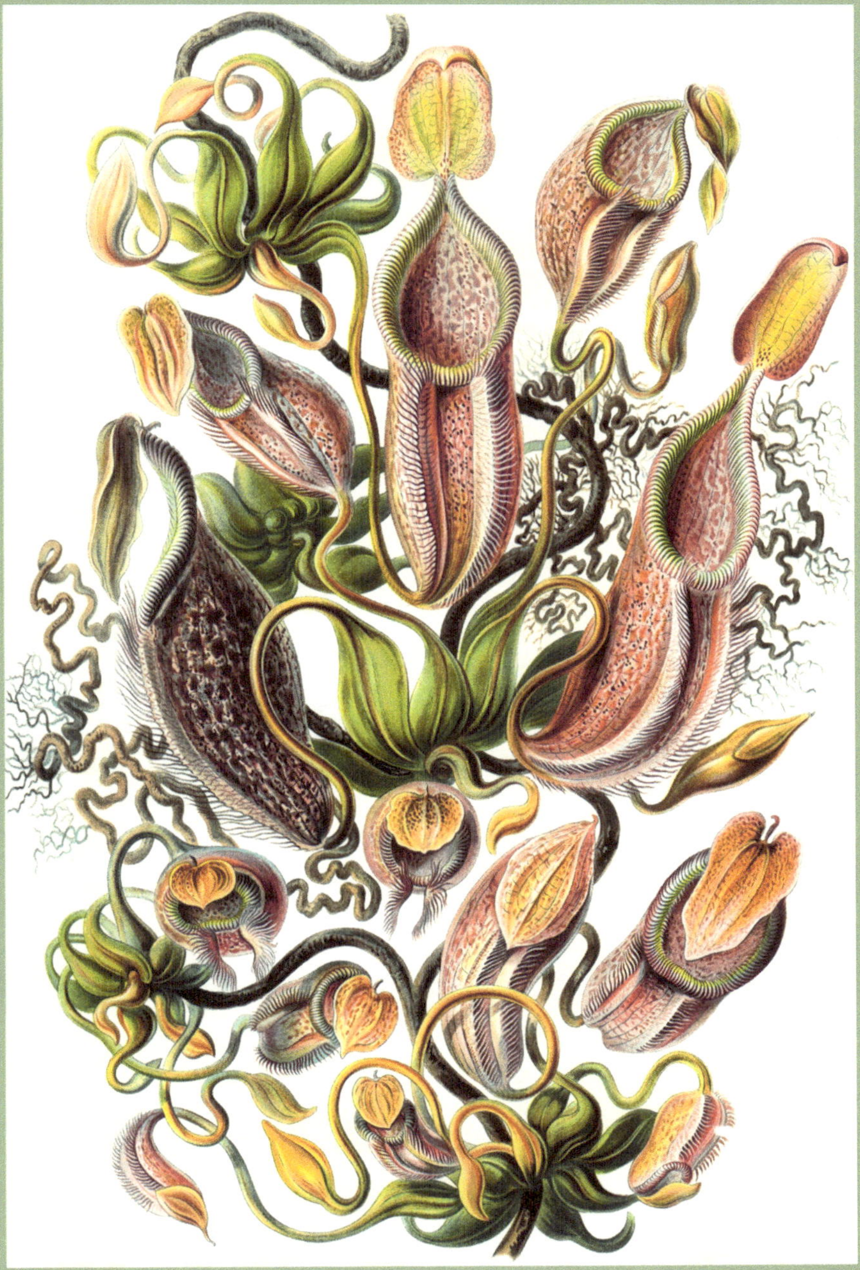

Ernst Haeckel
Kunstformen der Natur

'Art Forms of Nature'

THE FIBONACCI SEQUENCE IN PLANTS

The patterns and structures found in the plant world make a fascinating study. An understanding of the Fibonacci sequence discovered in 1202, can help the artist enter this intriguing world, and it can be important to understand when approaching some subjects. The sequence is a close mathematical relative to the golden ratio, and is achieved by adding the two previous numbers to make the succeeding developmental sequence. The Fibonacci formula explains the arrangement of parts in many natural phenomena including the plant world. It can be observed in the arrangement of petals in a rose, the arrangement of the small flowers at the centre of a sunflower, the seed arrangement of cones and many more. In some plants it is difficult to observe, but there are plants where the sequence is very apparent such as in the arrangement of sections in a pineapple. The sequence is most easily observed in: Cones, Pineapples, Cacti, Cycads and composite flowers such as the sunflower.

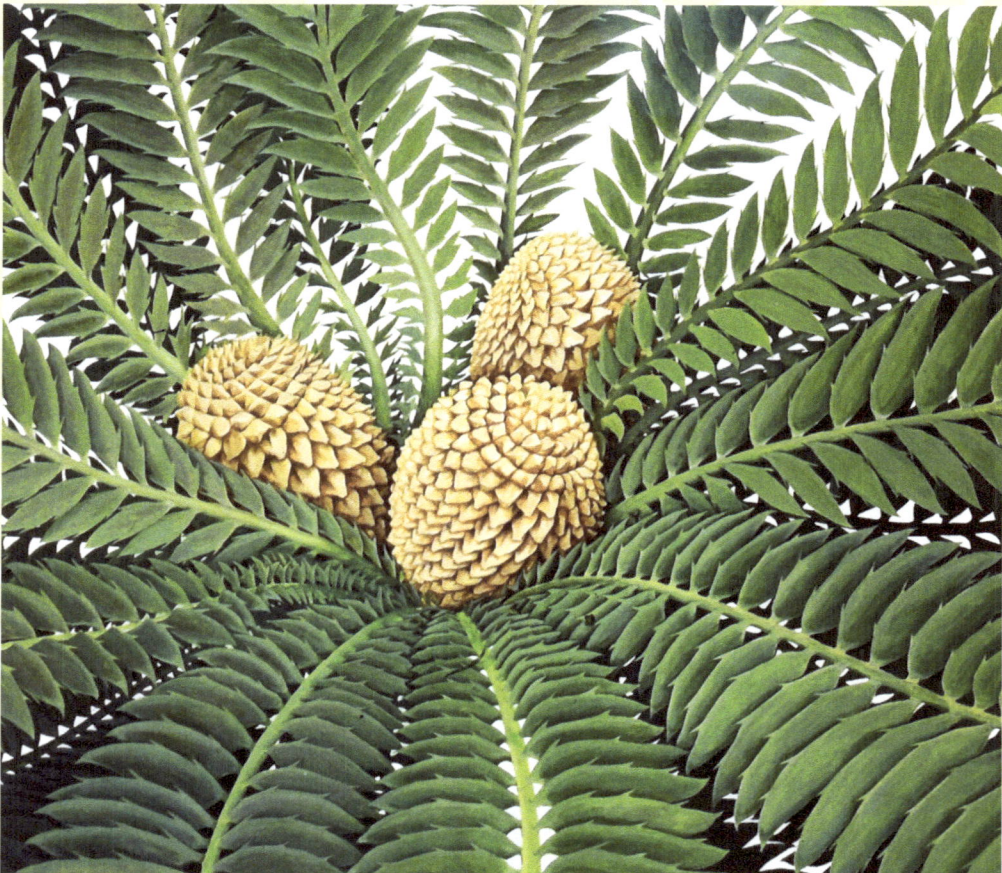

Rita Parkinson
Left: *Cycas* enphalartos
Gouache
Right above: *Araucaria bidwilli*.
Bunya Bunya Pine Cone
Gouache
Right: *Ananus Comosus*
Pineapple
Gouache

THE SEQUENCE

The Fibonacci Sequence works as a series of numbers: 0, 1, 1, 2, 3, 5, 8, 13, 21, 34 ....
The next number is found by adding up the two numbers before it. The 2 is found by adding the two numbers before it (1+1). Similarly, the 3 is found by adding the two numbers before it (1+2), and the 5 is made by adding (2+3), and so on to infinity. The next number in the sequence above is (21+34) = 55

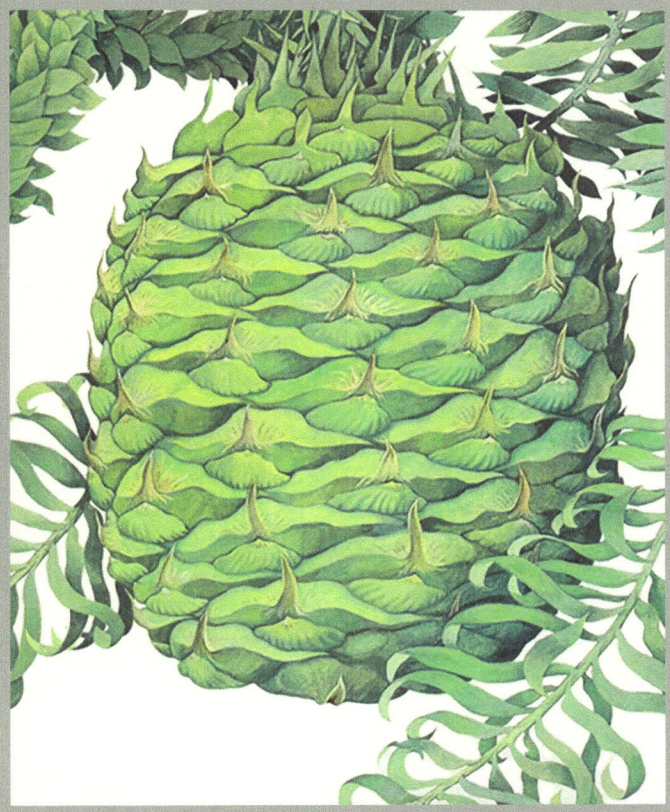

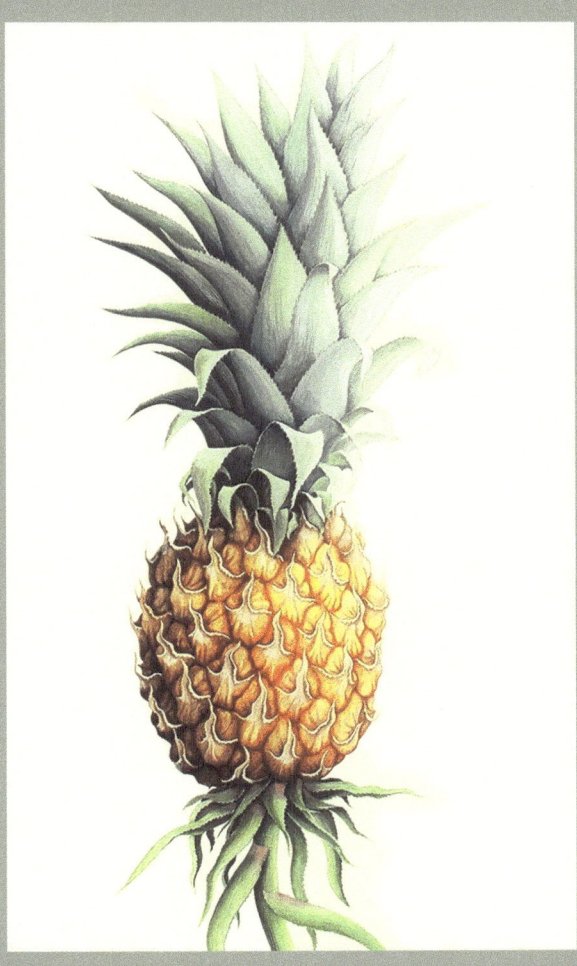

AN EVOLUTIONARY PLOY

This efficiency in pattern of development seems to be programmed into the growing process. One can see it in the rosettes of cacti and succulents, where the separate segments are arranged to allow valuable rainfall to be retained and directed to the root system. In the cone form, starting at the axis, the seeds spiral outwards in an angle that follows the sequence in an arrangement that enables the most effective positioning of as many seeds as possible to be packed into the given space that provides maximum exposure to the sun. If the placement of the angles is not accurate it would not happen so efficiently. As it is, the sequence of spirals in each direction must follow the pattern accurately.

ANATOMY OF A PLANT

The use of the cross section is a staple devise in botanical illustration and is used as a means of accurately describing significant parts of a plant's anatomy. Such details are often, very small when seen in the context of the entire plant. When the subject matter warrants it, a particular feature is enlarged and rendered out of scale with the main illustration as an aid to comprehension, and usually arranged along the base of the illustration. The cross section images on these pages differ from this convention by enlarging the sectional view to such an extent that they become the entire picture. In these images the plant is still examined in an anatomical manner but the illustration focuses on specific functions, describing them diagrammatically and to scale.

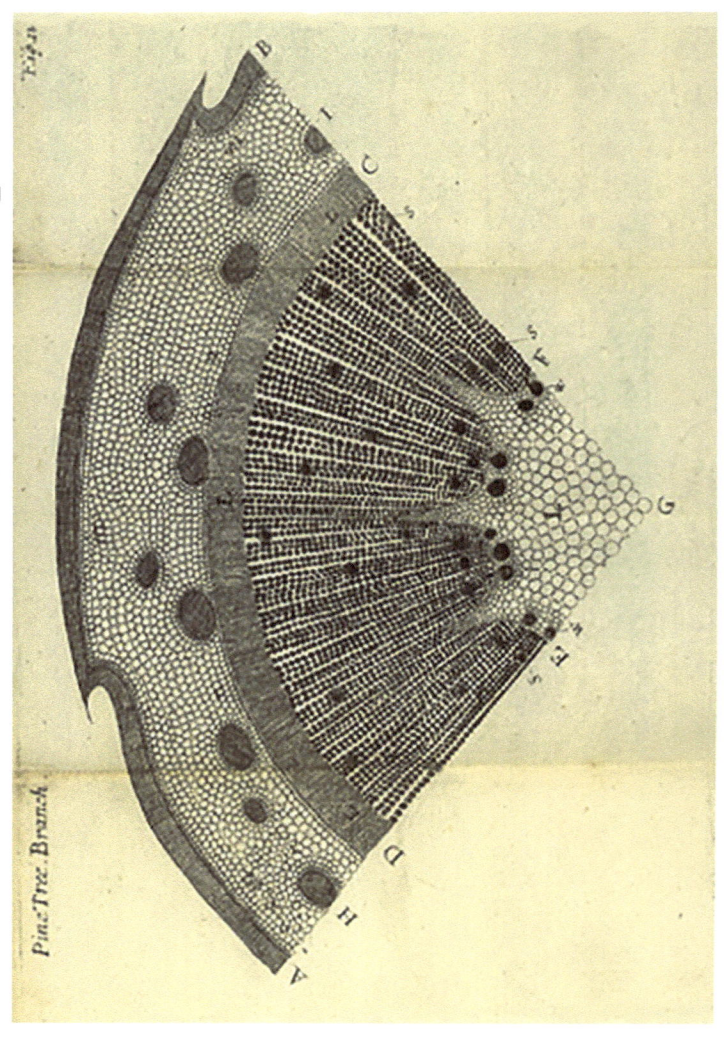

Nehemiah Grew   Cell structure of Pine tree branch

NEHEMIAH GREW. 1641-1712

Nehemiah Grew was an English botanist who together with the Italian, Marcello Malpighi, are considered the co-founders of plant anatomy. Grew and Malpighi, working independently, at similar times came to similar conclusions about the function of sap and its resemblance to the system of circulation of the blood in the animal world. Grew approached his botanic studies from the standpoint of medicine, and it was his knowledge of anatomy that opened his mind to the processes within a plant. The work of these two men took place just as the Medieval Herbals were losing their influence and the forces of the Renaissance and reason were coming to the fore.

   His great work on the Anatomy of Plants, appeared in 1682. It was divided into four books, Anatomy of Vegetables, Anatomy of Roots, Anatomy of Trunks and Anatomy of Leaves, Flowers, Fruits and Seeds, and was illustrated with eighty-two plates.

ARTHUR CHURCH

When you first come across the paintings of Arthur Church, what strikes you is their simplicity of purpose, their clarity and the pure elegance of their design. Arthur Harry Church was an unlikely botanical illustrator. He was a reclusive professor of biology at Oxford University who never considered himself an artist. His illustrations were made to demonstrate how the reproductive structures of flowers work, in a pictorially straightforward way, that would make them simple for his student to understand. He devised his unique mechanistic style which verged on the diagrammatic, by very enlarged details of cross-sections, always depicted in perfect, magnified detail. His entire works encompassed an enormous variety of plant reproductive systems and in the process he made an important contribution in the field of botanical art and science.

Despite his purely pedagogical intentions his work has such a beautiful clarity of purpose, aligned with a natural pictorial sensibility that it would not be out of place in an art gallery today.

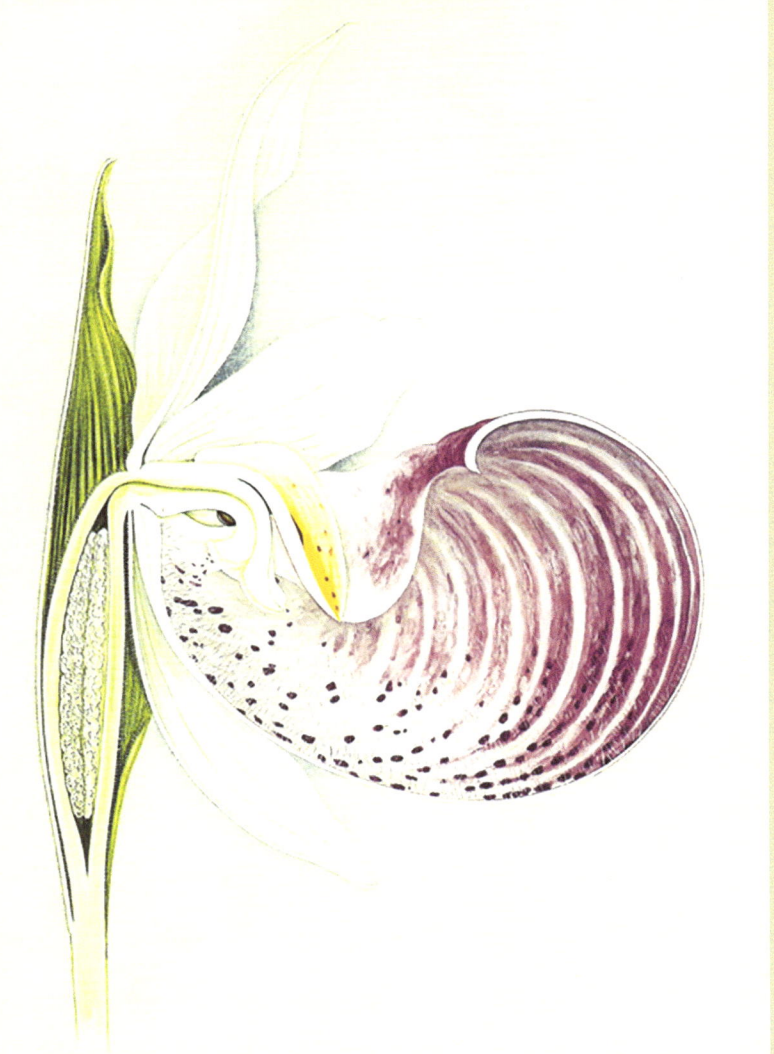

Arthur Church. *Cypridedium reginae* Lady's slipper orchid

Church described his book "Types of Flora Mechanism" published in 1908 as follows "They are limited to a hundred types as illustrating what may be termed in popular phraseology 'The Hundred Best Flowers' has been arranged for publication in the hope that it may prove useful, not only to other teachers and students, but also to all those who are interested in the study of the Natural History and problems of plant-life."

 Arthur Church "The Anatomy of Flowers". David Mabberley. Published by the Natural History Museum 2003.

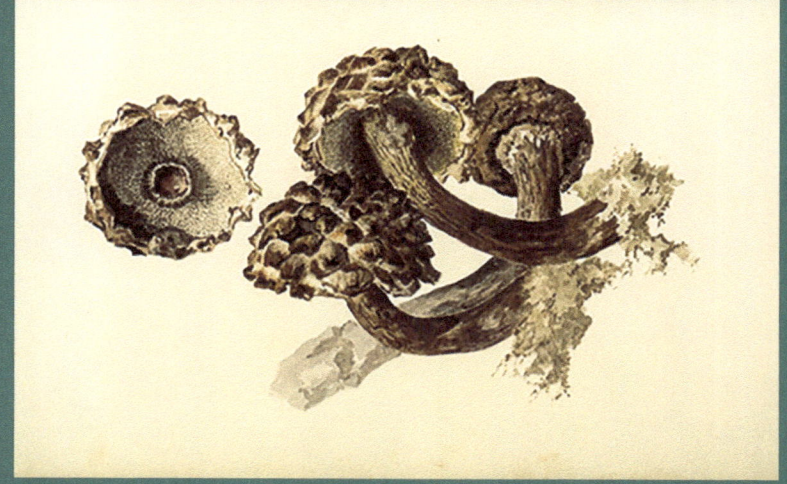

Strobilomces strobilaceus. Beatrice Potter

OTHER WORLDS

ALGAE

FUNGI

LICHENS

BRYOPHYTES

ALGAE Phycology

Phycology is the scientific study of Algae. It is a sub discipline of botany. Aquatic algae are found in both fresh and marine waters. They are simple plants that can range from the single-celled and microscopic of phytoplankton and other microalgae up the large seaweeds, such as sargassum and the giant kelp which is more than one hundred feet in length. They are very diverse and found almost everywhere on the planet. The seaweeds can be broadly divided between green, red or brown forms, depending on their nearness to the surface and the resulting level of photosynthesis that will influence the chlorophyll levels. The number of algae are conservatively estimated at 700,000 seaweed species and many more if you include the microalgae. Algae are probably the least illustrated of plant forms. This is understandable as the limited colour range may limit the appeal to many. But the real fascination lies in their unusual structures, the feathery waving fronds, the delicate filaments of this underwater world.

THE SEAWEEDS

The seaweeds are distinguished from the higher plants by a lack of a root system to take up nutrients. Their "roots" are called holdfasts that keep the algae anchored onto the rock surface. Algae take their food in through their leaf-like fronds which are surrounded by nutrient-carrying seawater. Algae have several features that make them unlike normal land-based flowering plants. As they do not flower they have to reproduce quite differently to the flowering plants. They have spores like the ferns, mosses, lichens and liverworts. Algae play a primary part in aquatic ecosystems including providing the foundation for the aquatic food chains and can be the first indications when things are out of balance.

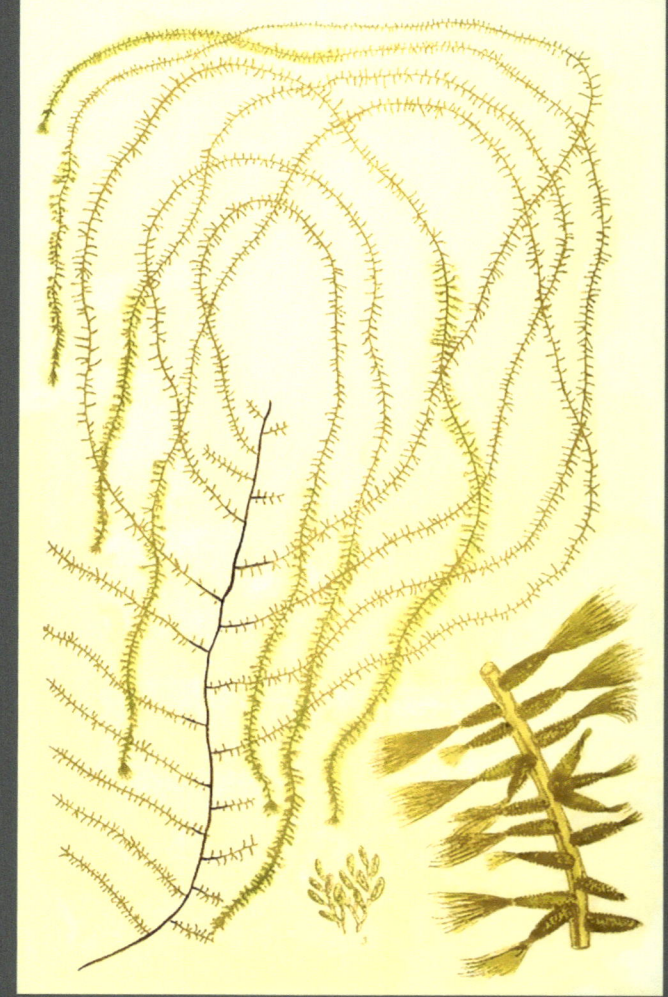

William Henry Harvey. 1811-1866

The masters of botanical illustration come in many guises. William Henry Harvey was an Irish botanist whose main area of interest was phycology. He was an authority on European, American, South African and Australian algae. His books, including Phycologia Australica (London, 1858-63) is a seminal work on Australian seaweeds and is still referred to today. It is a rare book now and you would be fortunate to come across a copy. Harvey was widely travelled and needed to be his own illustrator. He wouldn't be the first to do this, but he was a gifted one.

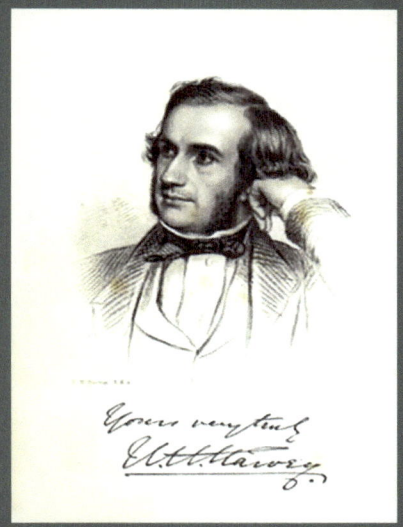

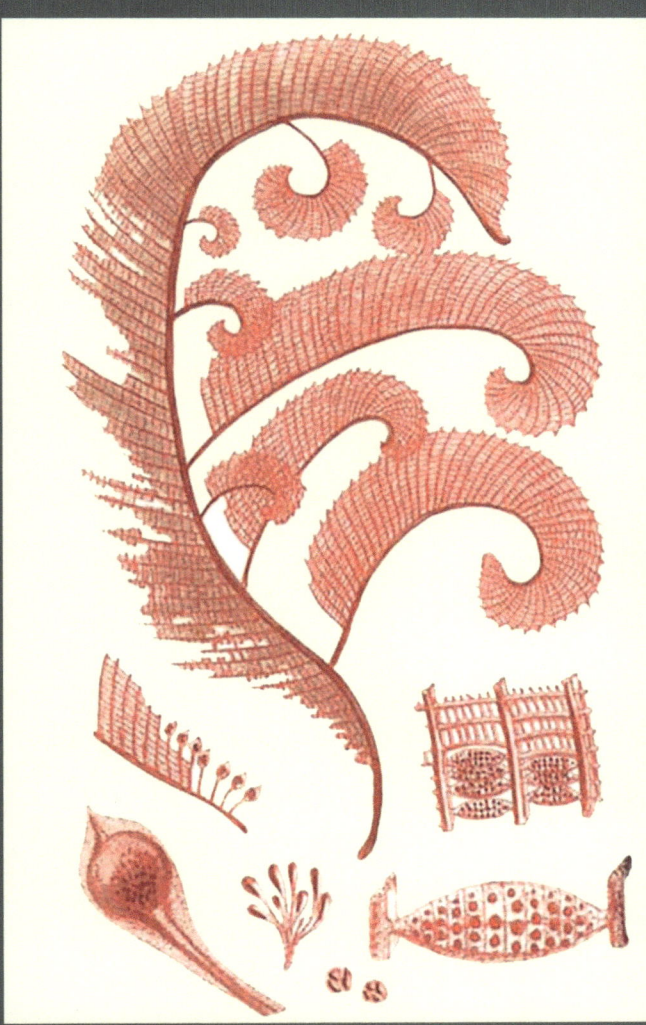

This begs the question, what exactly makes a good illustrator? Generally an illustrator, as opposed to an artist works to someone else. This person is the primary source of information whether they are a scientist or an author. The illustrators' job is to illuminate the subject. No more, no less. This brings us back to William Harvey. His illustrations are deceptively simple, but illustrate what needs to be known, and of course he knew exactly what that was, because he was the botanist and knew exactly what his peers would need to know. The result is that his illustrations seamlessly integrate all the essential elements pictorially, to accommodate the plate. There is nothing extraneous here. His complete knowledge of his subject informed his pictorial work and his natural skill as an illustrator created images that were a perfect meld of science and image.

Images from: Phycologia australica: Harvey, W.H. (1862).
Left: *Claudia elegans*
Far left: *Sporochnus apodus*

THE SEAWEEDS

MAKING A SPECIMEN

Unlike the majority of plants, an algae really does need to be made into a dried specimen in order for the illustrator to be able to observe the sample over a period of time. They are just too awkward, slippery and that pleasant aroma from the sea can quickly degrade. Making a dried specimen is not difficult. It is done by placing the cleaned specimen into a shallow tray of clean water. A piece of acid free paper is placed beneath it, and then slowly drawn out of the tray with the specimen remaining on the paper as you remove it. While you do this, you need to arrange the specimen with an instrument such as a kebab stick, in such a way as to create the optimum specimen for illustration purposes. The resulting specimen is then dried over several days. The result is a specimen that you can take time to observe and refer to at close range and then illustrate.

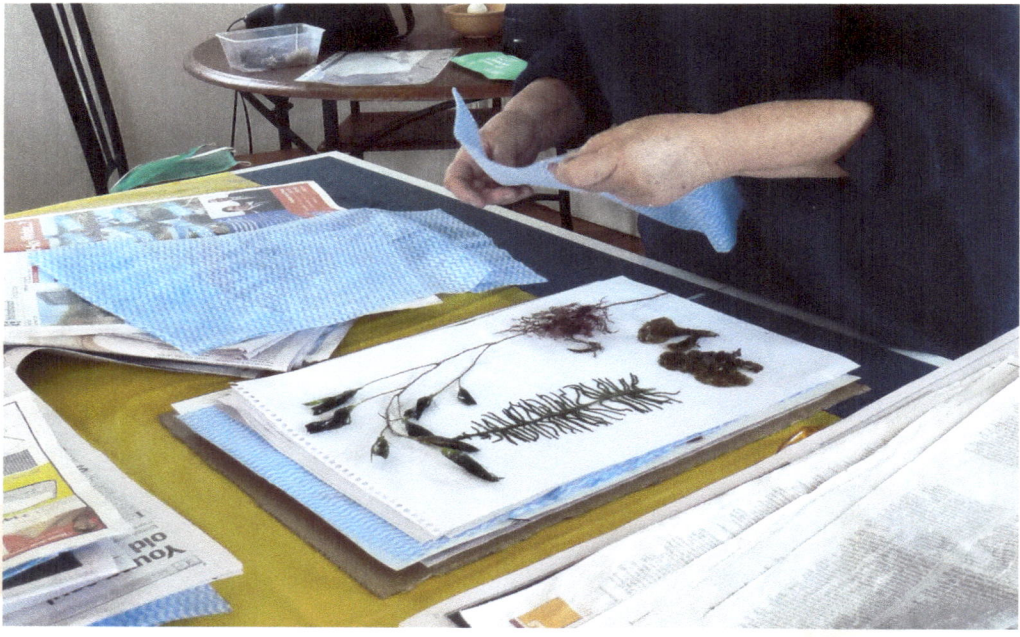

GETTING THE SCALE RIGHT

It is not always possible or desirable to illustrate a seaweed specimen to actual size. Seaweeds can vary enormously from the large kelps, to some very small examples of just a few centimeters that have some exquisite detailed forms. They simply cannot be understood if illustrated at their actual size. The illustrations on the preceding page by Harvey were not done to actual size, but to accomodate the plate, that is to make them comprehensible.

The main parts of an Algae that you should aim to include if possible in an illustration, are the holdfast, the stipe, the blade and the bladder floats if they are present.

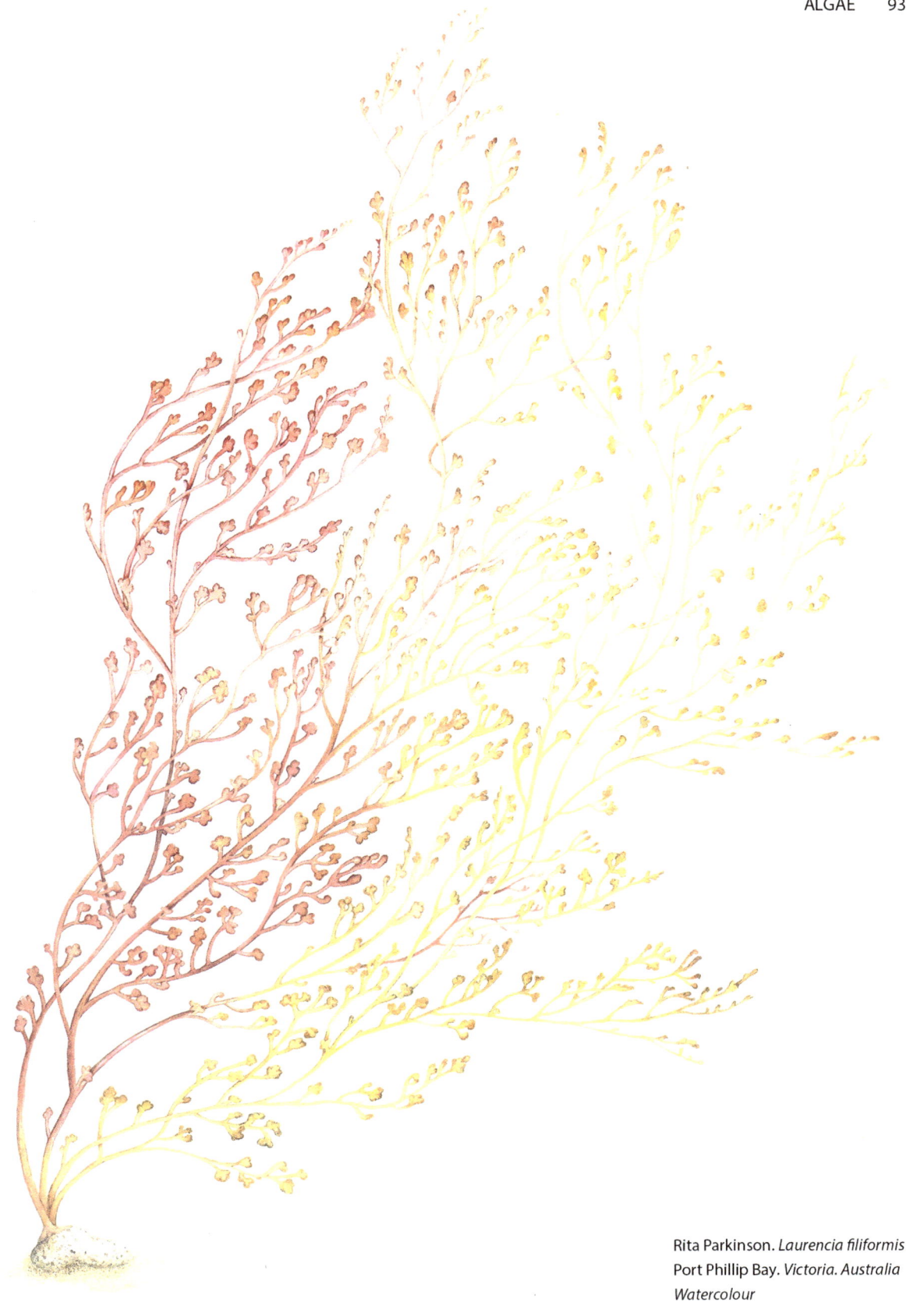

Rita Parkinson. *Laurencia filiformis*
Port Phillip Bay. *Victoria. Australia*
Watercolour

FUNGI

Fungi are a fascinating subject that has great appeal for some artists. They are a complete family, entirely separate from the plantae family. There are estimated to be over 1.5 million species. But this could be a conservative estimate. This makes the fungi family six times as diverse as the family plantae, and that means that very few of this vast field have been described so far. The family does include the yeasts and molds as well as the more familiar mushrooms but it is images of the macro fungi that we see most often. The mushrooms and sporocarps that you see are actually the fruiting bodies of the fungi. For the rest of the time the plant could be just membrane strings underneath the ground.

   This is another type of small world like the lichens and bryophytes, a miniature world with its own unique structures and systems. The strangeness of the structures, the soft spongy textures, the underside lined with tiny gills, the earthy colours and patterns provide subtle aesthetic images. The blemishes of the forms and the detritus of the ground can provide a counterpoint to these weird and wonderful structures of nature.

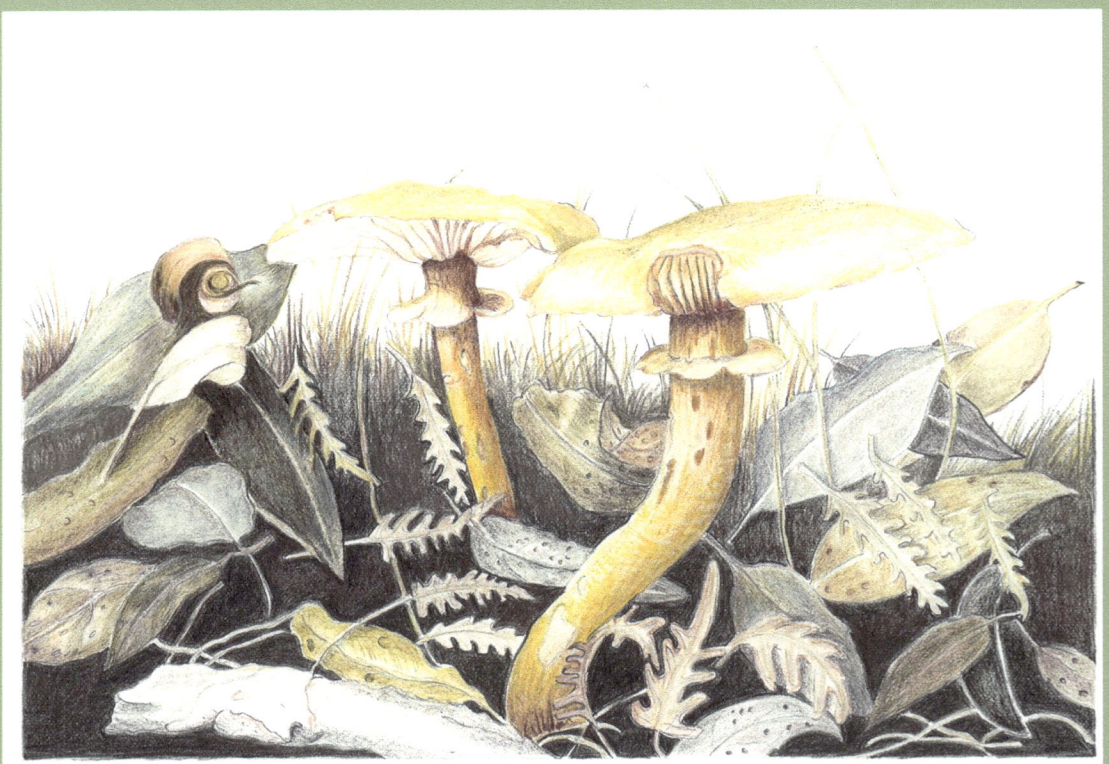

Marlene Hurt. Fungi and leaf litter. Grampians N.W. Victoria. Australia. Coloured Pencil

Beatrice Potter 1866-1943.

It was the landscape of the English Lake District that inspired Beatrix Potter to create her famous children's book illustrations, but it also inspired her other, less well-known, passion - botany. Beatrice Potter is of course best known for her inspired cosy world of the creatures of the countryside that she created for children. A large part of the reason they were so successful was because she was a gifted naturalist, and could channel her illustrations with a level of truth not available to most of us.

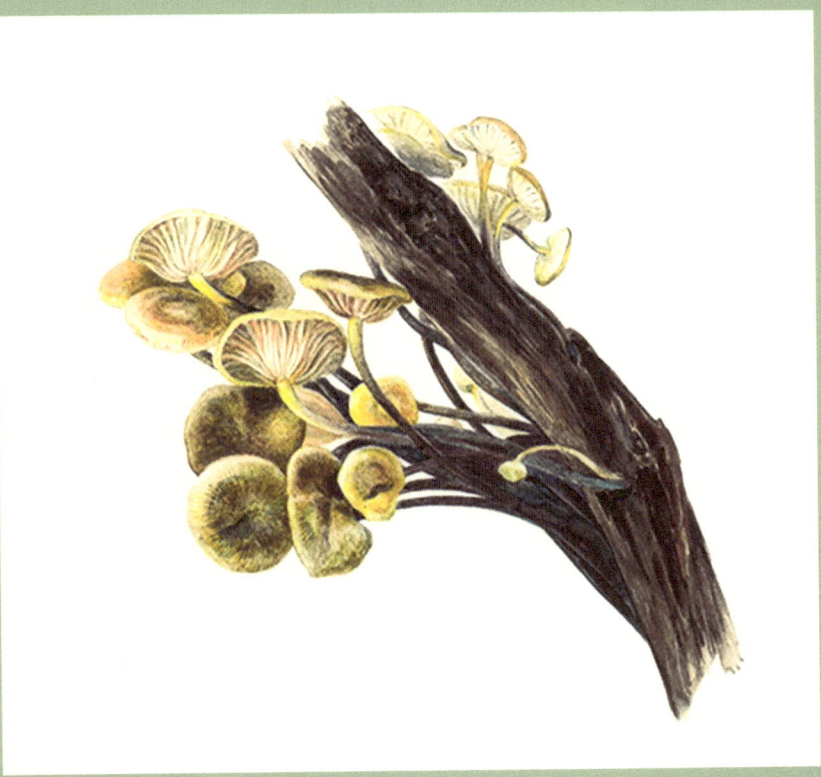

Beatrice Potter. *Flamulina veluptipes.* Watercolour

The Mycologist

Her work in Mycology, the study of fungi, is still referenced today. She conducted experiments with the germination of fungi and lichens and even wrote and presented a paper on the subject to The Linnean Society of London, the world's oldest, active society concerned with the biological sciences. Her paper was accepted for reading, after a peer review, at an open meeting of the society, however, for unknown reasons, it was not published. She had plenty of respected scientists and mycologists backing her paper, and it is unclear why it was rejected, but the Linnean Society eventually apologized for her treatment many years later. The paper itself, unfortunately, has been lost.

 Beatrix Potter: A Life in Nature. 2008. Linda Lear

MINIATURE WORLDS

Lichens together with the bryophytes are among the inhabitants of a miniature world that mostly pass unnoticed. But there they are on the tree trunk, the soil, and rocks and together they provide a beautiful backdrop for the larger plants. This miniature world, so common in our everyday life and taken for granted, can really surprise us when the spotlight is thrown upon it and this strange world of unique forms and textures is opened up to us.

THE LICHENS

An important aspect of lichen ecology is the concept of microhabitat. Large scale habitat descriptions are important in lichen study, as there are lichens that can be found only in rain forests and others that are confined to arid landscapes. The very idea of 'habitat' is usually associated with the large scale. However with lichens you must also think of habitat on the micro scale, on the surfaces where they exist.

  Lichens have a complex biology. They are stable, self-supporting associations between fungi and either algae or cyanobacteria. It is the fungus that forms the majority of the biomass of the lichen. Lichens never have leaves or organs that look like leaves, so their appearance is different from the bryophytes.

  Lichens and bryophytes are another minuscule world that has its avid aficionados. The more they delve, the more they are fascinated. When lichens are painted life size, this will usually give the priority to its local habitat. But if they are painted to an enlarged size, then the unique shapes and fine details are revealed and that has the means to really surprise us. Lichens come in some wonderful colours, from the subtle greys through to oranges, reds and intense ochre yellows.

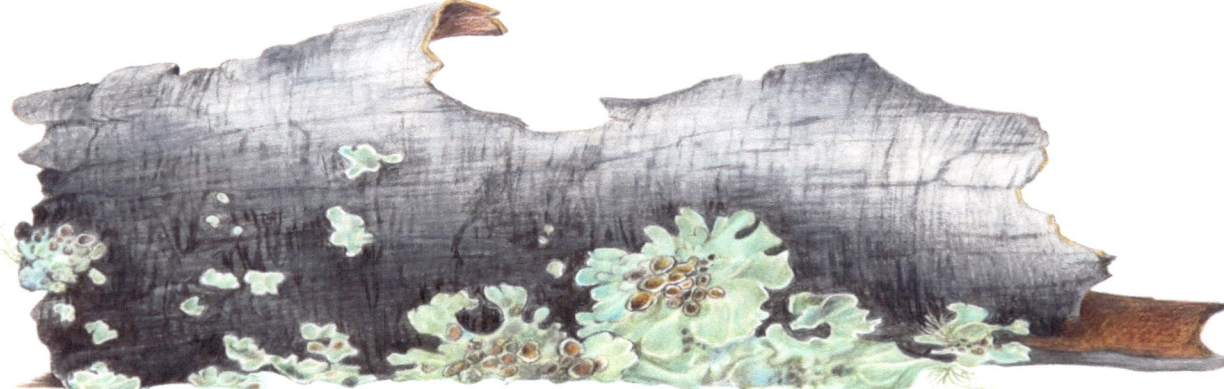

Dolores Sk-Malloni. *Xanthoparmelia. Parmeliceae.* Foliose Lichen

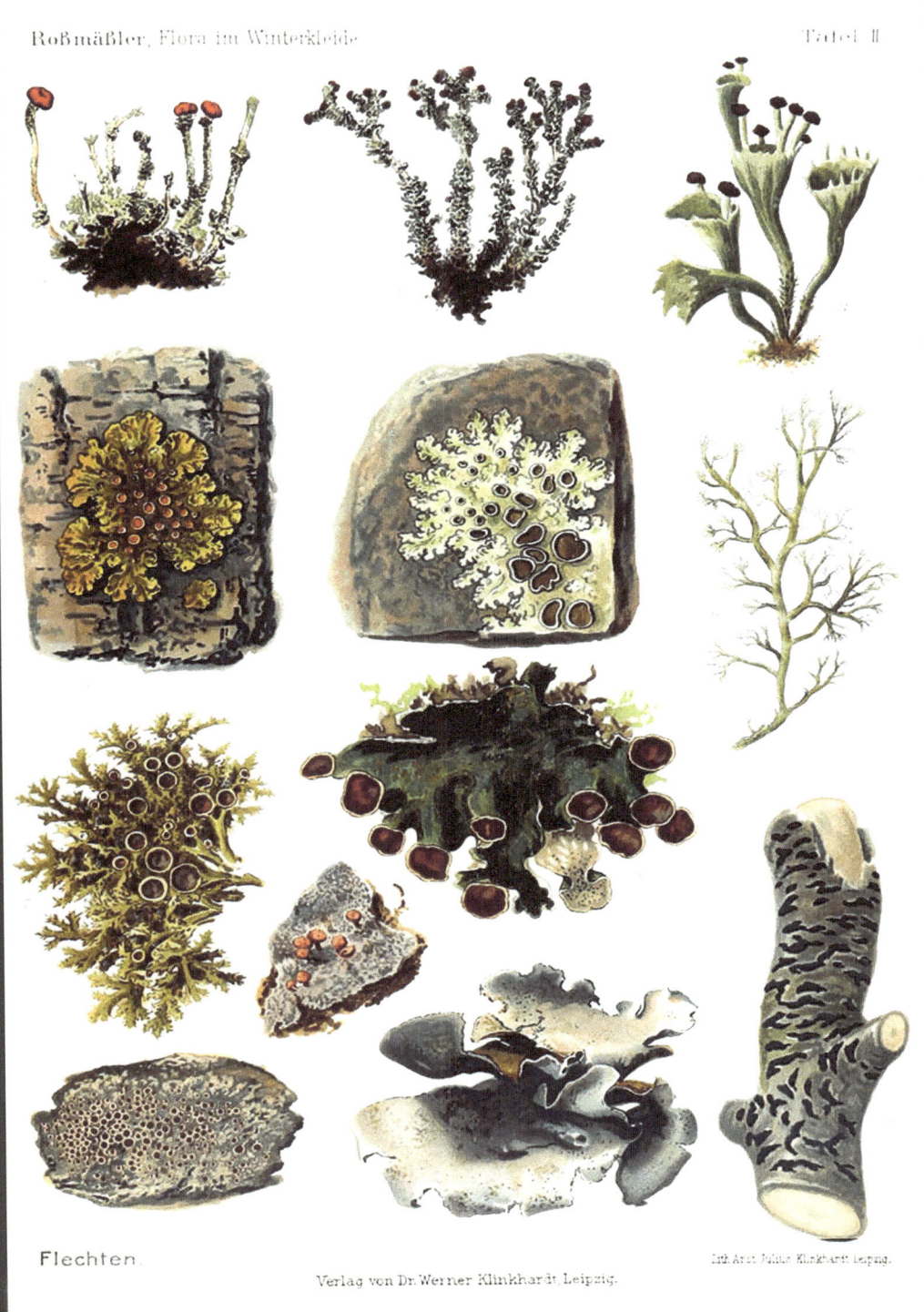

Roßmäßler, Flora im Winterkleide.   Tafel II

Flechten.

Verlag von Dr. Werner Klinkhardt, Leipzig.

Lith Anst Julius Klinkhardt, Leipzig.

Adolf Rossmassler. Educational Chart of Lichens.
Flora im Winterkleide 1908

BRYOPHYTES

MOSS, LIVERWORTS, HORNWORTS

Bryophyte is the collective term for mosses, hornworts and liverworts. While there are marked differences between these groups of organisms, they are related closely enough to warrant the single term bryophyte. They are all small species, usually covering less than a metre and some microscopic. They are normally associated with moist conditions but can tolerate a broader range including from dry to exposed or the shady. Bryophytes are non-vascular plants, so they do not have the types of tissues to develop roots. They are spore-producing, rather than seed-producing plants and they are all without flowers.

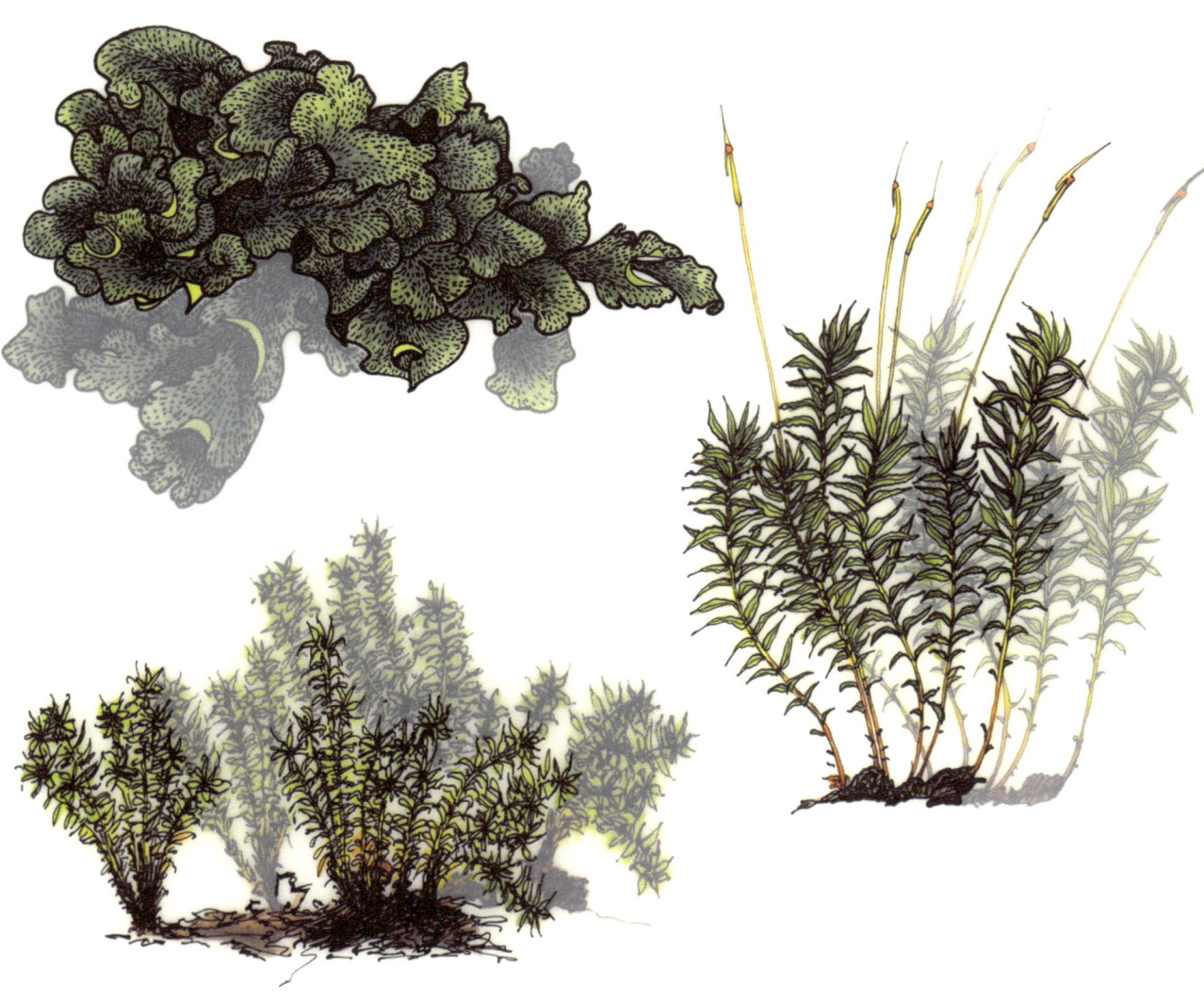

MOSSES (Bryophyta)

The differences between the three are complex. In simple terms: The mosses have thin stems around which simple leaves branch out. The leaves of moss frequently have a midrib. Capsules can be roundish or long, coloured on a long green stalk.

LIVERWORTS (Marchantiophyta)

The liverworts are either made up of a thallus or leafy stems. Unlike many mosses, liverwort leaves do not have midribs. Capsules are roundish and black on a translucent stalk.

HORNWORTS (Anthocerophyta)

The hornworts have a irregular lobed or branching bodies, known as thalli, the tissue of which is not organised into organs. Capsules are long and like needles.

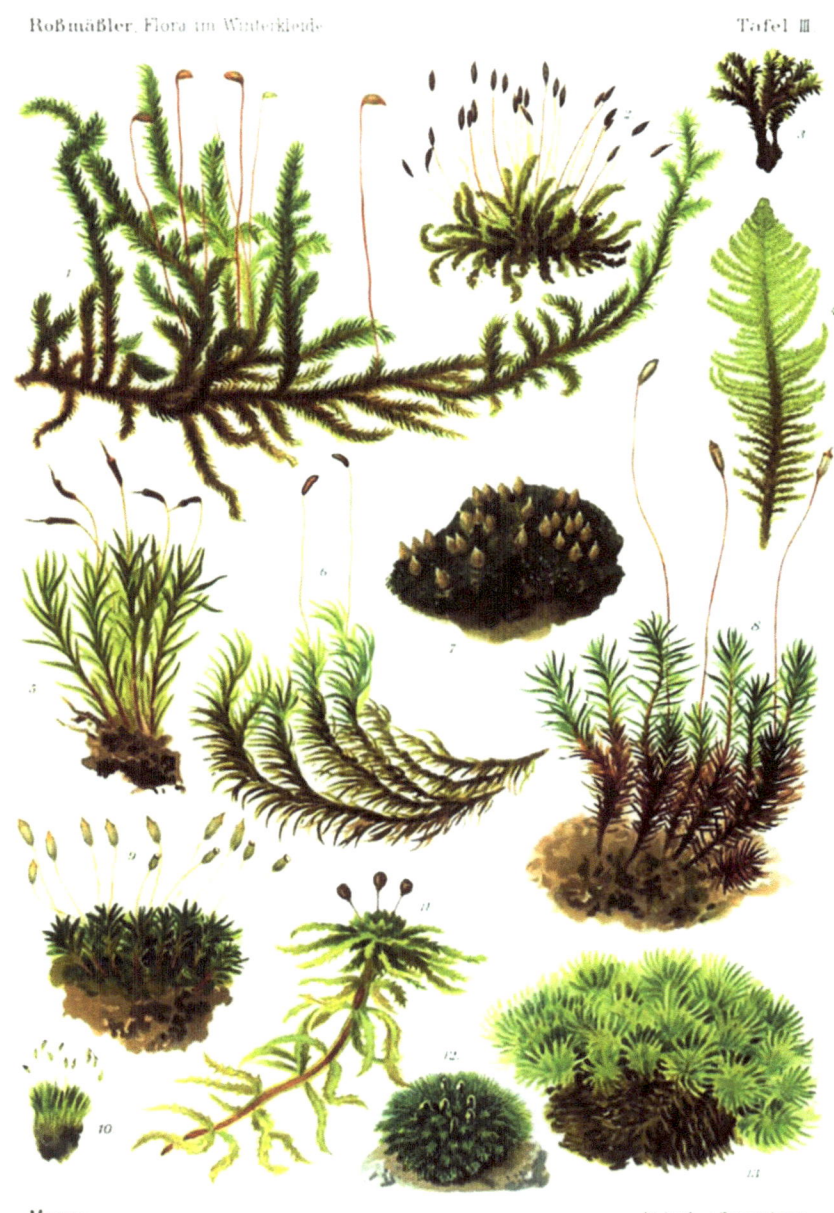

Dolores Sk-Malloni. Watercolour on film.
Left: *Atrichum androynum* (Moss)
Far left above: *Lunularia cruciata* (Liverwort)
Far left below: *Tortula antartica* (Moss)

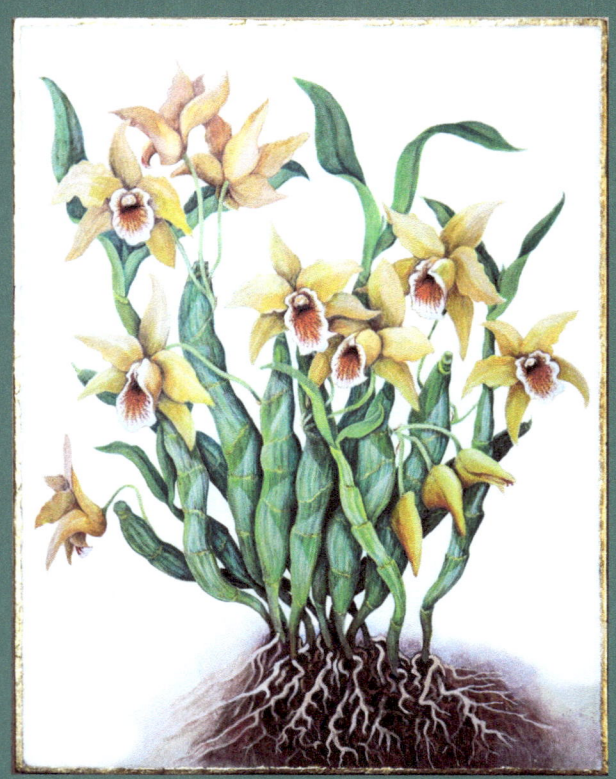

Rita Parkinson
Cymbidium. cv. Hybrid native Australian orchid
Tempera on panel. Gilding

STUDIES IN STYLE

A JAPANESE AESTHETIC

A 16th C. FLORELEGIA

THE FLORAL MOTIF
The Gilded Canopy
A Design for Ceramics

BLACK AND WHITE

A STILL LIFE

STYLE

The concept of style entails a distinctive manner of expression, a particular look brought about by influences of time and place and purpose. In Botanical art to preference style over substance would mean a diminishment of its illustrative and scientific purposes, and that isn't what we normally do.

But the influence of flowers is a strong influence in itself, in the applied arts. Floral motifs have always been such a strong source for design, and you will find them in many cultures and through many periods. This is no more so, than in the field of textiles and ceramic designs in architectural details, wallpaper, carpets, gift wraps. Etc.

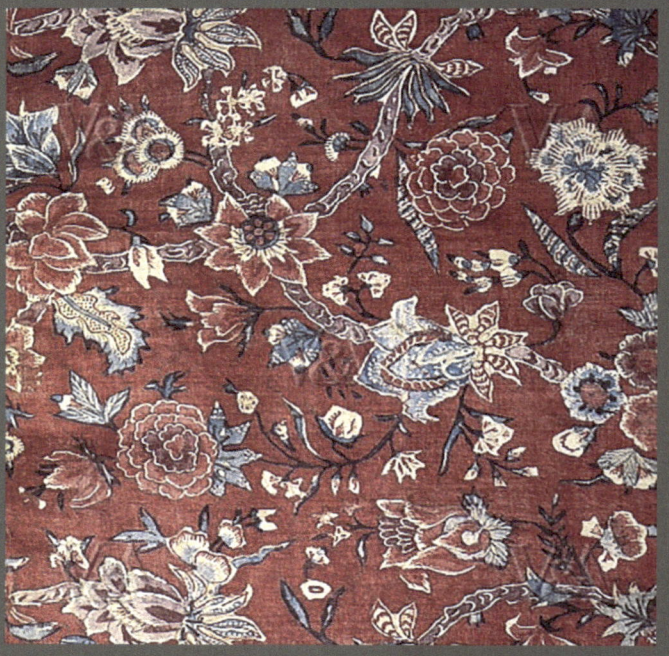

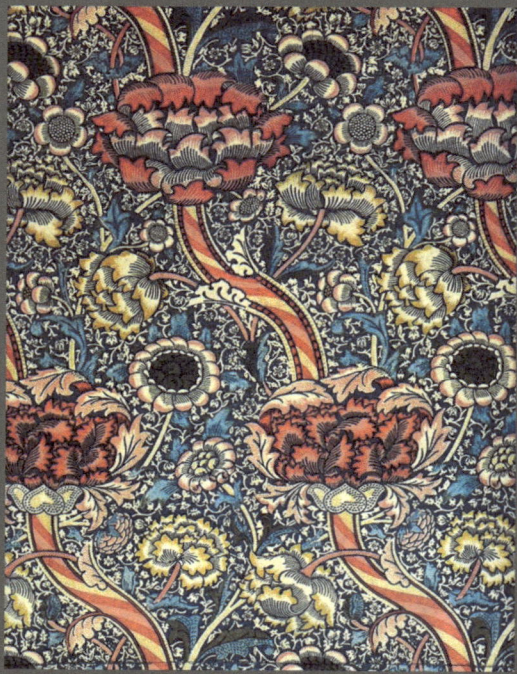

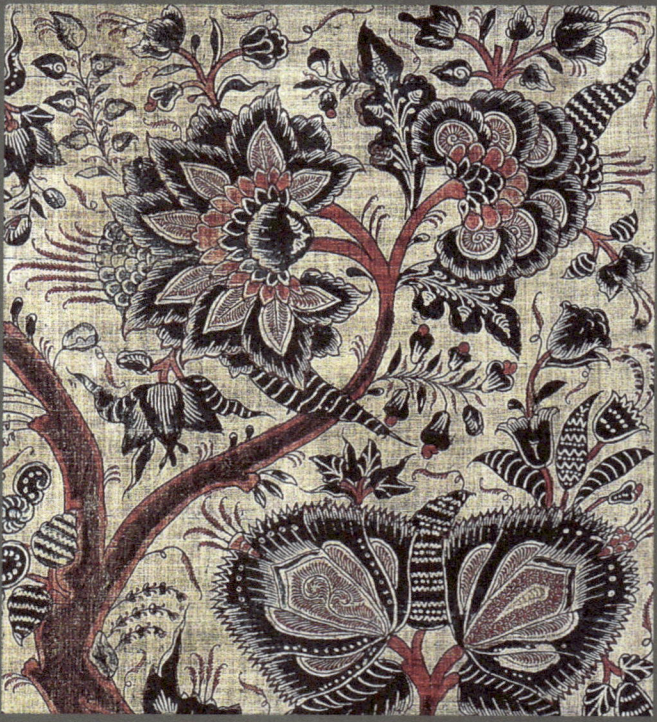

Top: Indian textile
Above: Indian Chintz design
Left: William Morris design. 19C English

THE FLORAL MOTIF

Designs based on flowers have been a popular sources of subject in the field of textiles. The floral print had its origins in Asia. Traders brought these ornately floral designed fabrics to Europe, where they became very desirable.

In the Far East, Japan and China had produced for centuries, wonderful floral designs, including designs in their beautiful silks. These fabrics with floral designs began to appear in the late Middle Ages. Italian merchants traded regularly with Ottoman textile manufacturers and brought their sumptuous woven velvets to Europe. Of course, in time the Italians weavers worked out how to copy these complex velvets and began to produce their own ornate heavy and stylized textiles. In time, other European manufacturers discovered the secrets of production and began to copy these fabrics to suit European tastes.

Chintz fabrics, once so synonymous with English interiors, had their origins in India. Chintz is a glazed cotton cloth printed with small, multi-colored floral motifs. It was exported to Europe by Dutch and British merchants. Again, it was copied by British manufacturers and they began to print their own chintzes. The developments of the Industrial Revolution of the nineteenth century saw textile production increased tenfold, and machine printed chintzes flooded the market and were used extensively in women's day dresses and fabrics for interiors.

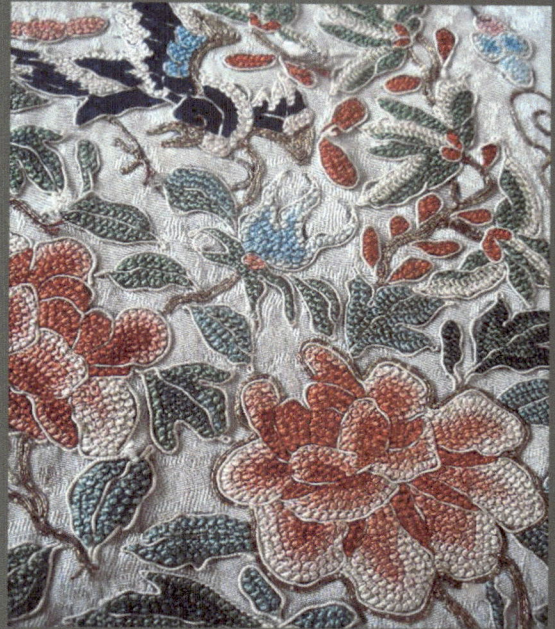

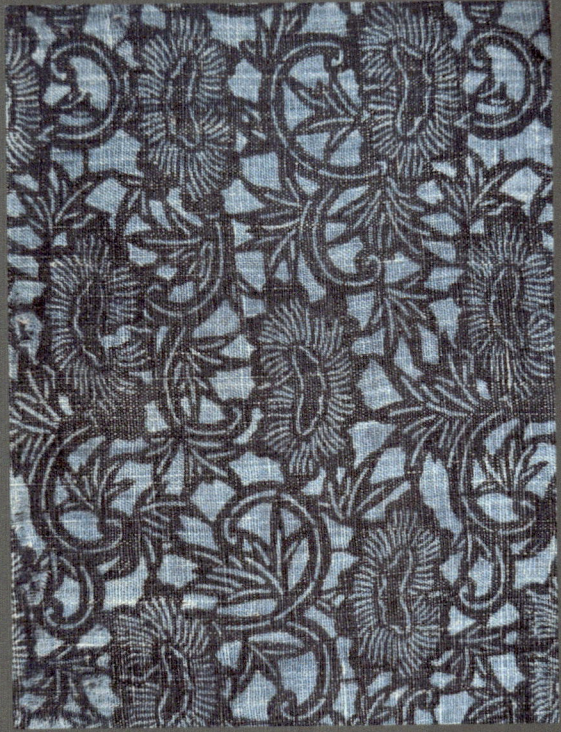

Top: Chinese embroidered silk
Below: Japanese printed fabric

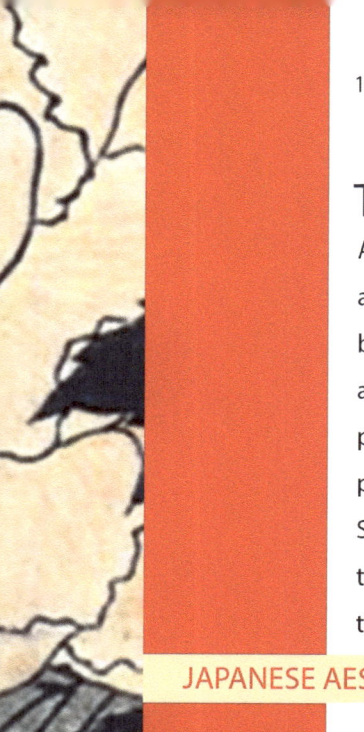

THE INFLUENCE OF JAPAN

A botanical illustration must be true to its subject. It needs to be exact in specific forms, colours and accurately represent the correct size. Close observation and accuracy is one of the first things a botanical art student has to learn. The emphasis is on painting exactly what you see and dismissing any subjective response. But the question is, if any of us can do this outside of our own cultural paradigm. Do artists from a different cultures view the world in a different visual way? Do different perceptions of visual balance, viewpoints and even choice of subjects, alter that idea of accuracy? So do we actually, with our different cultural emphasis, paint our subjects exactly as we 'see' them. In Japan, aesthetic appreciation developed as a way of life that integrates with everyday things, rather than in the west where aesthetics is a matter of art philosophy.

JAPANESE AESTHETIC CONCEPTS

Wabi
Sabi
Wabi-Sabi

Kanso
Shibui

Fukinsei

Shizen

Seijaku
Ma

Wabi expresses the transience of life and the ephemeral nature of all living things.

Sabi is the appreciation of patina and age, as a natural consequence of life.

Wabi-Sabi combines the two concepts and represents the appreciation of things ephemeral and incomplete and sometimes flawed.

Kanso The beauty of simplicity, expressed in a natural manner. The elegance of understatement.

Shibui objects appear to be simple overall, but they include subtle details, such as textures, that balance simplicity with a complexity that causes its aesthetic value to grow over the years.

Fukensei is the art of asymmetry or visual balance. Nature itself should be expressed as a relationships that is asymmetrical yet balanced. This is an important concept of Ikebana.

Shizen represents naturalness as being an absence of pretense or artificiality. In a Japanese garden, the viewer perceives the garden is man-made but is created to express a natural environment.

Seijaku expresses tranquility, calmness, stillness and solitude.

Ma is the negative space necessary within which something can stand out. The pure, and essential void between all 'things'. A minimalist total lack of clutter.

JAPONISM

Ukiyo-e, 'pictures of the floating world', was a genre of art that flourished in Japan from the 17th to the19th centuries. Its artists produced woodblock prints and paintings of subjects such as portraiture; kabuki actors and sumo wrestlers; scenes from history and folk tales; travel scenes and landscapes; flora and fauna. Ukiyo-e was central to forming the West's perception of Japanese art in the late 19th century, especially the landscapes of Hokusai and Hiroshige. From the 1870s Japonism became a prominent trend in Europe and had a strong influence on the early Impressionists such as Degas, Manet, and Monet and artists such as Toulouse-Lautrec.

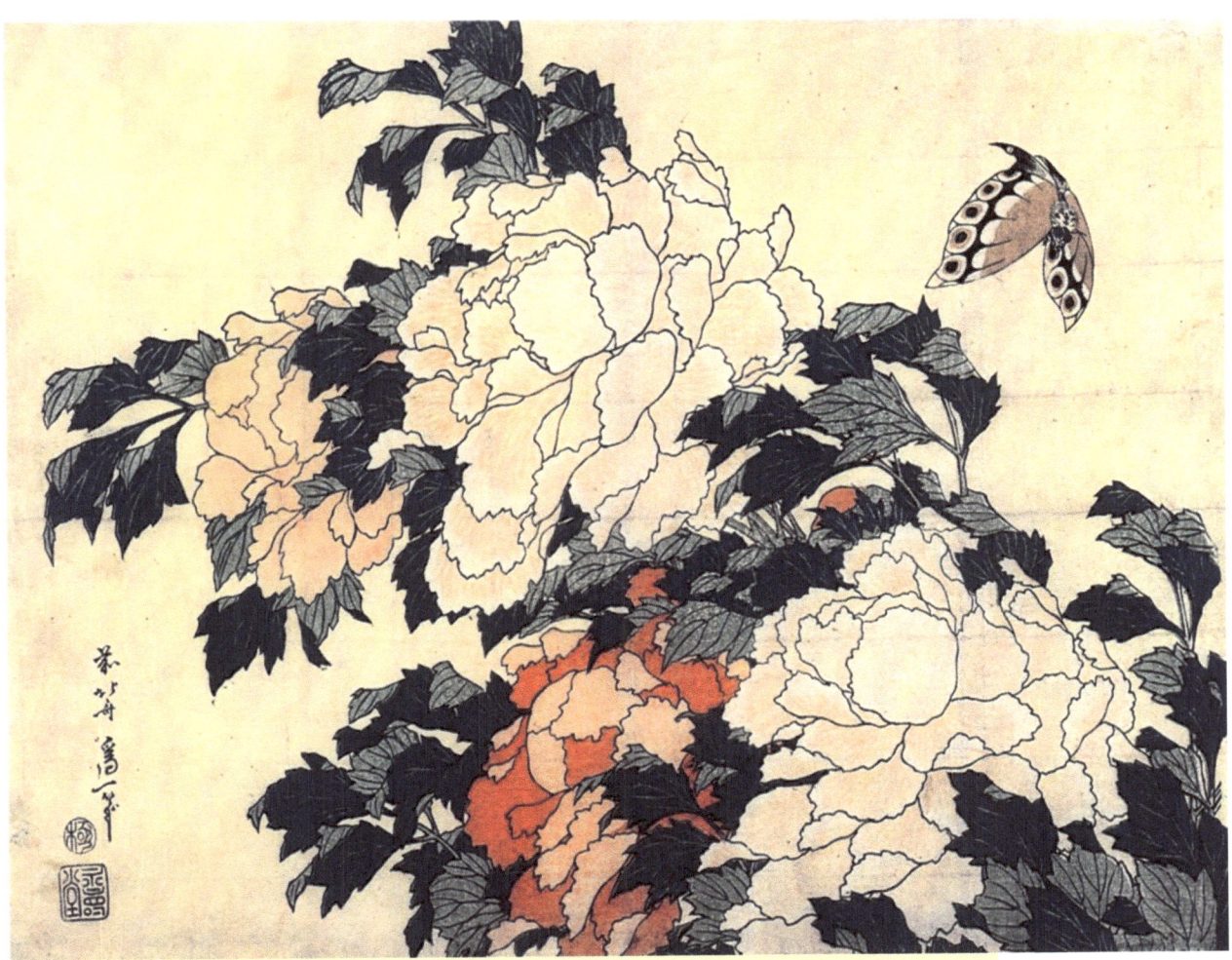

Hokusai. Katsushika
Peonies with Butterfly.
Woodblock print

The Japanese art of making prints was unique in that the woodblock print was not developed to be a reproduction of an already existing work of art, but a work of art in itself. From the beginning of the art of printmaking in Japan, in the 17th century, artists began to transform printing techniques into a complex process of wood carving techniques that could produce complex multi-coloured images. The first block was designed as a key print. This would be created by carving out everything but the raised outline. It would then be printed and would produce a black outlined key print. After this multiple blocks would be produced, one for each colour. They would then be printed using the key print to properly align each stage.

The wood block print gave Japanese culture a unique means of expression and it combined perception with culture and a philosophy of life.

JAPANESE STYLE

Japanese art has had an influence on European artists since it first came to notice. Artists were fascinated by the lack of perspective and shadow, the flat areas of strong color, and the compositional freedom gained by placing the subject off-centre, quite often with a low diagonal axis to the background. In general Japanese style tends toward a paring down to essentials, an attempt to capture the basic form and characteristics of a specific subject. The style of art called 'Ukiyo-e', the Floating World, came to be known to Westerners in the 19th century, mainly through the woodcut print which possessed a very distinctive, dramatic ways of using line and color in landscape, portraiture, and other subjects. Ukiyo-e prints had an important effect on the work of Western artists of the time.

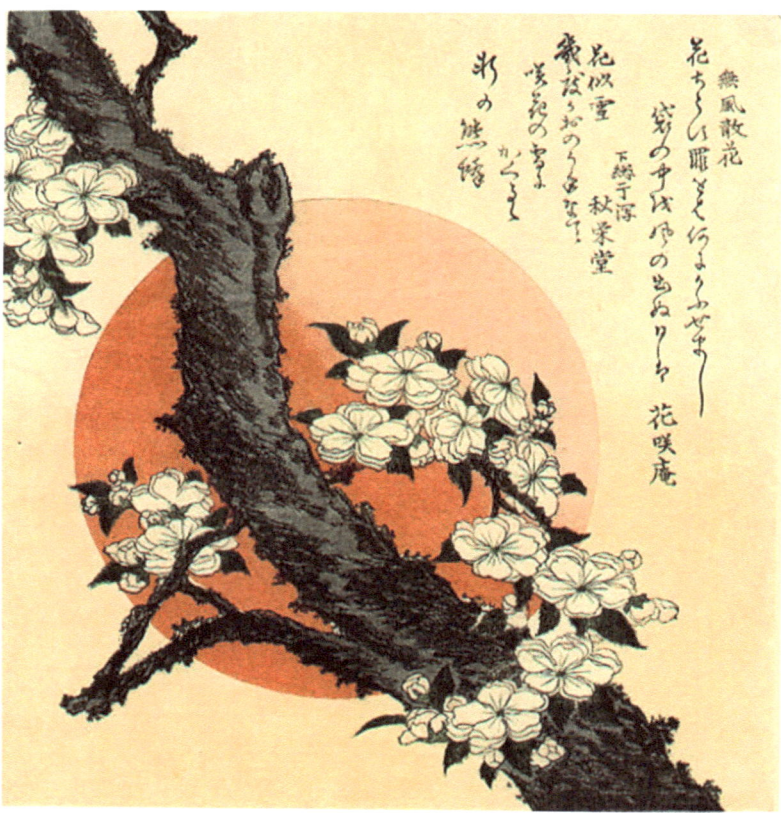

The style of Japanese art allowed for greater spontaneity and individuality. Although Japanese landscapes and panoramic scrolls, like Chinese painting featured shifting perspective, many works focused on intimate and close-up subjects, allowing more explicit perspective and lighting effects. Favorite subjects would be portraits of individuals, scenes of daily life, studies of plants and animals. In this image of the famed cherry blossom, Hokusai uses the contrast of texture of the branch to highlight with the delicate forms of the blossom.

Hokusai. Katsushika
Cherry blossoms.
Woodblock print

Dolores Sk-Malloni. *Rhododendron indicum 'Ruzicon'.* Azalea. From the Bonsai Series

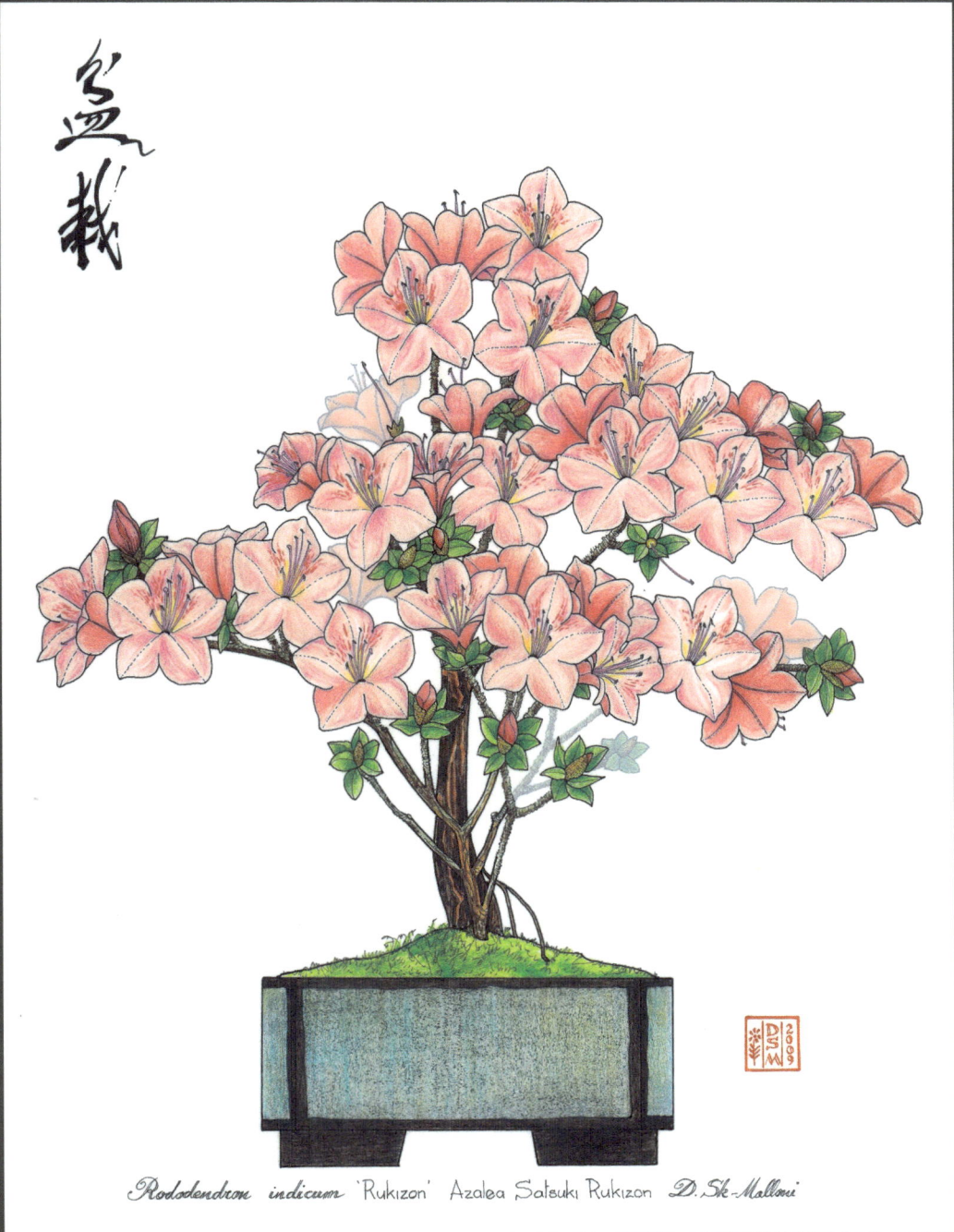

Rhododendron indicum 'Rukizon' Azalea Satsuki Rukizon D. Sk-Malloni

The image of an Azalea from a 'Bonsai series' references the subject matter from a very Japanese perspective, both in the form of a bonsai and the choice of the Azalea, a favorite Japanese species. The treatment is also a reference to Japanese style, with the use of black outlines reminiscent of the woodblock print, with the virtually flat colour, the direct perspective and ultimately a sense of 'Kanso', the beauty of simplicity, expressed in a natural manner, the elegance of understatement.

A JAPANESE AESTHETIC

The painting of two entwined Convolvulus was one of a set of works presented in a group exhibition in Melbourne called 'Botanicasia'. The premise of the exhibition was to focus on flora that originated in Asia. Plants that probably many of us are very familiar with, but may not appreciate their Asian roots. There were plenty of appealing subjects to select from. You could choose from the peonies, the chrysanthemums, the orchids and the irises, the bamboos and the hydrangeas and many more.

But what interested me most was the links with the very different aesthetic qualities of the Asian visual tradition, and this is what I wanted to explore. The inspiration here is the Japanese stylistic elements of the woodblock. Flowers were often a source of subject for this genre. So this meant incorporating some of their main elements, the sense of vitality and plant characterization, the flat colorations, the different viewpoints.

The picture includes two species of convolvulus, and seemed to sum all this up, with its chaotic cascading colourful, yet simple quality.

Rita Parkinson
Ipomoea indica. I. lacunose
Convolvulaceae
Acrylic on board

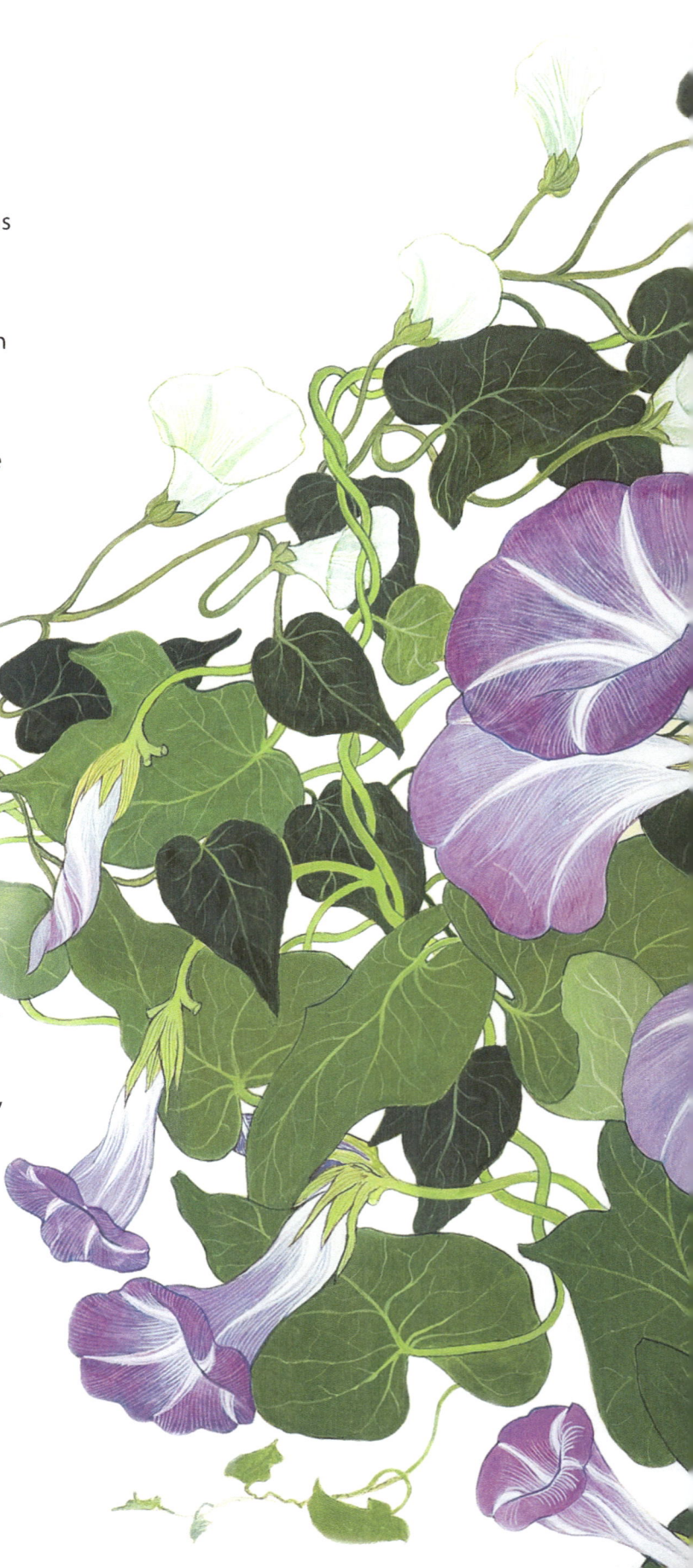

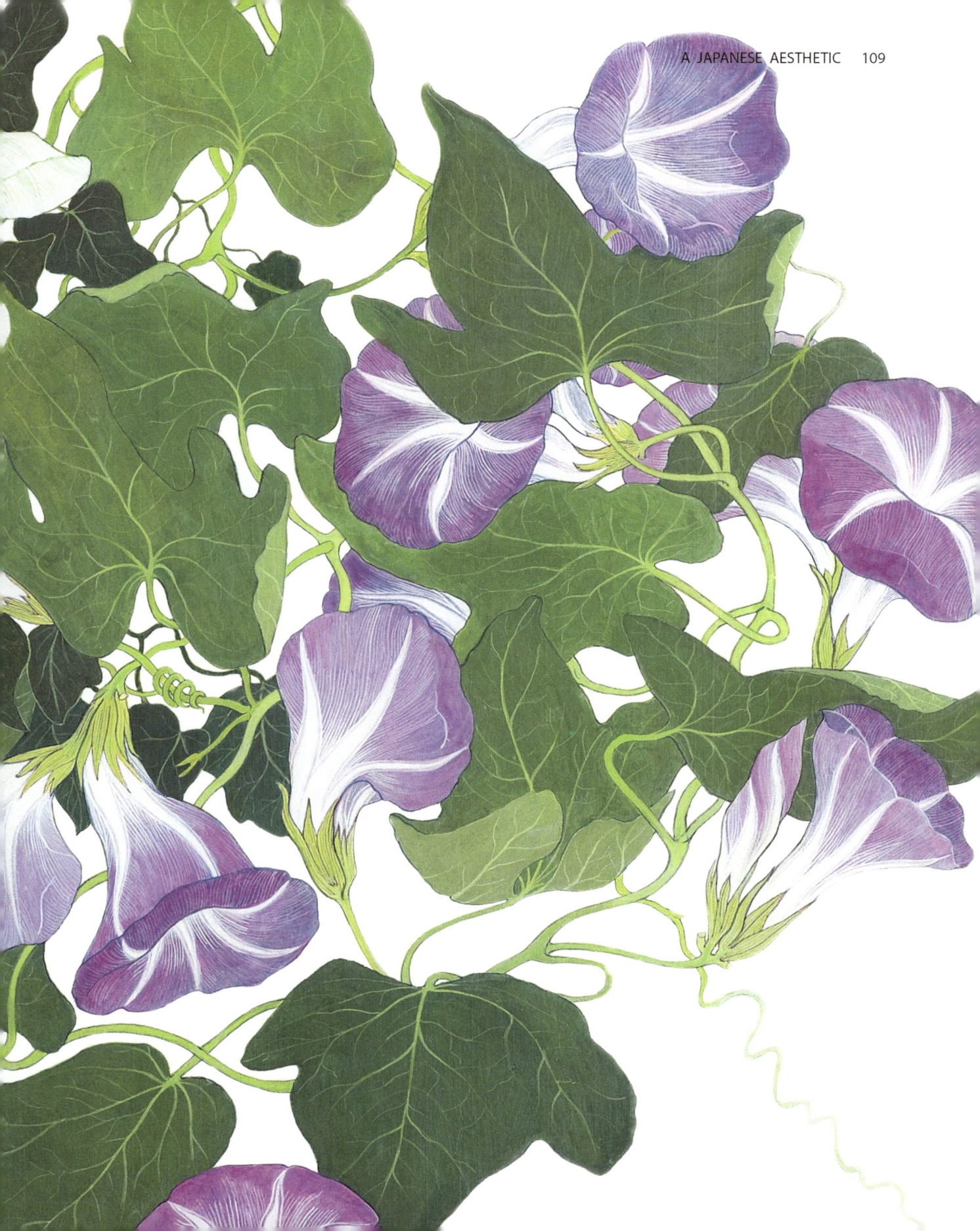

In the Style of 16th Century Florilegia

Early Florilegia evolved from a genre of flower books that dated back to the 15th century, when herbals were the main source of plant information. Herbals described the culinary and medicinal uses of plants. They were printed with a text accompanied with illustrations of flowers, usually by simple woodblock prints. As printing techniques advanced, and new plants began to arrive in Europe in the 16th century, wealthy individuals and botanic gardens commissioned artists to record the beauty of these exotics. Engraved plates were made from the paintings and published as a Florilegia- a book of flowers. They flourished in the 17th century when expeditions from far afield presented ever more rare and exotic plants to portray.

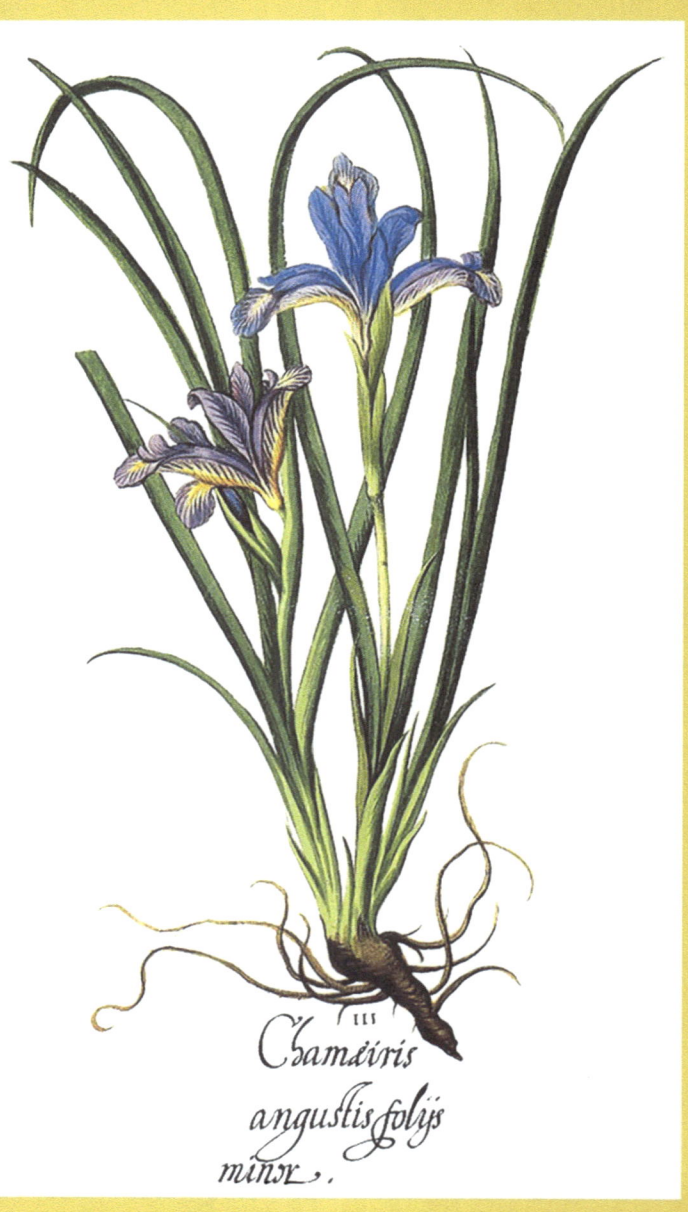

'Hortus Eystettensis 1613. Basilus Besler.
Chamaeris angustis foliis minor
Beardless purple iris

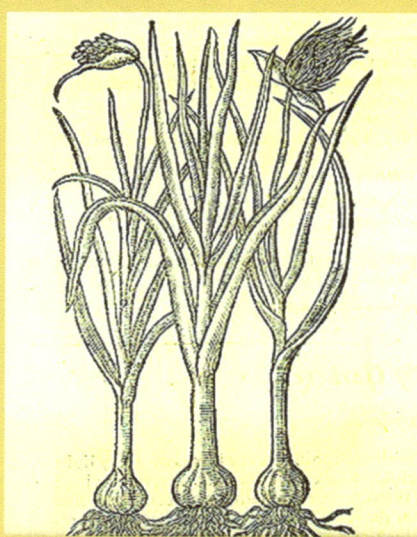

Herbal. John Gerad. 1597.
North American Plants
Wood Block Print.

FEATURES OF EARLY FLORILEGIA

1. Images created to be easily transposed to the engaving process.
2. They displayed a sense of formality, suited to the times.
3. A centralized composition used as a forceful element of emphasis.
4. A style of decorative simplification.

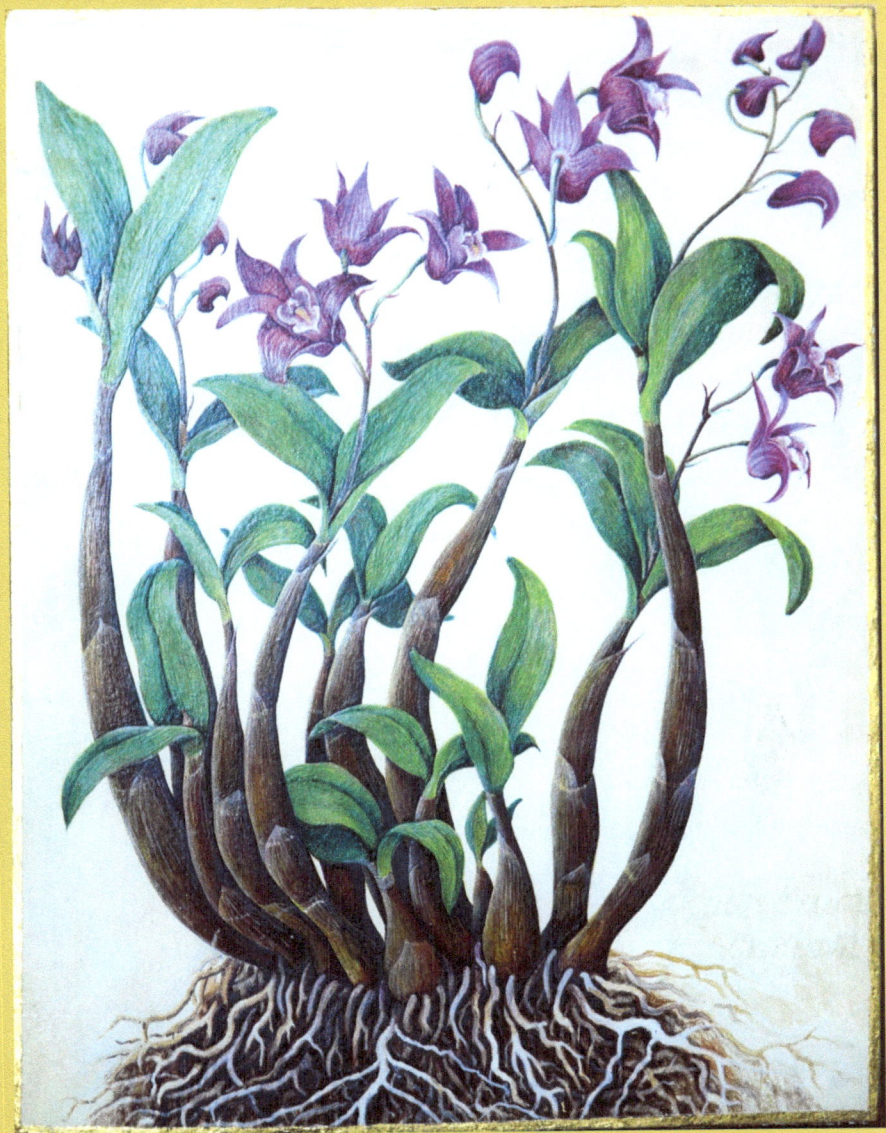

Rita Parkinson.
Dendrobium kingianum.
Tempera on board. Gold leaf.

This painting of native orchids was inspired by 16 century florilegia. It is executed in tempera with a gold leaf edging. The composition is based on decorative simplicity using a direct eye level centalized position.

THE FLORAL MOTIF

Studies in the applied arts are not the usual focus of a botanical illustration course. But they can be a useful and enjoyable side trip. The emphasis will be very different, as there will be a greater emphasis on composition. There will be a need to edit down to the essential details, while keeping some essential qualities of the plant. All of which can enhance useful skills for an illustrator, by a set of useful design excercises that have the capacity to enhance their normal practice.

Floral subjects have always been used as an ornamental theme in the decorative arts. It can be found in many cultures, from the design of textiles, architectural elements through to ceramics. The interplay of influences on motifs runs through many cultures and periods. For instance the familiar late Victorian floral design styles of William Morris, with their vibrant patterns in surface design were a direct descendant of a much longer tradition in Indian textiles.

THE PAINTED CEILING

The two panels featured on this page are a part of the painted ceiling at London's Natural History Museum. They were designed as an intrinsic part of the architectural design. The ceiling is covered with hundreds of panels of plants of all descriptions, painted in rich colours and finely gilded. The plants themselves tell stories that bring to life the times in which the museum was founded, the Victorian age of Empire. There are plants pictured that influenced agriculture and commerce or simply brought pleasure to many. These beautifully designed tiles reflect an era when exotic plant specimens flooded into Britain, sparking public interest in botany and horticulture.

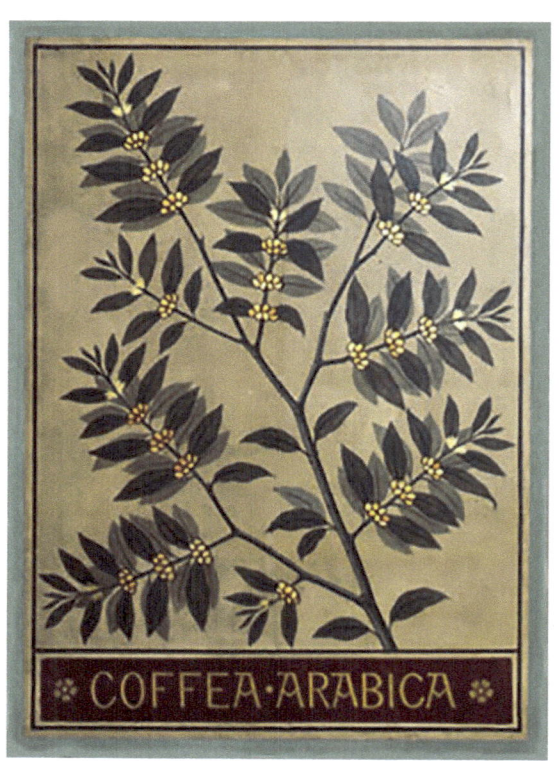

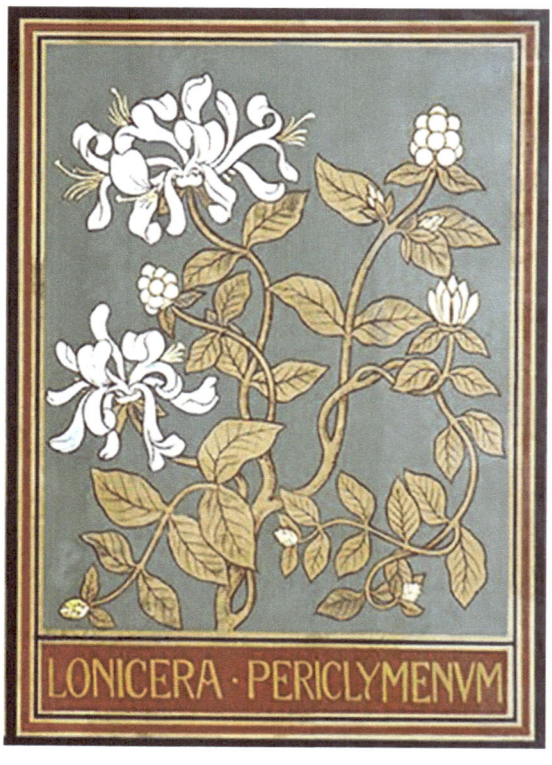

A GOLD LEAF WORKSHOP

The famous ceiling of the Natural History Museum in London, inspired a workshop held on the other side of the world in Melbourne, Australia. The Museum in London is a Victorian era Institution, built at the height of Empire. The design of the panels was highly stylized. They were worked in flat colours, with dark outlines and highlighted with gold gilding. The workshop used similar parameters, usually working from a previous completed work. But however stylized the finished work needed to be, it was important that, despite the simplification in the design process the plants remained readily identifiable.

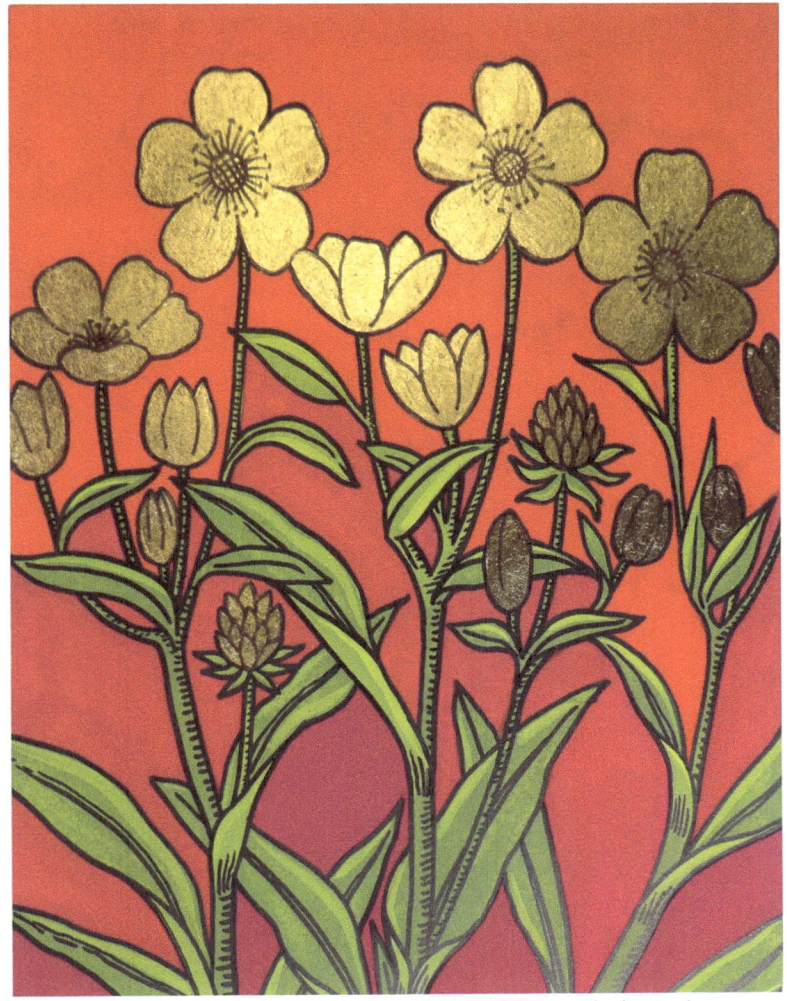

Dolores Sk-Malloni. *Ranunculus lingua*. Anenomes Acrylic. Gold leaf gilding

THE DESIGN PROCESS

The students were asked to base their design work on a pared down former composition, into a simplified design, incorporating the essential elements of their chosen plant. The flat background colour was then added, and the black outlines detailed in. The final stage was the addition of gold leaf gilding, which magically lifted the whole design, by giving every work a magical glow. The whole design process was a new experience for many students and all the resulting works were successful, with an emphasis on balanced design and a focus on the essential character of the plant.

Opposite: Two panels from the painted ceiling.
Top: *Coffea arabica*. Coffee
Below: *Lonicera periclymenum*. Honeysuckle

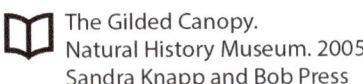 The Gilded Canopy.
Natural History Museum. 2005
Sandra Knapp and Bob Press

CERAMICS and the floral motif

Nothing illustrates the cross fertilation of influences on design as the story of porcelain. The techniques of porcelain production were invented by the Chinese, who in time brought to the process a very high level of technique in materials and production. The whole industry evolved into a very successful export trade. Europeans were fascinated by the designs that flooded into Europe, so different to the ceramics that were available to them. So important was this industry to the Chinese, that the secrets of their techniques were jealously guarded. Of course, the Europeans set about discovering these secret practices. They finally succeeded in 1708, in Saxony in Germany, where the Meissen Company was the first to develop and sell their own porcelain, in time developing their unique style. Other companies followed suit, such as Sevres in France and Spode and Wedgewood in England, each in their own way creating pieces suited to their own market.

WORKSHOP - A Design for Ceramics

The illustrations on this page were done as demonstrations for a workshop which aimed to use our more traditional botanical works as a source for designs. The use of floral motifs on ceramics is something we are all very familiar with in our everyday lives. During the workshop students looked at various traditions of ceramic ornamentation to help develop their own work. They considered various templates of vases or plates, from different cultures and traditions, and then had to organize their design to be pictorially balanced on the shape. The emphasis had to be in describing the essential elements of their chosedn plant in a simple but decorative way. It was important for the plant to be recognizable.

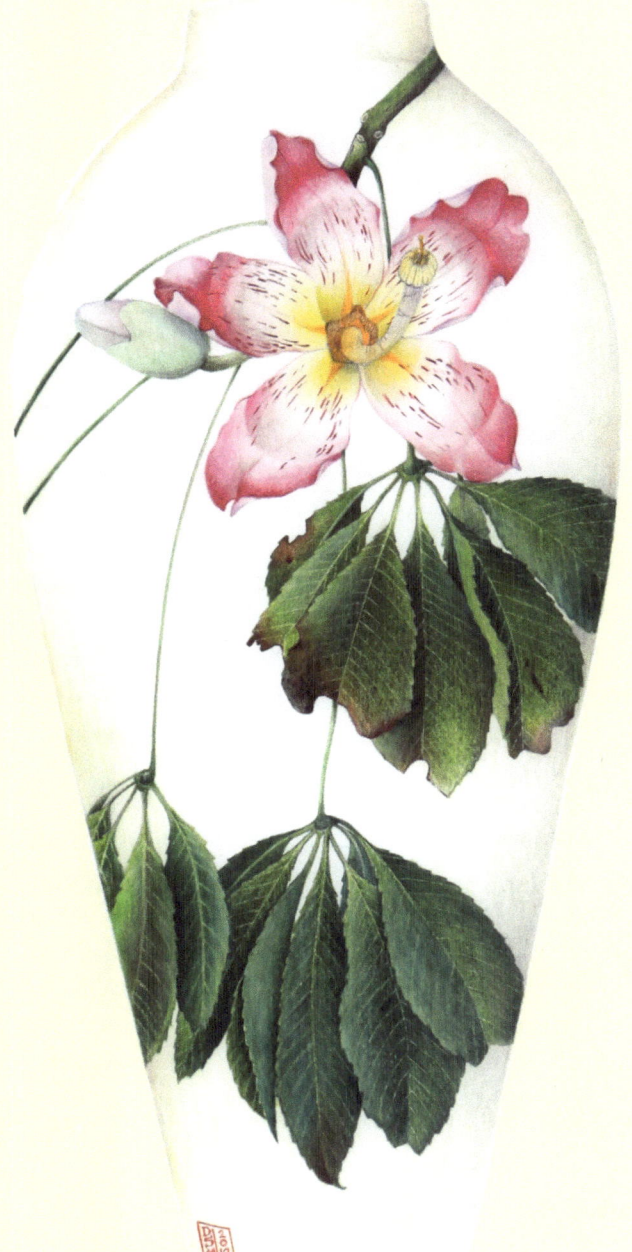

Rita Parkinson
The Grevillea Plate
Design developed from the work:
Grevillea robusta

Dolores Sk-Malloni
Image on Vase developed from the work:
Chorisia speciosa. The Silk Floss Tree

BLACK AND WHITE

The origins of botanical art lie in the black and white image, in the early woodcuts of medieval herbals. Today a botanical artist might choose the black and white mode, but more for aesthetic reasons. There are artists who really love to work in black and white because there is a special quality about these works. Part of it is that an absence of colour can give a focus to the sharpness of the tonal contrasts, and that brings an emphasis to form and sculptural qualities.

There are a few media that work well in botanical subjects. The most common would be the good old graphite pencil, through its various grades. There is also graphite powder, which can produces some wonderful soft velvety blacks. Then there is pen and ink and pen and wash. In earlier times this would have been a dip pen but today is usually a technical pen. A black coloured pencil can also work very well. Then there are other media that you occasionally come across, usually coming from traditional printing methods such as wood engravings, etchings and scratchboards.

One of the biggest influences on black and white imagery is one that we take for granted. In the the earlier part of the 20th century, black and white imagery was everywhere. You would have seen it all around in photographs and in films. So it entered the lexicon through all of those early photographs, black and white films and later on early television. And in a way we got used to it.

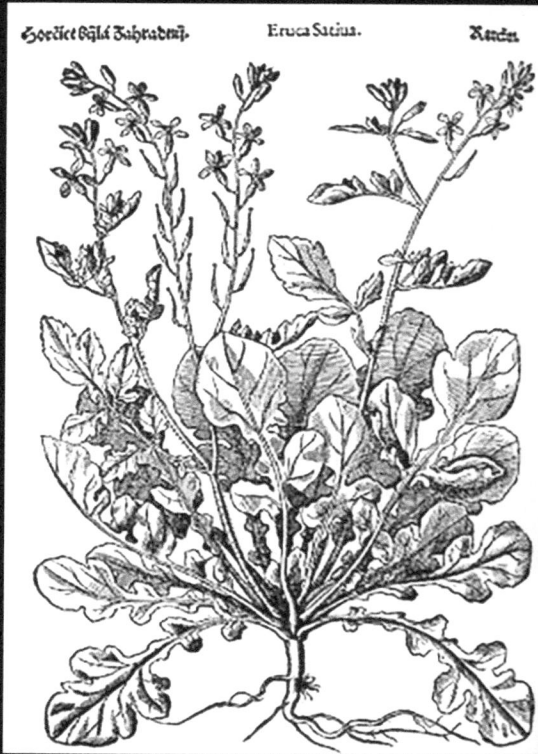

Many artists never consider any drawing media beyond the graphite pencil with all its grades from the H's to the upper B's. This is a pity as it can be difficult to get the really strong blacks with a graphite pencil when you need to get a good contrast. Using other media can produce the rich, dark blacks that will get you that good range of tone that can give you subtle contours and volume. Other media to try all have their own qualities, their strengths and difficulties and there's no way to find out which one is for you without a little experimentation. So it's worth trying a few to see which feels right for you.

GRAPHITE PENCIL / GRAPHITE POWDER
CHARCOAL / SCRATCHBOARD
PEN AND INK / PEN AND WASH
TECHNICAL PENS
WOODCUTS / WOOD ENGRAVING

Rita Parkinson *Telopea specioissima* Waratah.   Technical drawing pen and ink

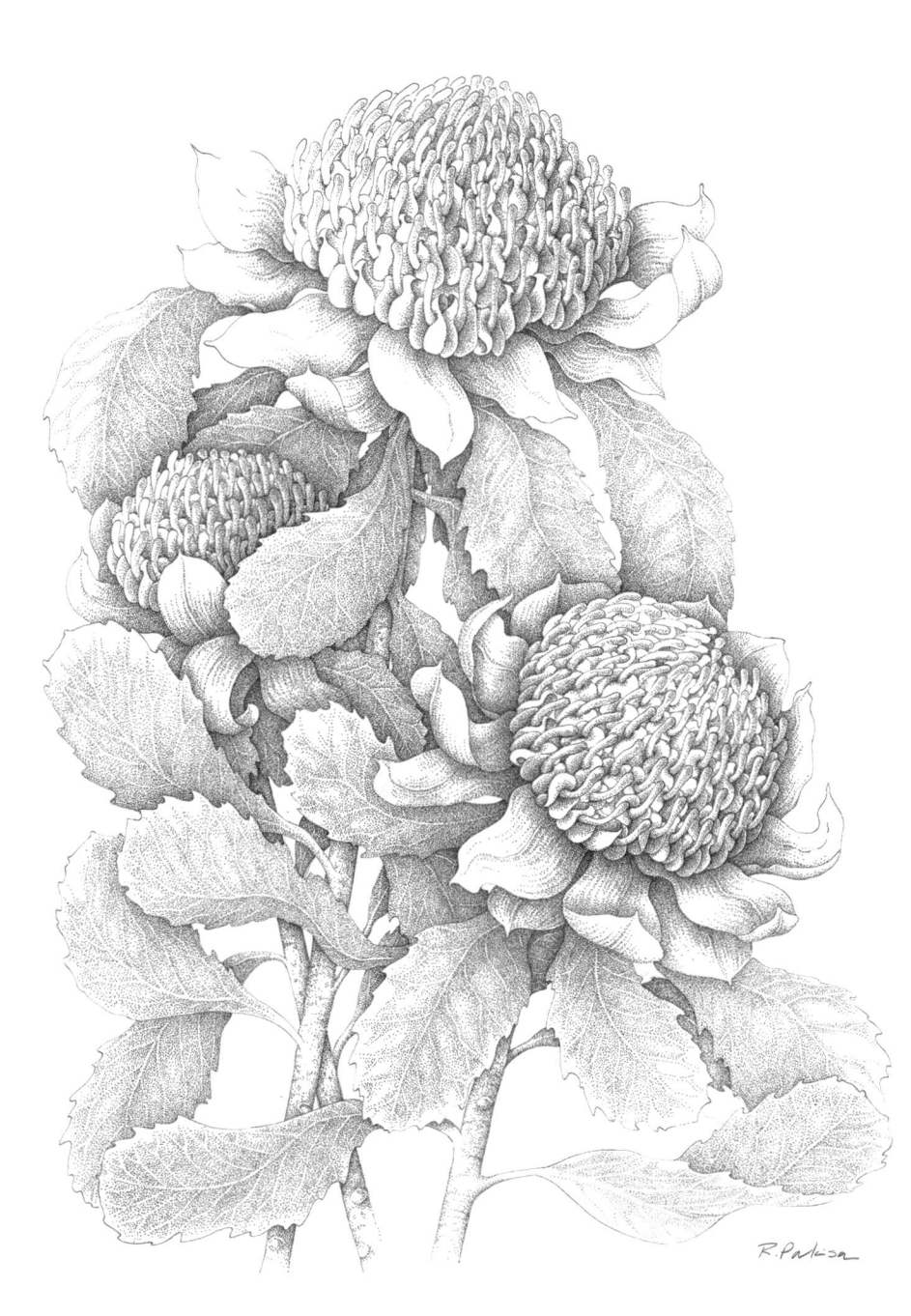

The method used in this image is the dot method of using ink and a technical pen. This technique is usually confined to black and white scientific illustration. But there's no good reason why that should be so. The method creates its tonal areas by increasing the number of dots in a specific area. The more dots the darker the area becomes. Line is also used to delignate forms.

STILL LIFE

A still life painting would normally come under the umbrella of the fine arts, rather than botanical illustration. But genres do overlap and can be influenced by many different contexts. As a result, where nature's wares form the subject matter, the Still Life is often accepted as a form of botanical art for exhibition purposes. The Still Life has a long tradition, but its heyday is considered the Dutch still life tradition that began in the 1500's. The Dutch genre was rich in symbolism. Themes of transience were common, and the depiction of subjects at their peak would often be accompanied by a hint to the future and the finite qualities of nature. Flowers were a perfect visual metaphor for the idea of the temporary nature of life. The genre was one of virtuoso illusionism, by artists of enormous technical and mimetic skills. Other countries such as Italy and France developed their own traditions within the genre.

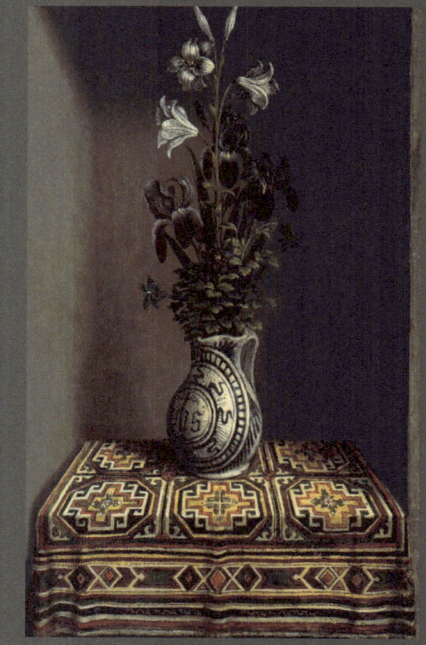

Hans Memling. Flowers in a Jug. c 1485
Oil on Panel.

Michelangelo da Caravaggio. Basket of fruit. c1599. Oil on canvas

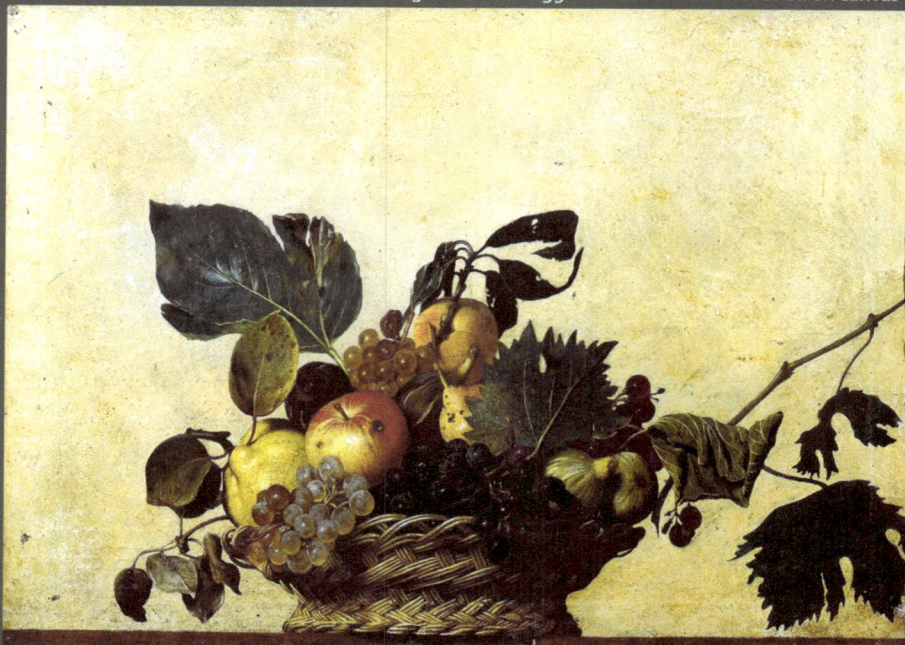

The artists of this period were very skilled when it came to presenting their heightened forms of reality. They used insects, ants, butterflies, and spiders, not as you might expect, as illustrations of pollinators, but as a devices to create reference points. They used the imperfections in their subjects in the same way. The viewer was not permitted to just look, but encouraged to observe and reflect carefully.

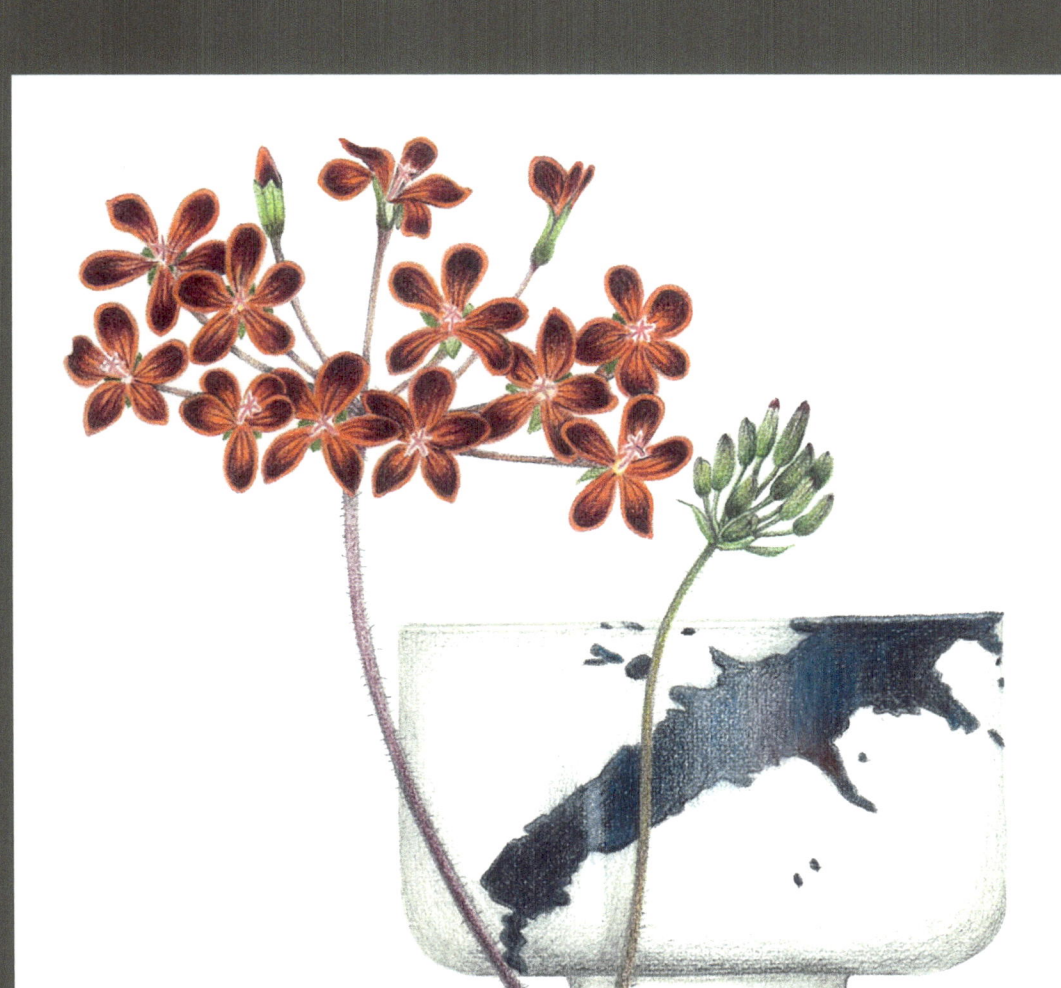

Dolores Sk-Malloni
Pelargornium ardens
Japanese ceramic
Coloured pencil

Traditional subjects in the art of the 16th and 17th century, were usually chosen from grand themes, either of religious subjects or from the classical world. But unlike these subjects, the Still Life enabled simple everyday objects to be elevated. It could be a group of red peppers, food on a kitchen table or a vase of simple flowers. They were all considered worthwhile subjects. Although the genre was steeped in symbolism, the majority of people of the time would be well versed in these visual metaphors. Today we don't usually take our Still Lives that seriously, but it is worth remembering that depicting an apple with a worm hole, or a wilting flower past its prime, does hold a visual message and as illustrators we need to be aware of this.

INDEX

Further Reading

The Anatomy of Flowers. Arthur Harry Church. David Mabberley. 2000

Kunstformen der Natur (Artforms in Nature). Karl Blossfeldt. 1928

A Life in Nature. Beatrix Potter: Linda Lear. 2006

The Brother Gardeners: Botany, Empire and the Birth of an Obsession. Andrea Wulf. 2009

The Invention of Nature. Alexander von Humboldt's New World. Andrea Wulf. 2015

Fern Fever. The Story of Pteridomania. Sarah Whittingham. 2012

The Flora Graeca Story: Sibthorp, Bauer, in the Levant. David Mabberley. 1998

The Gilded Canopy. Natural History Museum. Sandra Knapp and Bob Press. 2005

Tulipomania. Mike Dash. 2000

Bibliography

Delineations of Exotick Plants cultivated in the Royal Garden at Kew. Franz Bauer. 1796–1803

The Genera and Species of Orchidaceous Plants. Franz Bauer. John Lindley. London.1830-1838

Genera filicum; Illustrations of the ferns, and other allied genera. Franz Bauer. William Hooker. 1842

Flora Graeca Sibthorpiana. Ferdinand Bauer. 1806-1840

Illustrationes Florae Novae Hollandiae. Ferdinand Bauer. 1813

Metamorphosis insectorum Surinamensium. Maria Sybella Merian.1705

Les Roses, 3 vols. Pierre-Joseph Redouté 1817–1824

Les *Liliacées,* 8 vols. Pierre-Joseph Redouté. 1802–1816

Choix des plus belles fleurs et de quelques branches des plus beaux fruits. Pierre-Joseph Redouté.1827

Anatomy of Plants. Nehemiah Grew. 4 Vols, Vegetables. Roots. Trunks. Leaves, Flowers, Fruits and Seeds. 1682.

Hortus Eystettensis. Basilius Besler.1613

The Naturalist's Library. Vol 3. Entomology. William Jardine.1840

Paxton's Flower Garden, 3 vols. John Lindley. Sir Joseph Paxton. 1850-53

Phycologia Australica. William Henry Harvey. London, 1858-63

Urformen der Kunst (Art Forms in Nature). Ernst Haeckel. 1899

the narratives

The subject of this book is the range of approaches that can be seen in the field of Botanical Art. The concept was to outline the diversity that lies within the discipline, from the classic works of today in the Linnean style, employed since the time of the Golden Age, through to works influenced by other significant artists. It considers the diversity of approaches developed for many reasons, whether from a scientific, horticultural or simply for exhibition purposes. An illustrator is an 'illuminator', one who brings light to their subject, and in order to do this proficiently, it's worth investigating the scope of the genre and its roots in such a remarkable past.

 The book is not intended to be either comprehensive or conclusive. There will always be a personal element, and you may well find elements missing that you consider should be included. The fact is there are many different ways to interpret a subject, within the conventions of the genre, and new ways yet to illuminate the study of plants.

 While writing the book, it did surprise me to find that some treatments were definitely out of fashion. You seldom see the 'habitat' picture today, which is surprising when ecological issues are such a major concerns. We don't see 'the chart', such an obvious means of conveying a lot of information. I wonder why?

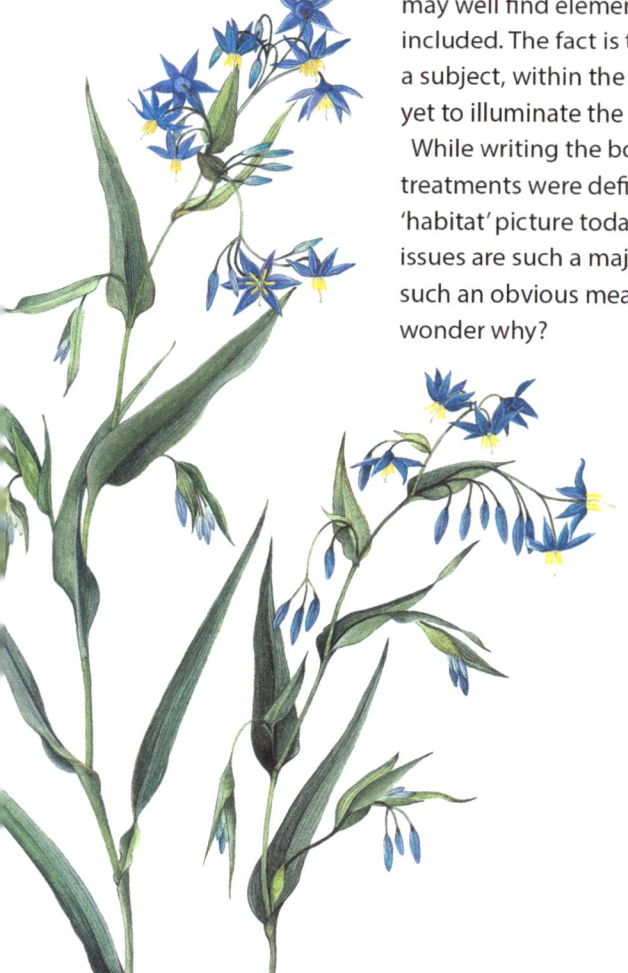